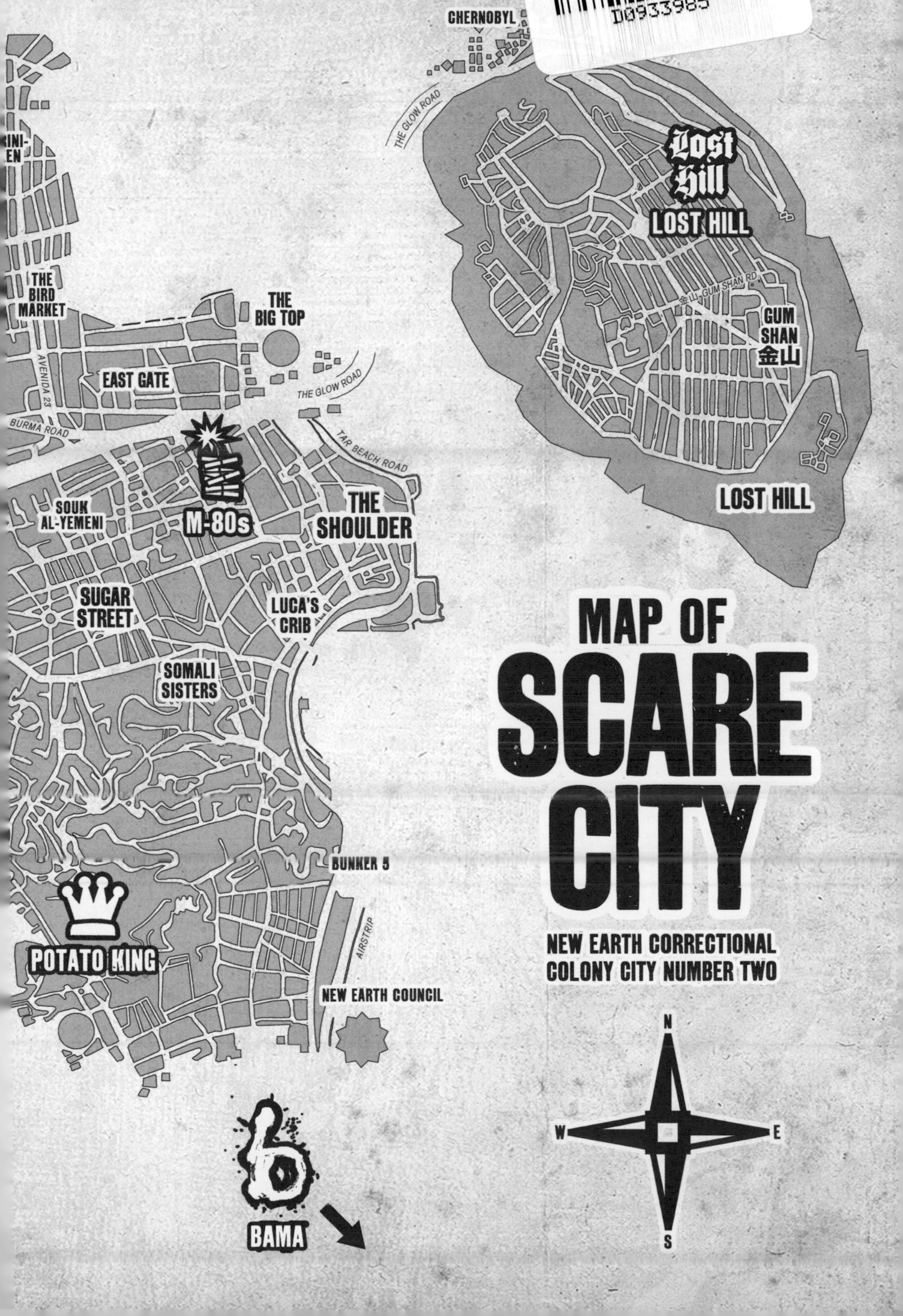
CHERNOBYL
THE GLOW ROAD
Lost Hill
LOST HILL
金山 GUM SHAN RD
GUM SHAN 金山
LOST HILL
THE BIRD MARKET
THE BIG TOP
AVENIDA 23
EAST GATE
THE GLOW ROAD
BURMA ROAD
TAR BEACH ROAD
SOUK AL-YEMENI
M-80s
THE SHOULDER
SUGAR STREET
LUCA'S CRIB
SOMALI SISTERS
BUNKER 5
AIRSTRIP
POTATO KING
NEW EARTH COUNCIL
BAMA
MAP OF SCARE CITY
NEW EARTH CORRECTIONAL COLONY CITY NUMBER TWO
N
W
E
S

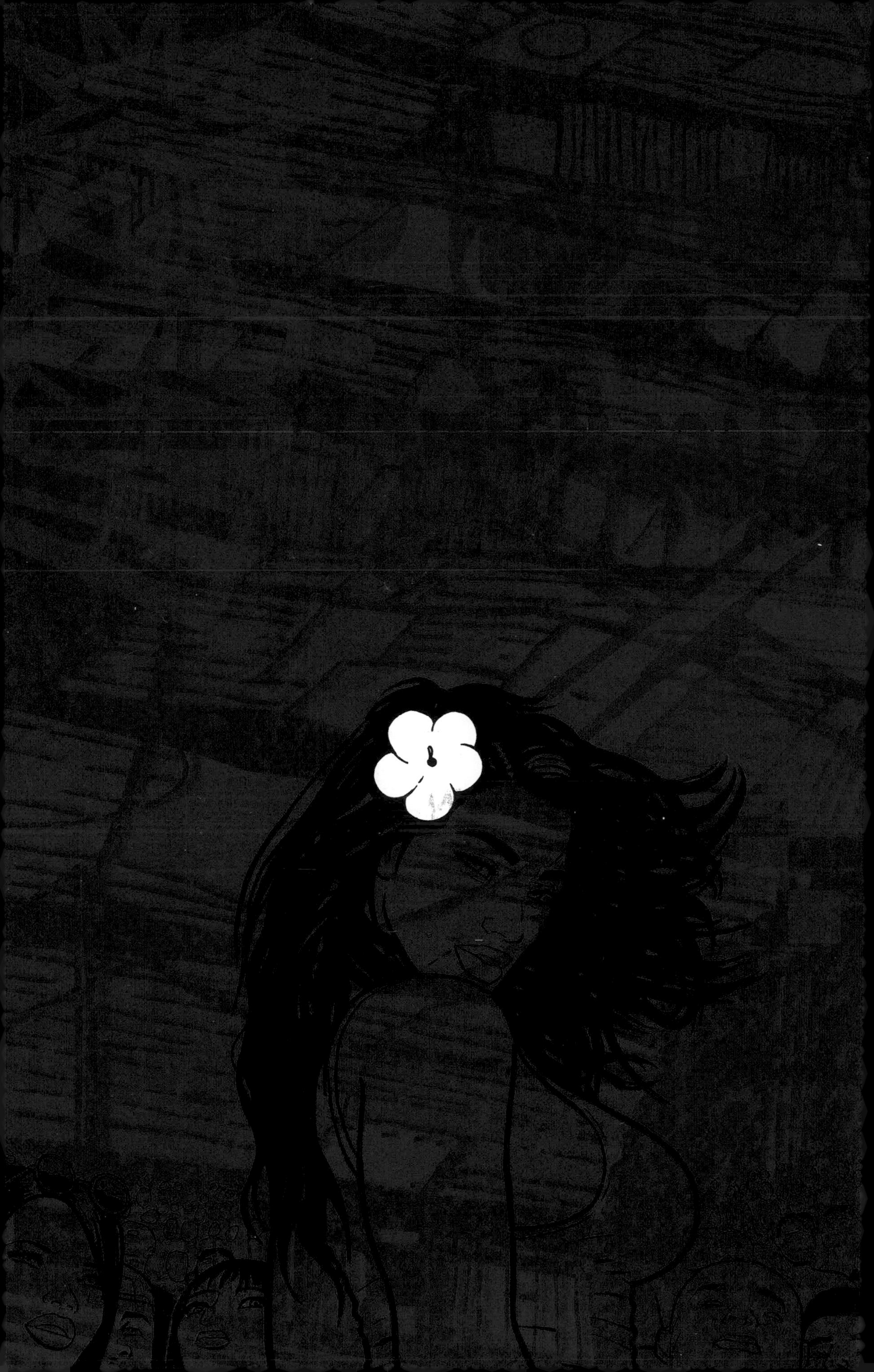

CONCRETE PARK

VOLUME 2: R-E-S-P-E-C-T

WRITTEN BY

TONY PURYEAR AND ERIKA ALEXANDER

ARTWORK, COLORS,
AND LETTERS BY

TONY PURYEAR

CREATED BY

TONY PURYEAR, ERIKA ALEXANDER, AND ROBERT ALEXANDER

TEAM CONCRETE PARK

COLOR ASSISTANT AND INTERN: ALEXANDRA QUINBY
COLOR ASSISTANT: ALICIA BURSTEIN
LEGAL: LICHTER, GROSSMAN, NICHOLS,
ADLER & FELDMAN, INC.

3D VEHICLE MODEL "WEAZEL" BY CHRIS "DZFIRE" LOCKE.
3D MECH MODEL "BE02K10" BY MESTOPHALES.
BASKET DRESS DESIGN BY LAURA SIRKIN BROWN.

VISIT CONCRETEPARK.COM

DARK HORSE BOOKS

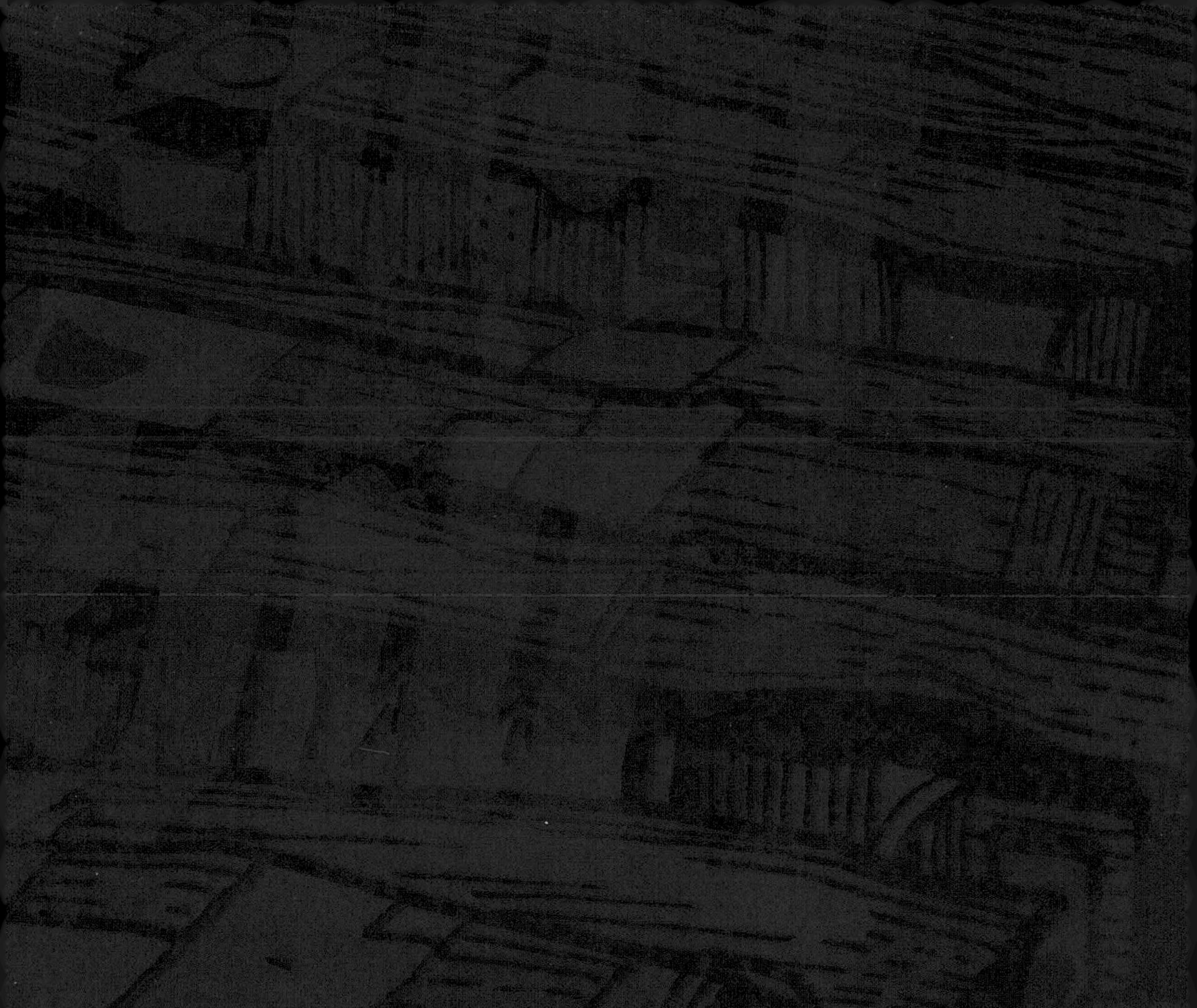

Publisher .... MIKE RICHARDSON
Editor .... PHILIP R. SIMON
Assistant Editor .... ROXY POLK
Designers .... RICK DeLUCCO WITH NICK JAMES
Digital Production .... CHRISTINA McKENZIE

CONCRETE PARK VOLUME 2: R-E-S-P-E-C-T
Text and illustrations of Concrete Park™ © 2014, 2015 Concrete Park, Inc. All other material, unless otherwise specified, is © 2015 Dark Horse Comics, Inc. Dark Horse Books® and the Dark Horse logo are registered trademarks of Dark Horse Comics, Inc. All rights reserved. No portion of this publication may be reproduced or transmitted, in any form or by any means, without the express written permission of Dark Horse Comics, Inc. Names, characters, places, and incidents featured in this publication either are the product of the author's imagination or are used fictitiously. Any resemblance to actual persons (living or dead), events, institutions, or locales, without satiric intent, is coincidental.

PUBLISHED BY
DARK HORSE BOOKS
A DIVISION OF DARK HORSE COMICS, INC.
10956 SE MAIN STREET
MILWAUKIE, OR 97222

DARKHORSE.COM | CONCRETEPARK.COM

TO FIND A COMICS SHOP IN YOUR AREA, CALL THE COMIC SHOP LOCATOR SERVICE TOLL-FREE AT 1-888-266-4226.

FIRST EDITION: APRIL 2015
ISBN 978-1-61655-633-4

10 9 8 7 6 5 4 3 2 1

PRINTED IN CHINA

MIKE RICHARDSON PRESIDENT AND PUBLISHER • **NEIL HANKERSON** EXECUTIVE VICE PRESIDENT • **TOM WEDDLE** CHIEF FINANCIAL OFFICER • **RANDY STRADLEY** VICE PRESIDENT OF PUBLISHING • **MICHAEL MARTENS** VICE PRESIDENT OF BOOK TRADE SALES • **SCOTT ALLIE** EDITOR IN CHIEF • **MATT PARKINSON** VICE PRESIDENT OF MARKETING • **DAVID SCROGGY** VICE PRESIDENT OF PRODUCT DEVELOPMENT • **DALE LaFOUNTAIN** VICE PRESIDENT OF INFORMATION TECHNOLOGY • **DARLENE VOGEL** SENIOR DIRECTOR OF PRINT, DESIGN, AND PRODUCTION • **KEN LIZZI** GENERAL COUNSEL • **DAVEY ESTRADA** EDITORIAL DIRECTOR • **CHRIS WARNER** SENIOR BOOKS EDITOR • **DIANA SCHUTZ** EXECUTIVE EDITOR • **CARY GRAZZINI** DIRECTOR OF PRINT AND DEVELOPMENT • **LIA RIBACCHI** ART DIRECTOR • **CARA NIECE** DIRECTOR OF SCHEDULING • **MARK BERNARDI** DIRECTOR OF DIGITAL PUBLISHING

TONY PURYEAR

Thanks to my two amazing co-creators, Erika Alexander and Robert Alexander, for the world and the fun and the struggle. Thanks to my parents, Leon and Dorothy Puryear, for loving every drawing I ever did—but insisting I try harder. Thanks to Lesley, my supportive sister. Thanks to the Zhang family of Shanghai and New York for believing in us. Thanks to Peter Nichols, the best entertainment lawyer in the game and my attorney of twenty years. Thanks to Mike Richardson, the gutsiest publisher in comics—and the nicest. Thanks to Philip Simon, a prince among editors. Thanks, Jim Gibbons. Thanks to the hard-working team at Dark Horse Comics. Thanks to Dan Farr for years of support and love. Thanks to Alicia Burstein and Daniel Presedo. Thanks to Alexandra Quinby. Thanks, again, and love to Erika, for making the world so beautiful.

ERIKA ALEXANDER

Thank you to Rachel Minard, Douglas Phillips, Barnes & Noble, Comics Bug, Black Cat Comics, Meltdown, Laramie Taylor, Sylv Taylor, Brandon Easton, John Jennings, David Walker, Michael Davis, Erica Watson, our social-media family on FB, Twitter, Instagram, and YouTube, Black Girl Nerds, the Visibility Project, Lisa Valdez, the Riemer family, Gary Morris of the David Black Agency, Kim Coles, Sheila Parham Lebwith, my brother Robert, and, of course, Mom. Finally, Tony, you're the Master and the Blaster.

ROBERT ALEXANDER

Thanks to Dyan, Erika, our families, and the visionary who made it all happen . . . Tony Puryear.

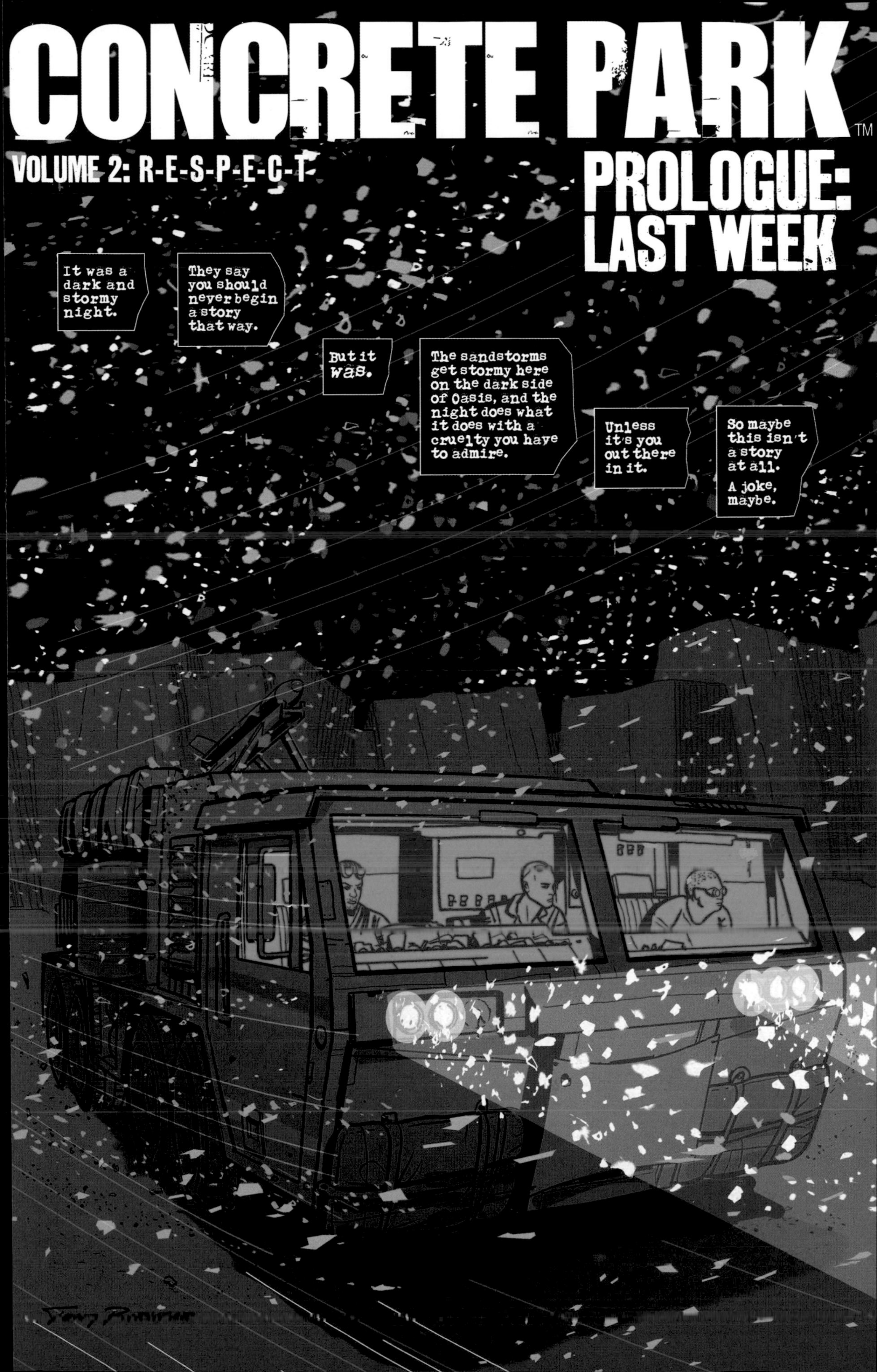
CONCRETE PARK™
VOLUME 2: R-E-S-P-E-C-T
PROLOGUE: LAST WEEK
It was a dark and stormy night.
They say you should never begin a story that way.
But it was.
The sandstorms get stormy here on the dark side of Oasis, and the night does what it does with a cruelty you have to admire.
Unless it's you out there in it.
So maybe this isn't a story at all.
A joke, maybe.

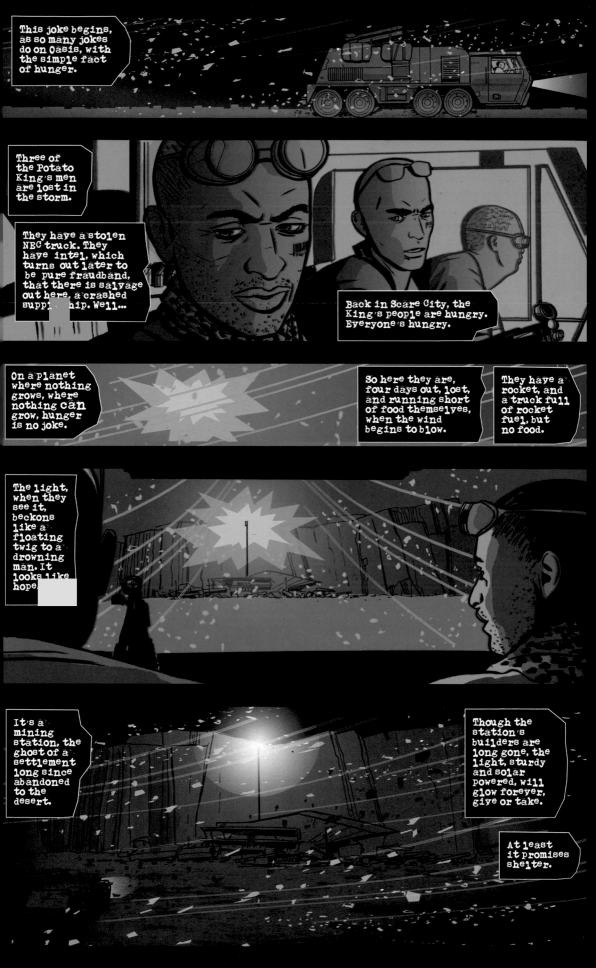

This joke begins, as so many jokes do on Oasis, with the simple fact of hunger.

Three of the Potato King's men are lost in the storm.

They have a stolen NEC truck. They have intel, which turns out later to be pure fraudband, that there is salvage out here, a crashed suppl[?] [?]hip. Well...

Back in Scare City, the King's people are hungry. Everyone's hungry.

On a planet where nothing grows, where nothing can grow, hunger is no joke.

So here they are, four days out, lost, and running short of food themselves, when the wind begins to blow.

They have a rocket, and a truck full of rocket fuel, but no food.

The light, when they see it, beckons like a floating twig to a drowning man. It looks like hope.

It's a mining station, the ghost of a settlement long since abandoned to the desert.

Though the station's builders are long gone, the light, sturdy and solar powered, will glow forever, give or take.

At least it promises shelter.

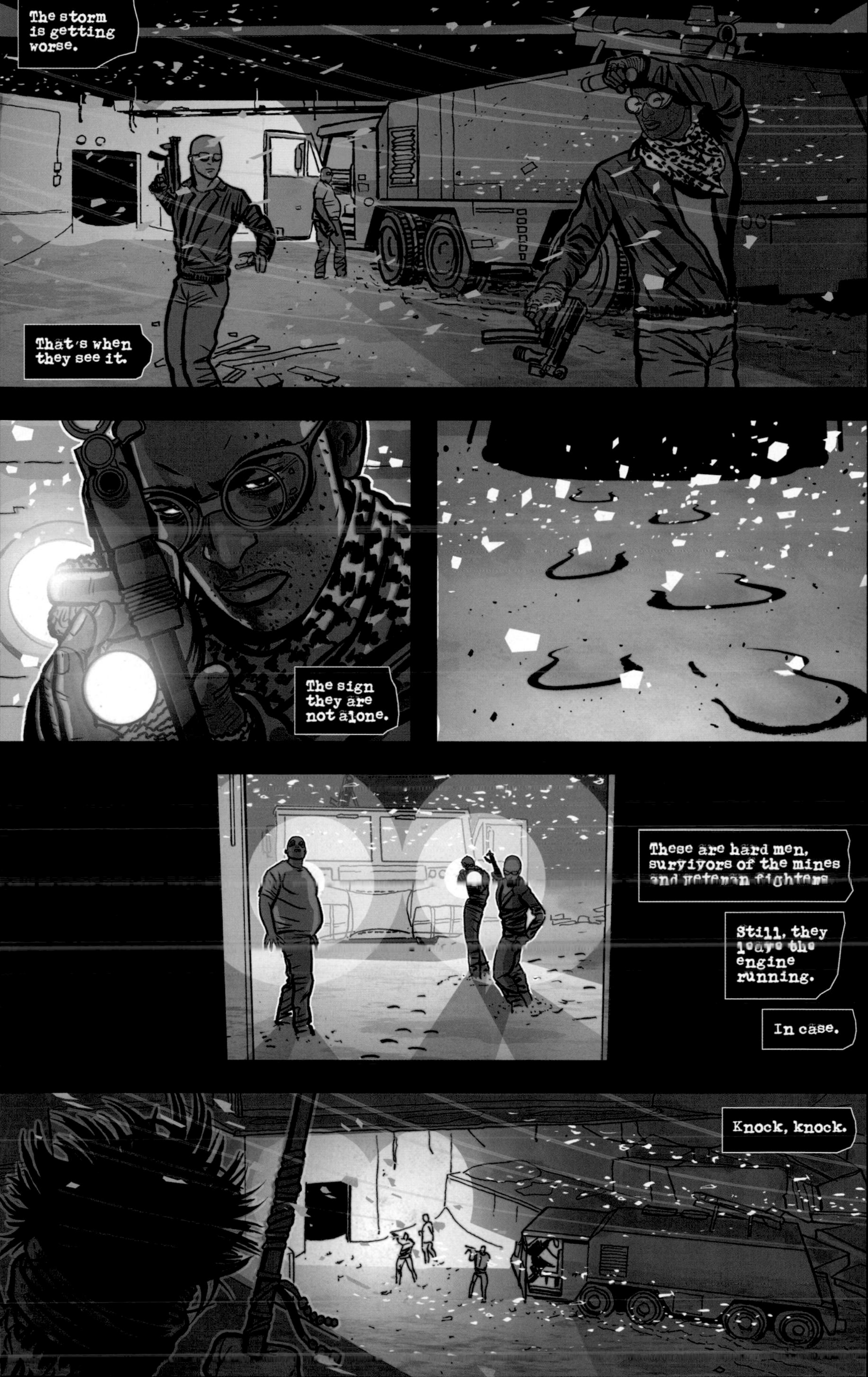
The storm is getting worse.
That's when they see it.
The sign they are not alone.
These are hard men, survivors of the mines and veteran fighters.
Still, they leave the engine running.
In case.
Knock, knock.

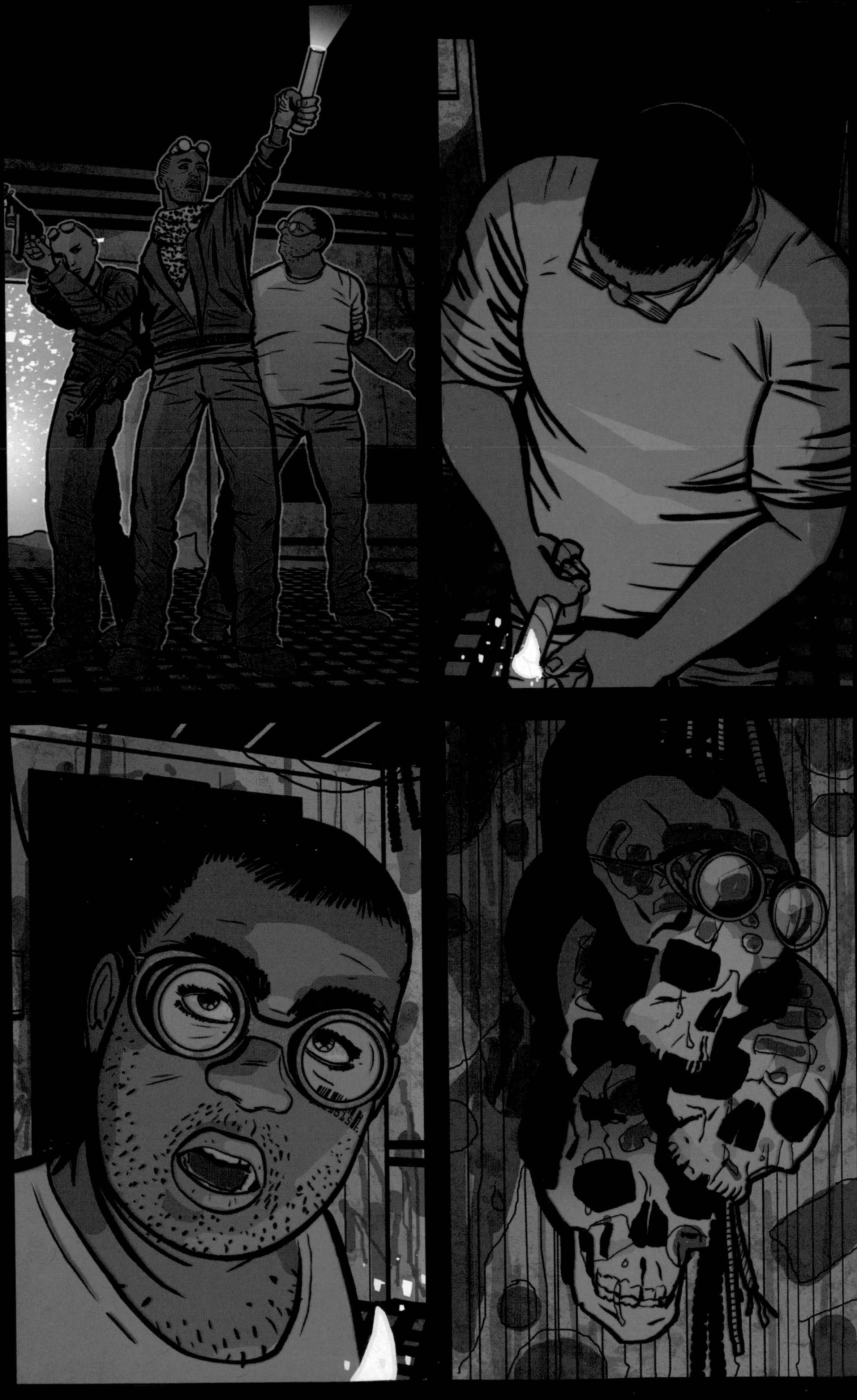

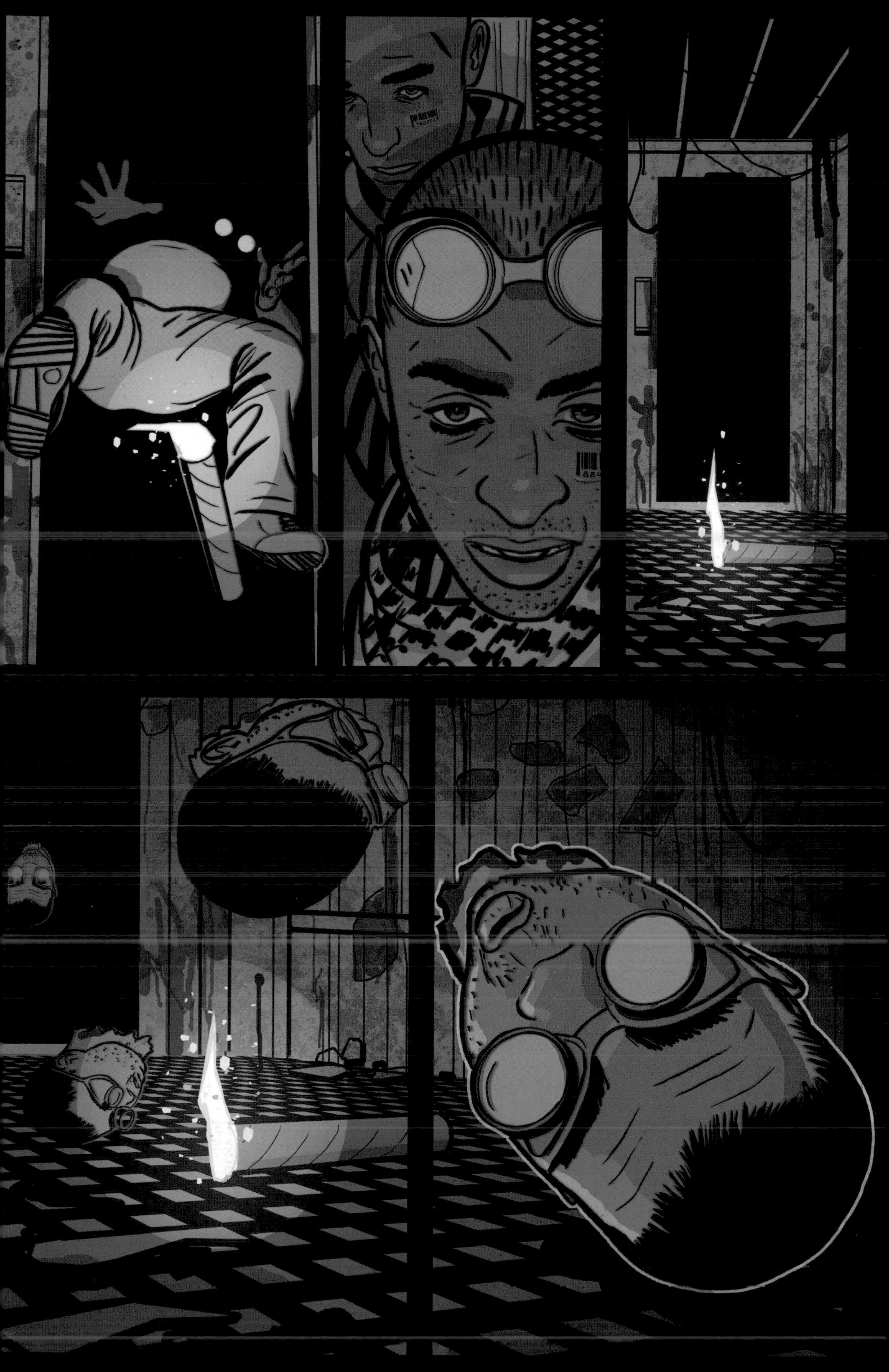

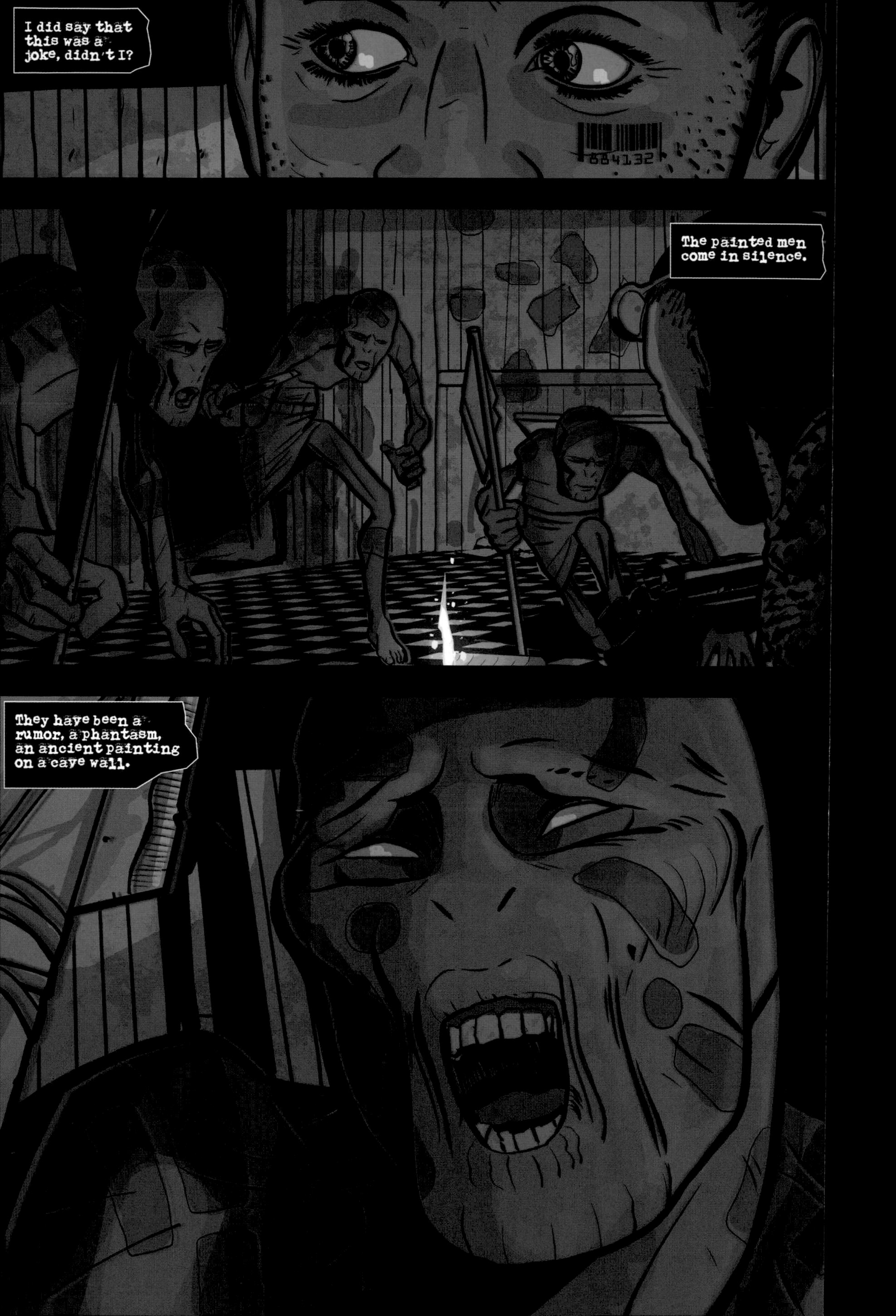
I did say that this was a joke, didn't I?
The painted men come in silence.
They have been a rumor, a phantasm, an ancient painting on a cave wall.

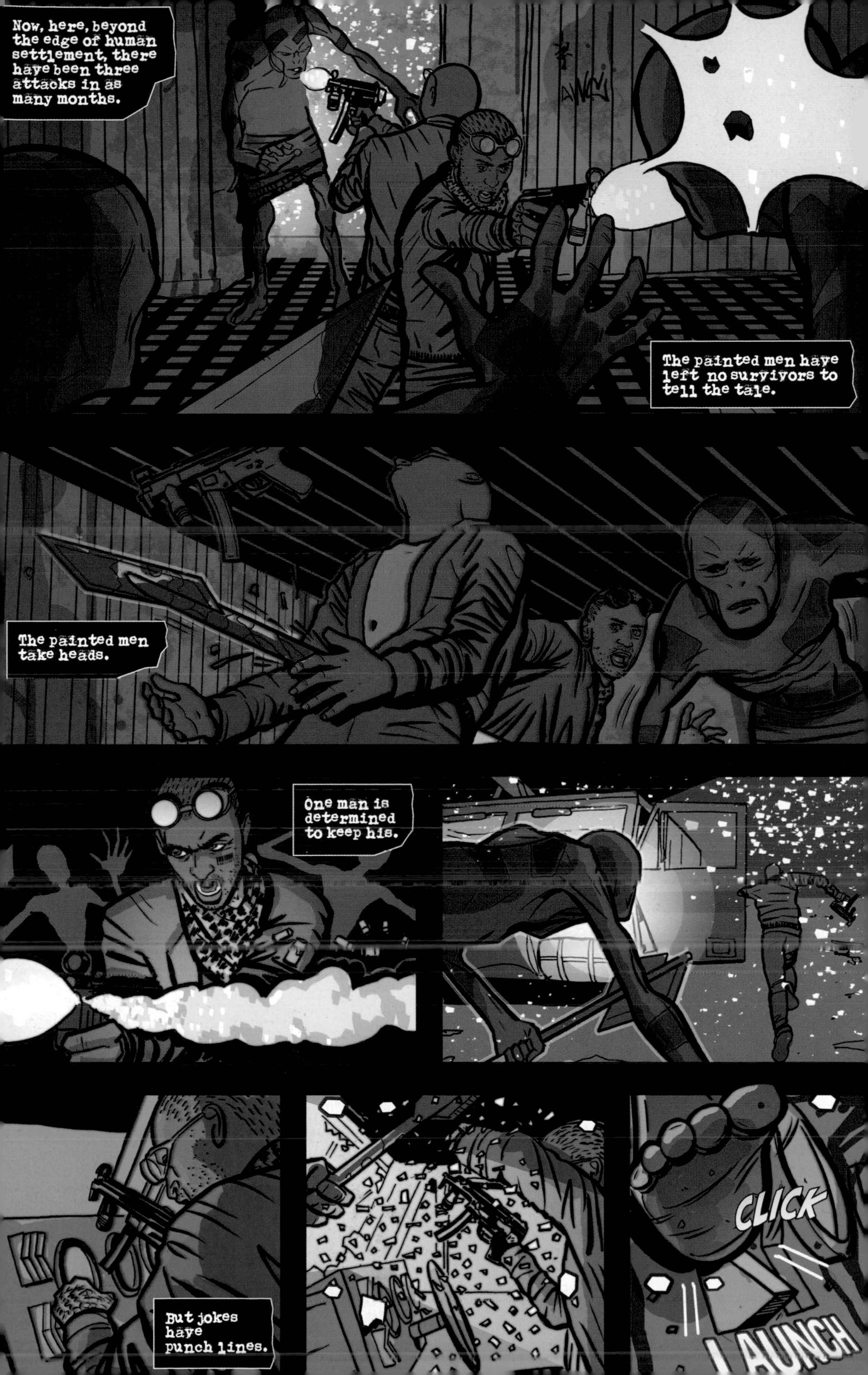
Now, here, beyond the edge of human settlement, there have been three attacks in as many months.
The painted men have left no survivors to tell the tale.
The painted men take heads.
One man is determined to keep his.
But jokes have punch lines.
CLICK
LAUNCH

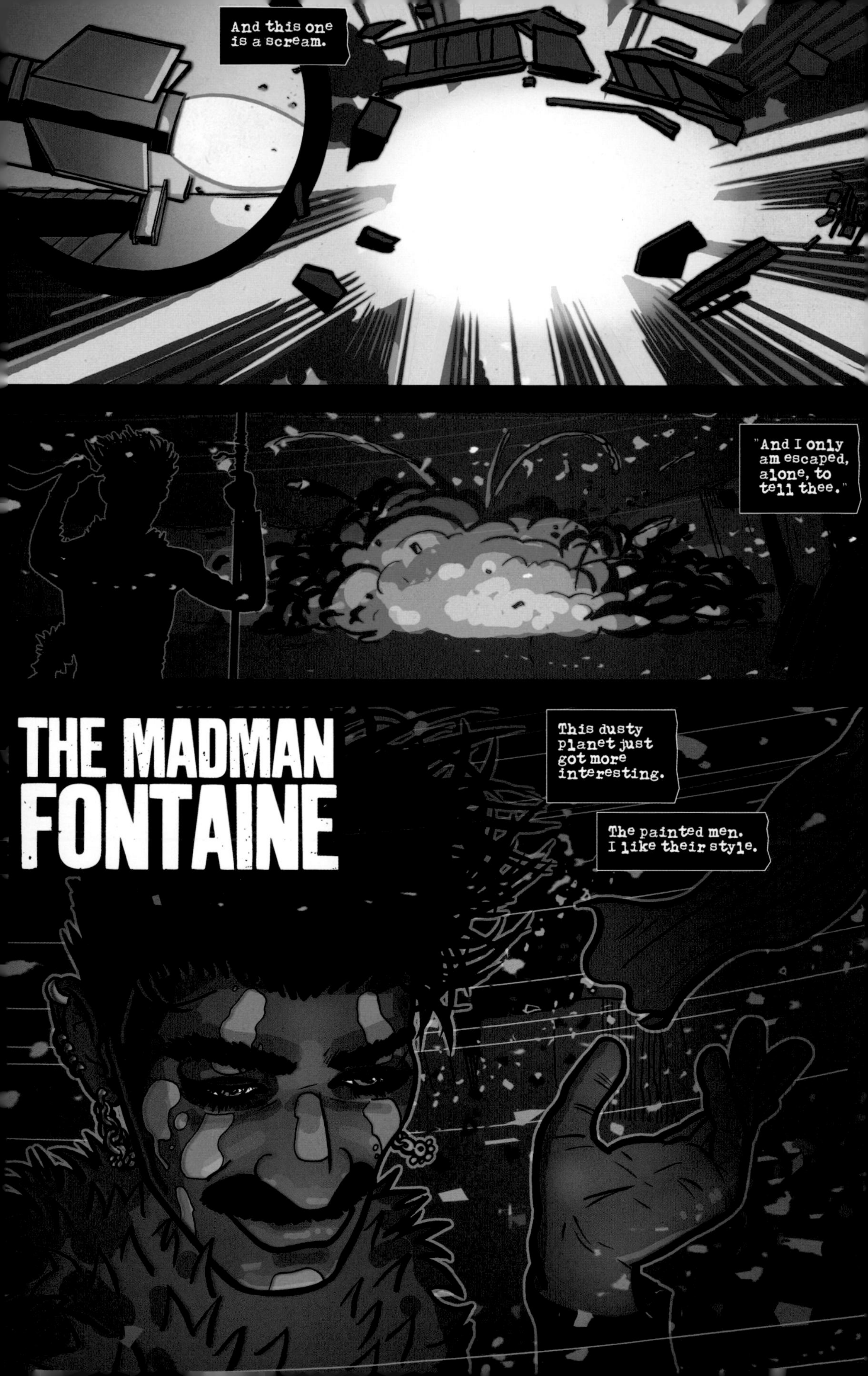
And this one is a scream.
"And I only am escaped, alone, to tell thee."
THE MADMAN FONTAINE
This dusty planet just got more interesting.
The painted men. I like their style.

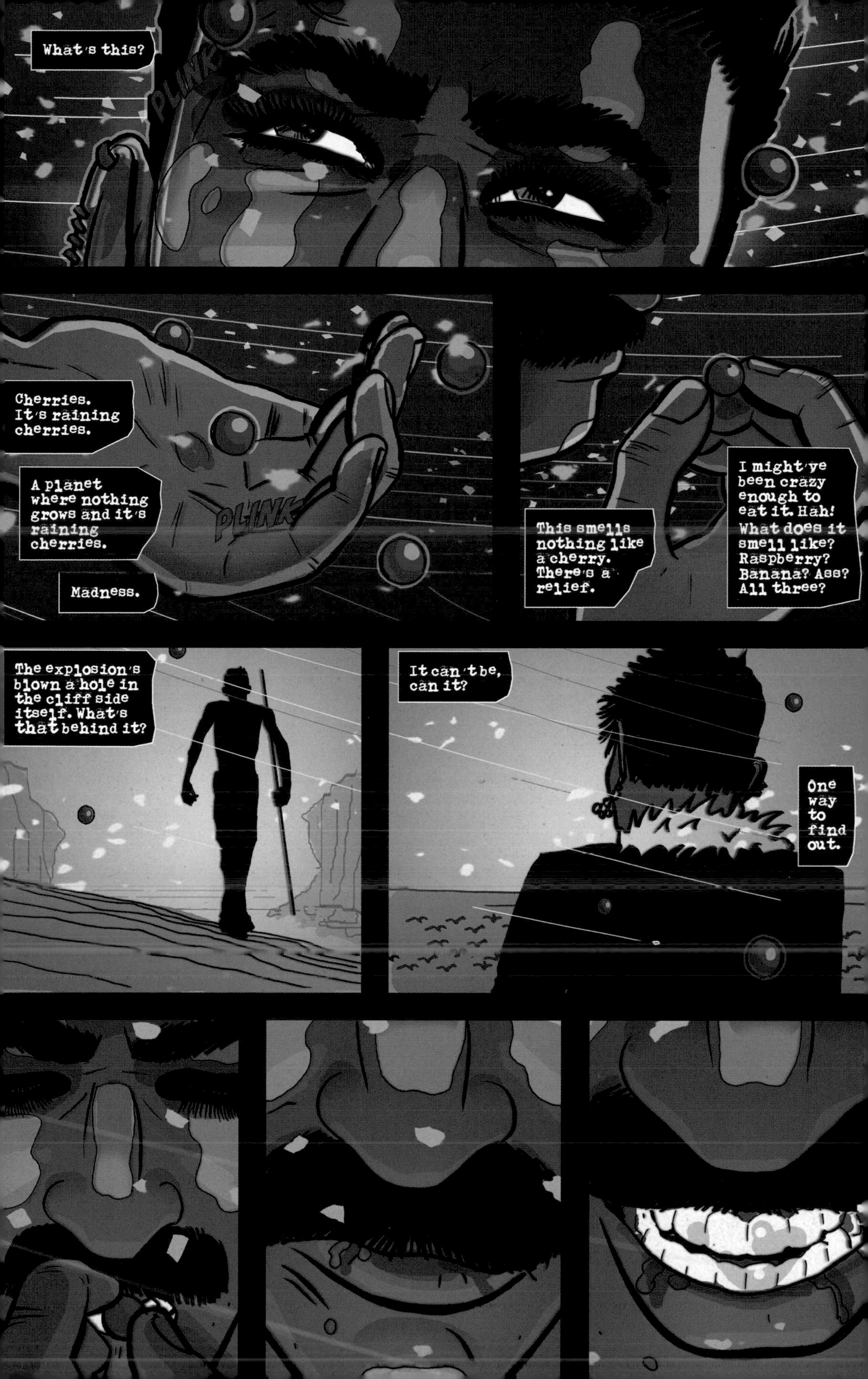
What's this?
PLINK
Cherries. It's raining cherries.
A planet where nothing grows and it's raining cherries.
Madness.
PLINK
This smells nothing like a cherry. There's a relief.
I might've been crazy enough to eat it. Hah! What does it smell like? Raspberry? Banana? Ass? All three?
The explosion's blown a hole in the cliff side itself. What's that behind it?
It can't be, can it?
One way to find out.

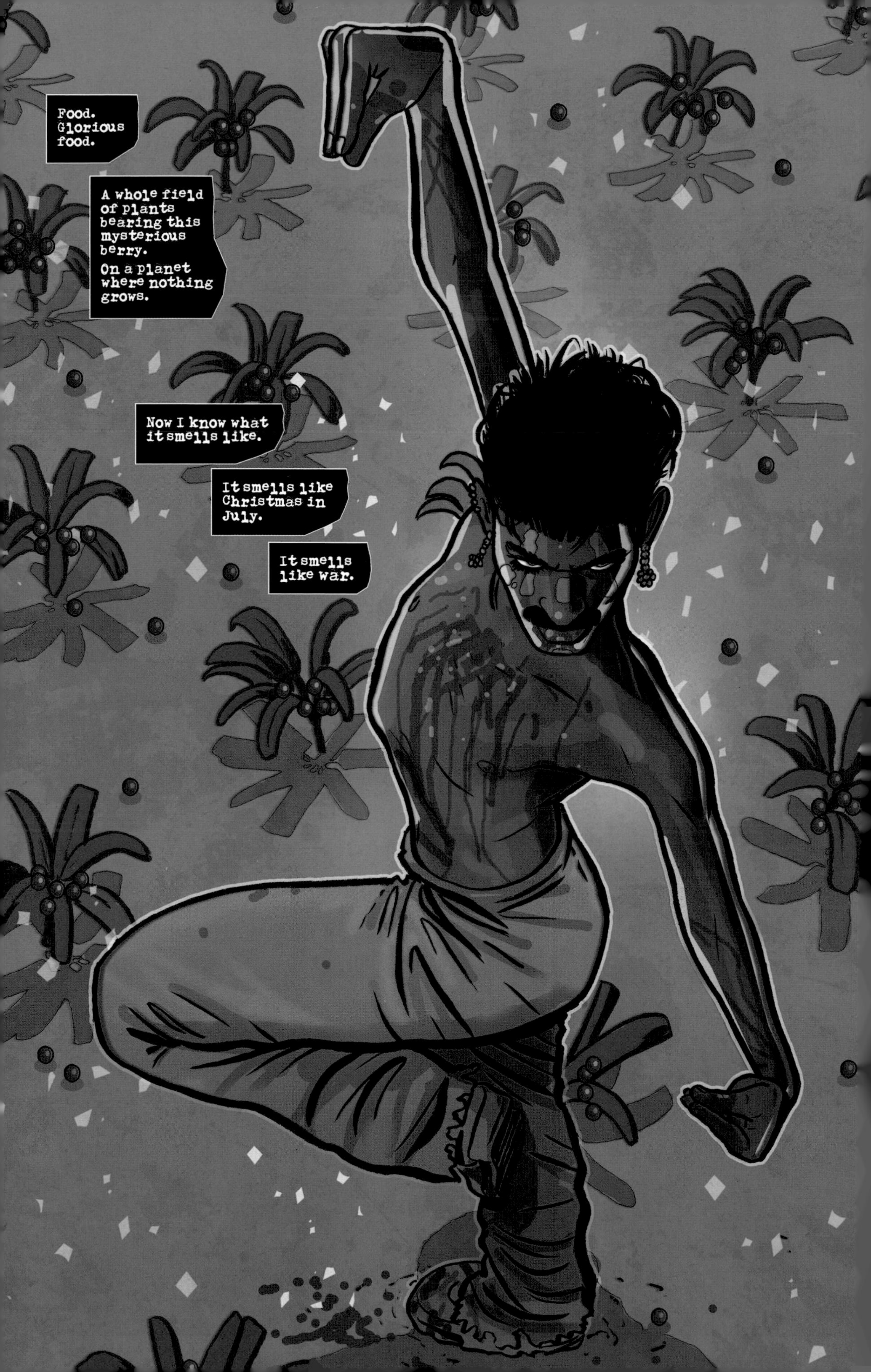

Food. Glorious food.
A whole field of plants bearing this mysterious berry.
On a planet where nothing grows.
Now I know what it smells like.
It smells like Christmas in July.
It smells like war.

"They say we'll die here. But see, I know something they don't. I know where we're going, and it's beautiful."
—Chavez

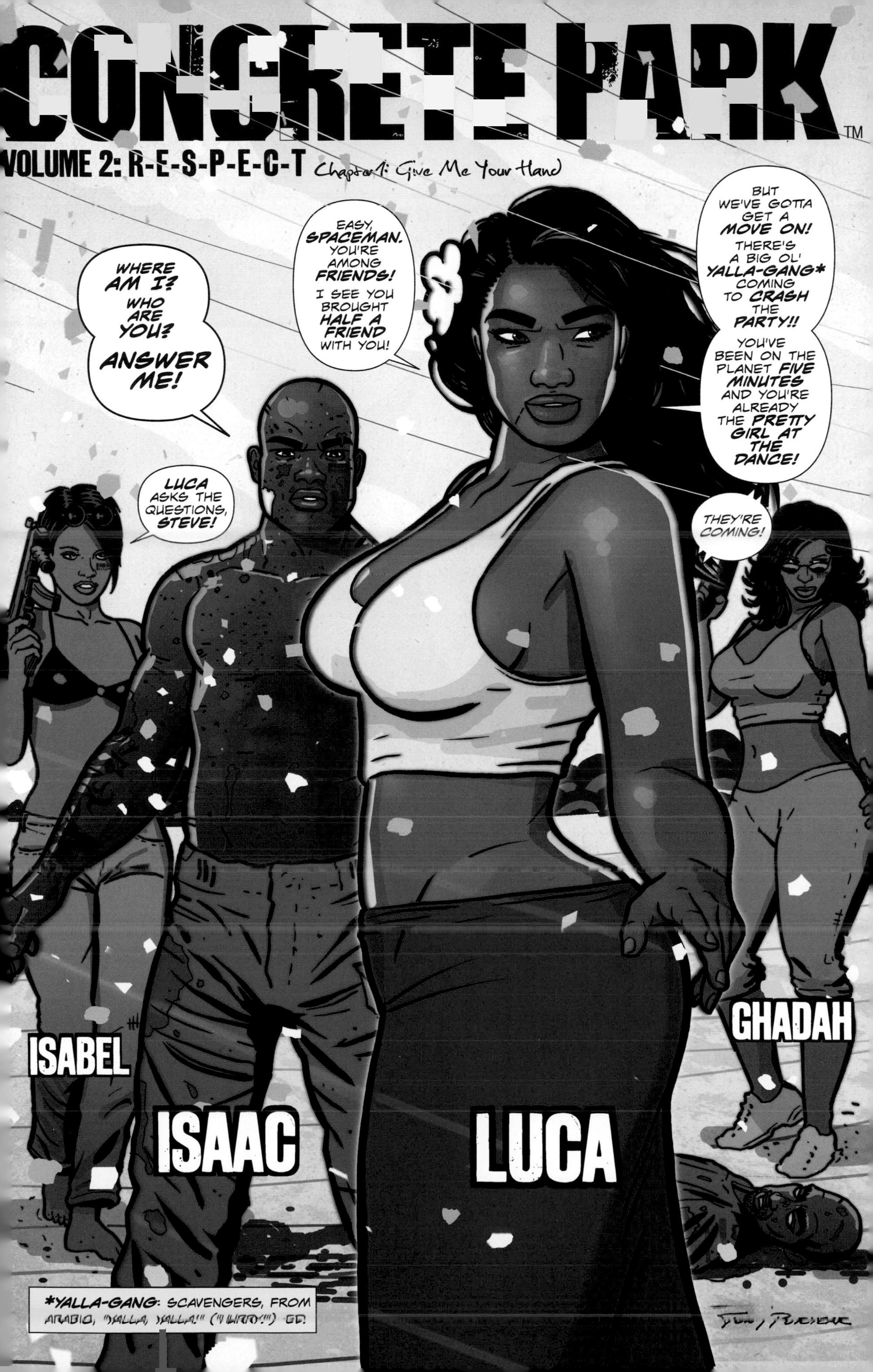
CONCRETE PARK™
VOLUME 2: R-E-S-P-E-C-T Chapter 1: Give Me Your Hand
WHERE AM I? WHO ARE YOU? ANSWER ME!
EASY, SPACEMAN. YOU'RE AMONG FRIENDS! I SEE YOU BROUGHT HALF A FRIEND WITH YOU!
BUT WE'VE GOTTA GET A MOVE ON! THERE'S A BIG OL' YALLA-GANG* COMING TO CRASH THE PARTY!!
YOU'VE BEEN ON THE PLANET FIVE MINUTES AND YOU'RE ALREADY THE PRETTY GIRL AT THE DANCE!
LUCA ASKS THE QUESTIONS, STEVE!
THEY'RE COMING!
ISABEL
ISAAC
LUCA
GHADAH
*YALLA-GANG: SCAVENGERS, FROM ARABIC, "YALLA, YALLA!" ("HURRY!") ED.

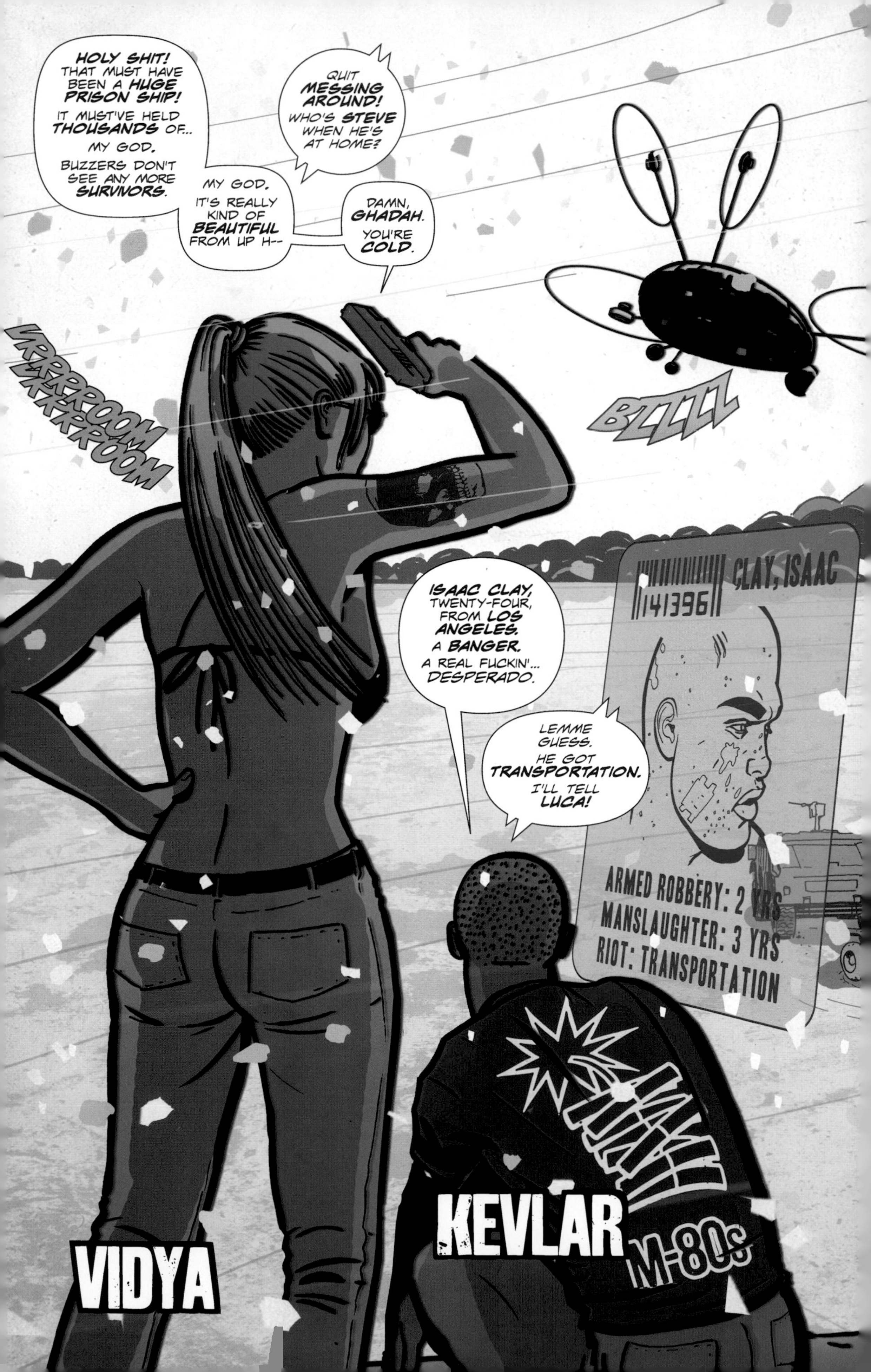
HOLY SHIT! THAT MUST HAVE BEEN A HUGE PRISON SHIP! IT MUST'VE HELD THOUSANDS OF... MY GOD. BUZZERS DON'T SEE ANY MORE SURVIVORS.
QUIT MESSING AROUND! WHO'S STEVE WHEN HE'S AT HOME?
MY GOD. IT'S REALLY KIND OF BEAUTIFUL FROM UP H--
DAMN, GHADAH. YOU'RE COLD.
VRRRROOM VRRRROOM
BZZZZ
ISAAC CLAY, TWENTY-FOUR, FROM LOS ANGELES. A BANGER. A REAL FUCKIN'... DESPERADO.
LEMME GUESS. HE GOT TRANSPORTATION. I'LL TELL LUCA!
CLAY, ISAAC
141396
ARMED ROBBERY: 2 YRS
MANSLAUGHTER: 3 YRS
RIOT: TRANSPORTATION
VIDYA
KEVLAR
M-80s

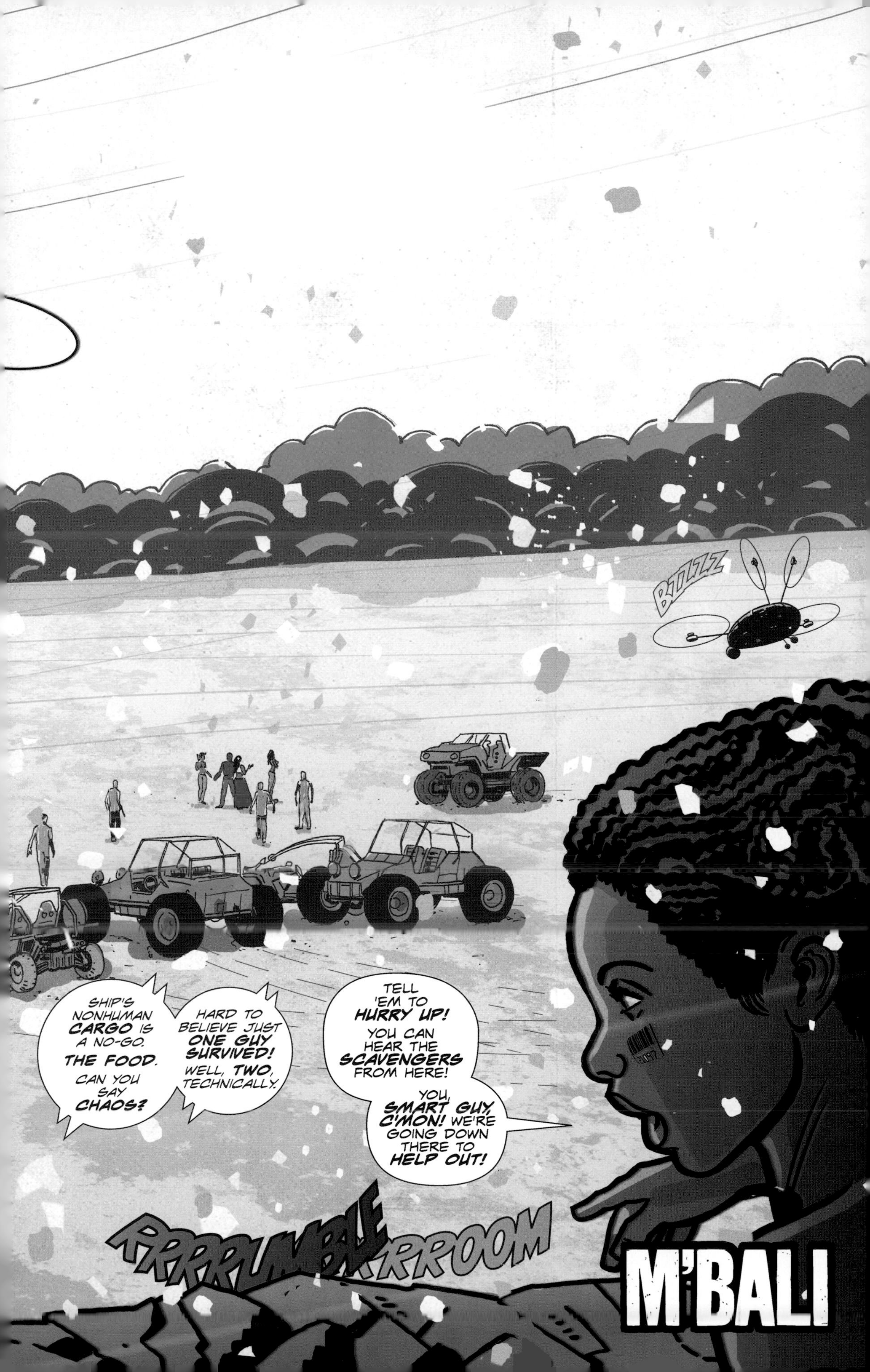
BZZZZ
SHIP'S NONHUMAN CARGO IS A NO-GO. THE FOOD. CAN YOU SAY CHAOS?
HARD TO BELIEVE JUST ONE GUY SURVIVED! WELL, TWO, TECHNICALLY.
TELL 'EM TO HURRY UP! YOU CAN HEAR THE SCAVENGERS FROM HERE!
YOU, SMART GUY, C'MON! WE'RE GOING DOWN THERE TO HELP OUT!
RRRRUMBLE
RRROOM
M'BALI

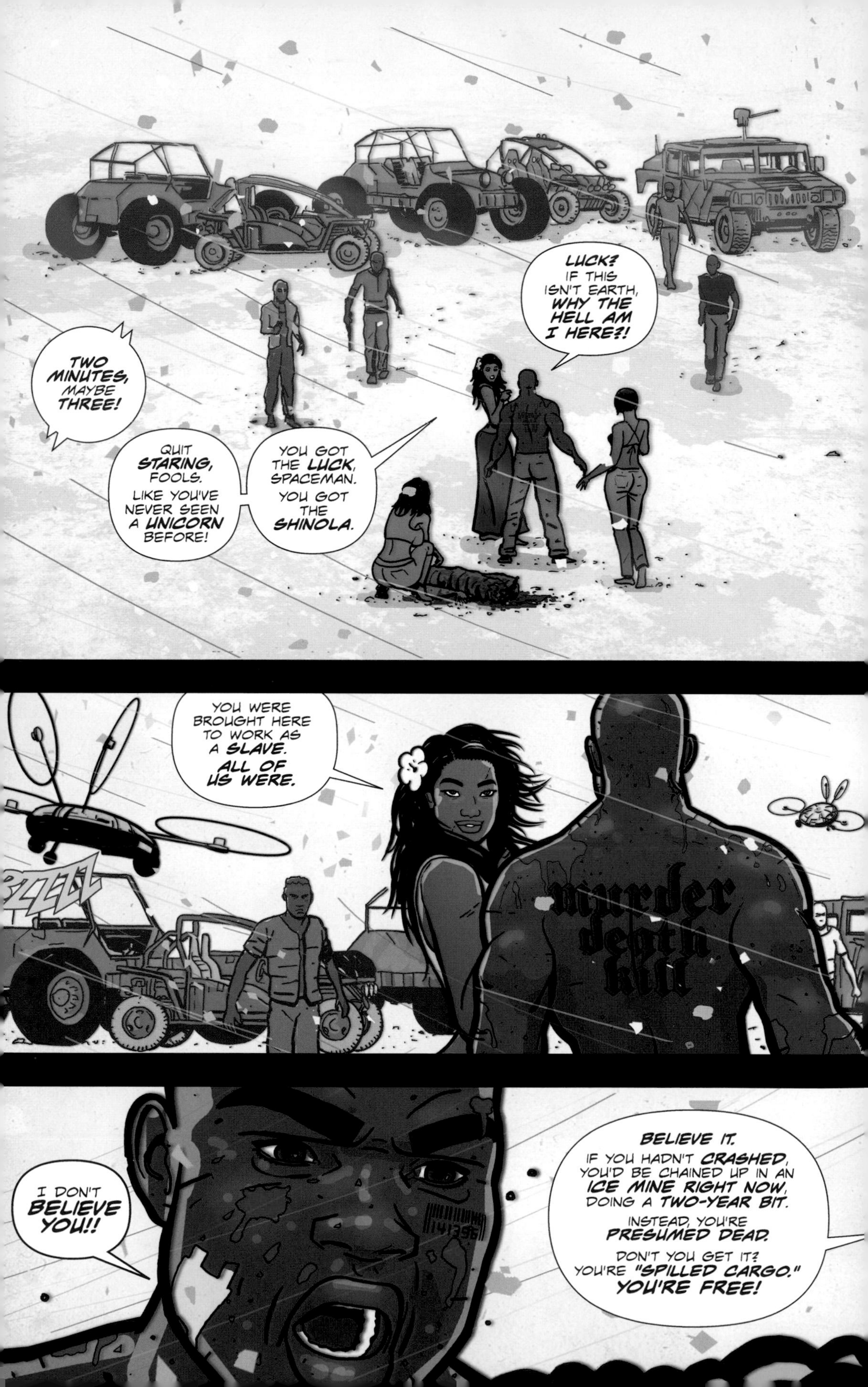
TWO MINUTES, MAYBE THREE!
QUIT STARING, FOOLS. LIKE YOU'VE NEVER SEEN A UNICORN BEFORE!
YOU GOT THE LUCK, SPACEMAN. YOU GOT THE SHINOLA.
LUCK? IF THIS ISN'T EARTH, WHY THE HELL AM I HERE?!
YOU WERE BROUGHT HERE TO WORK AS A SLAVE. ALL OF US WERE.
I DON'T BELIEVE YOU!!
BELIEVE IT.
IF YOU HADN'T CRASHED, YOU'D BE CHAINED UP IN AN ICE MINE RIGHT NOW, DOING A TWO-YEAR BIT.
INSTEAD, YOU'RE PRESUMED DEAD.
DON'T YOU GET IT? YOU'RE "SPILLED CARGO." YOU'RE FREE!

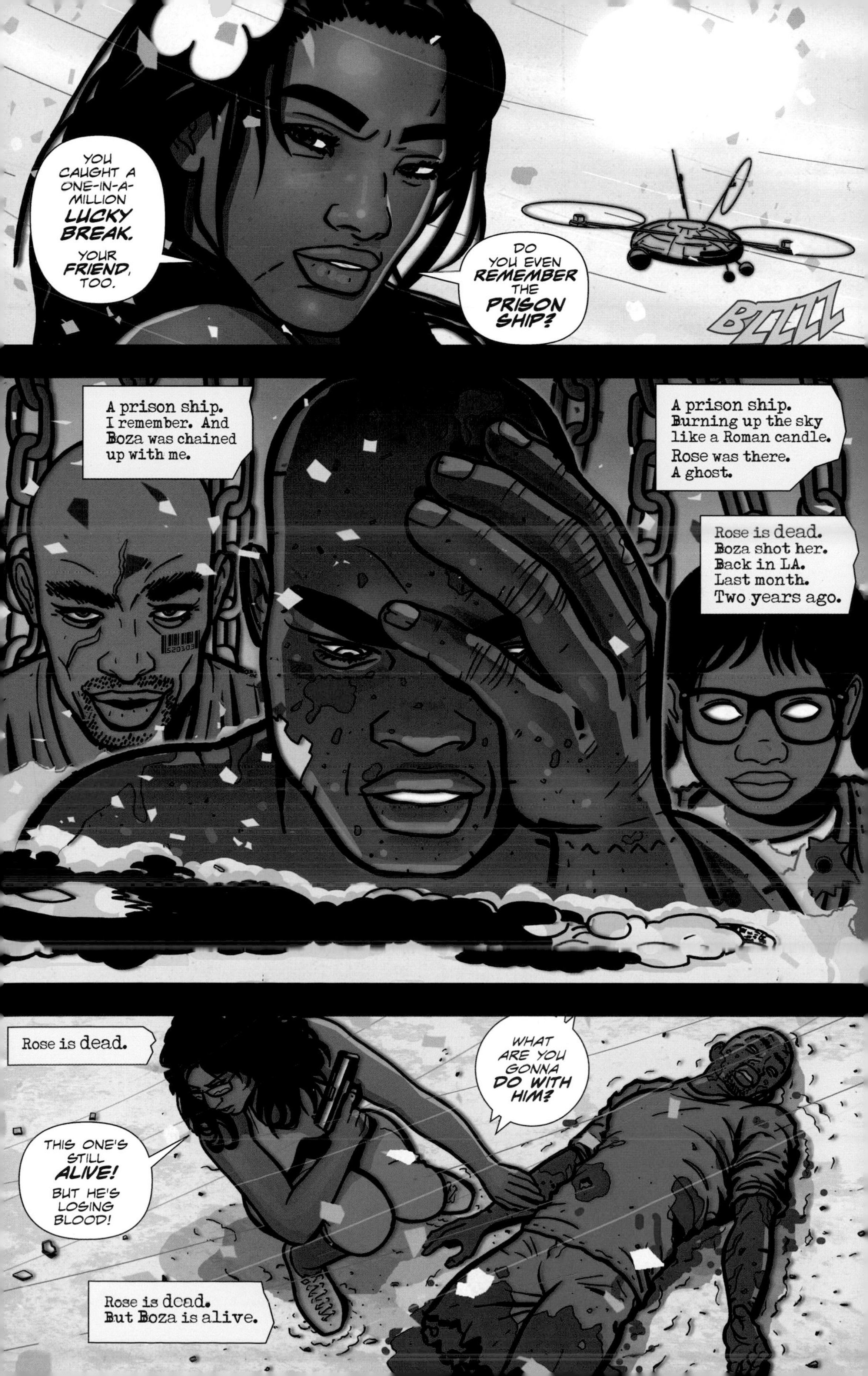
YOU CAUGHT A ONE-IN-A-MILLION LUCKY BREAK.
YOUR FRIEND, TOO.
DO YOU EVEN REMEMBER THE PRISON SHIP?
BZZZZ
A prison ship. I remember. And Boza was chained up with me.
A prison ship. Burning up the sky like a Roman candle.
Rose was there. A ghost.
Rose is dead. Boza shot her. Back in LA. Last month. Two years ago.
Rose is dead.
WHAT ARE YOU GONNA DO WITH HIM?
THIS ONE'S STILL ALIVE! BUT HE'S LOSING BLOOD!
Rose is dead. But Boza is alive.

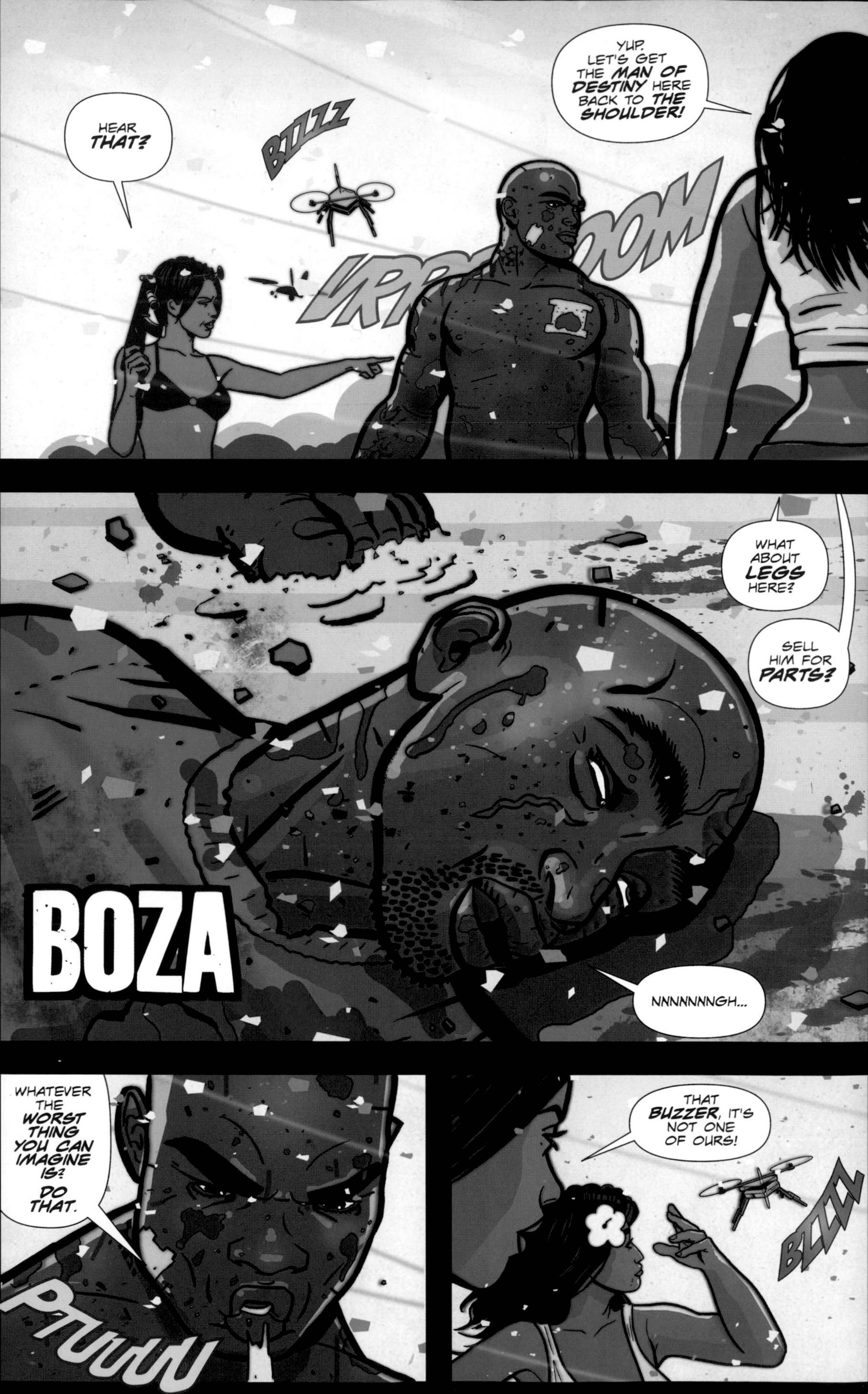
HEAR THAT?
BZZZZ
YUP. LET'S GET THE MAN OF DESTINY HERE BACK TO THE SHOULDER!
WHAT ABOUT LEGS HERE?
SELL HIM FOR PARTS?
BOZA
NNNNNNNGH...
WHATEVER THE WORST THING YOU CAN IMAGINE IS? DO THAT.
PTUUU
THAT BUZZER, IT'S NOT ONE OF OURS!
BZZZZ

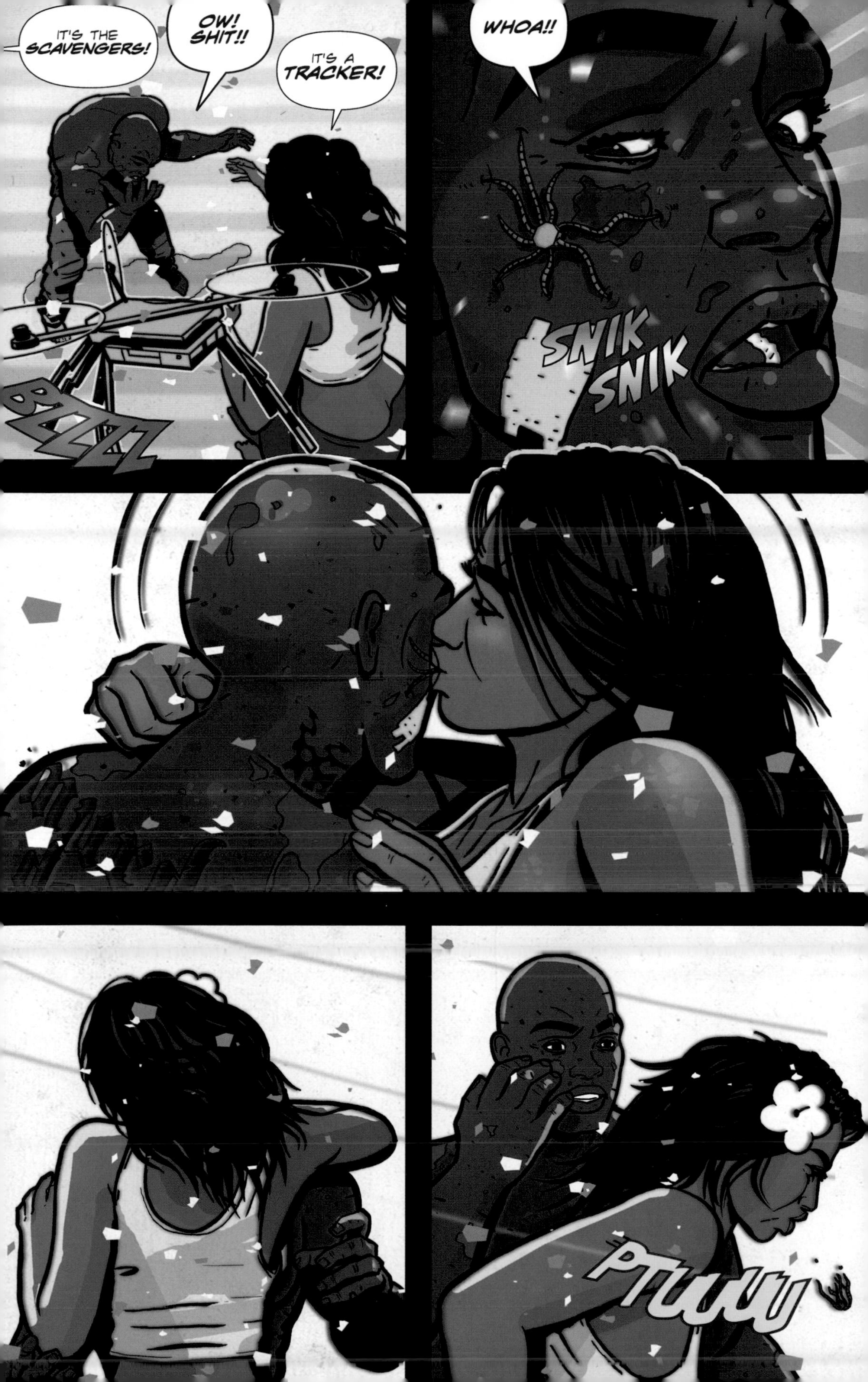
IT'S THE SCAVENGERS!
OW! SHIT!!
IT'S A TRACKER!
BZZZZ
WHOA!!
SNIK SNIK
PTUUU

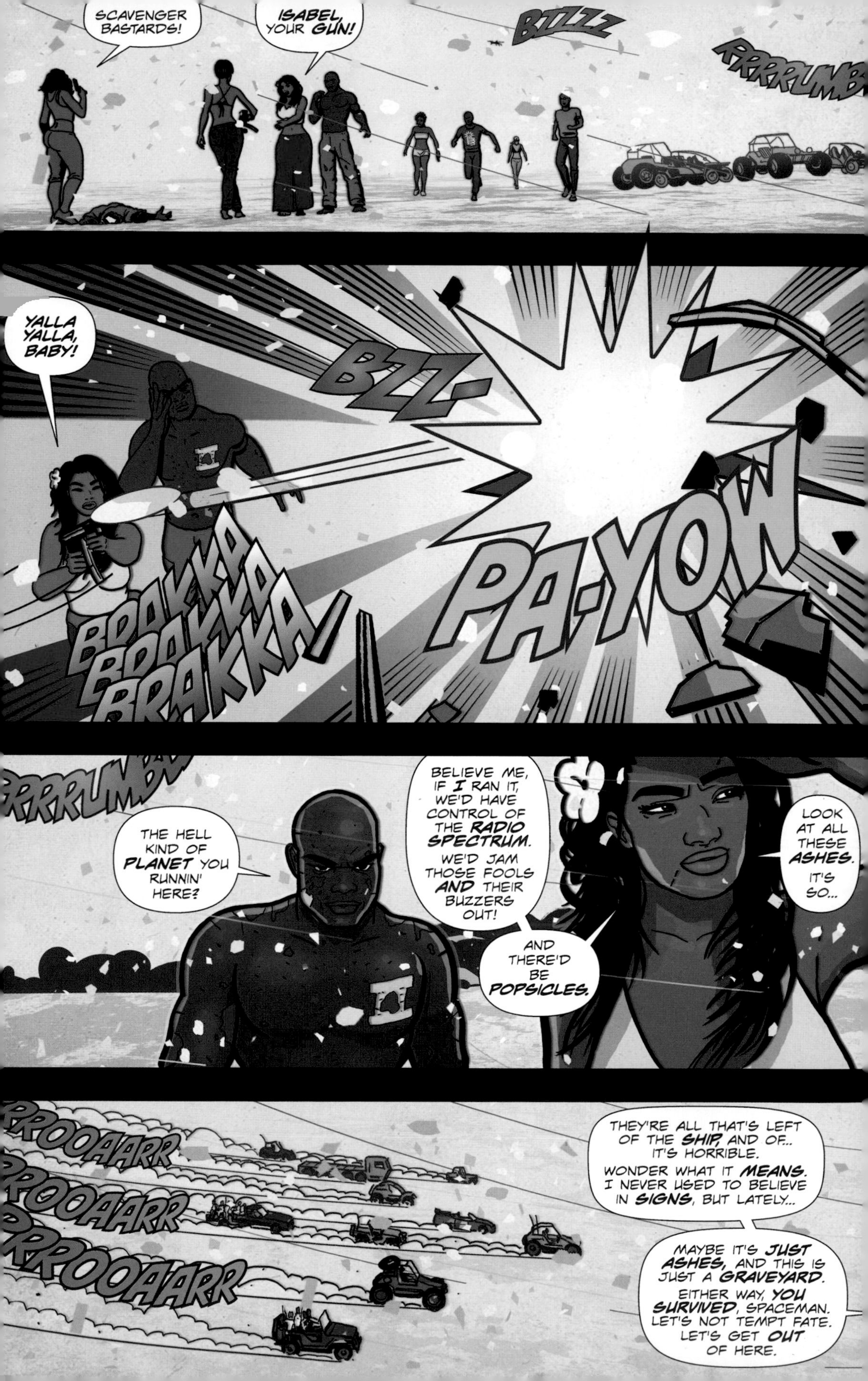
SCAVENGER BASTARDS!
ISABEL, YOUR GUN!
BZZZZ
RRRRUMB
YALLA YALLA, BABY!
BZZ-
BOOKKA BOOKKA BRAKKA
PA-YOW
RRRRUMB
THE HELL KIND OF PLANET YOU RUNNIN' HERE?
BELIEVE ME, IF I RAN IT, WE'D HAVE CONTROL OF THE RADIO SPECTRUM. WE'D JAM THOSE FOOLS AND THEIR BUZZERS OUT!
AND THERE'D BE POPSICLES.
LOOK AT ALL THESE ASHES. IT'S SO...
RROOAARR
RROOAARR
RROOAARR
THEY'RE ALL THAT'S LEFT OF THE SHIP, AND OF... IT'S HORRIBLE. WONDER WHAT IT MEANS. I NEVER USED TO BELIEVE IN SIGNS, BUT LATELY...
MAYBE IT'S JUST ASHES, AND THIS IS JUST A GRAVEYARD. EITHER WAY, YOU SURVIVED, SPACEMAN. LET'S NOT TEMPT FATE. LET'S GET OUT OF HERE.

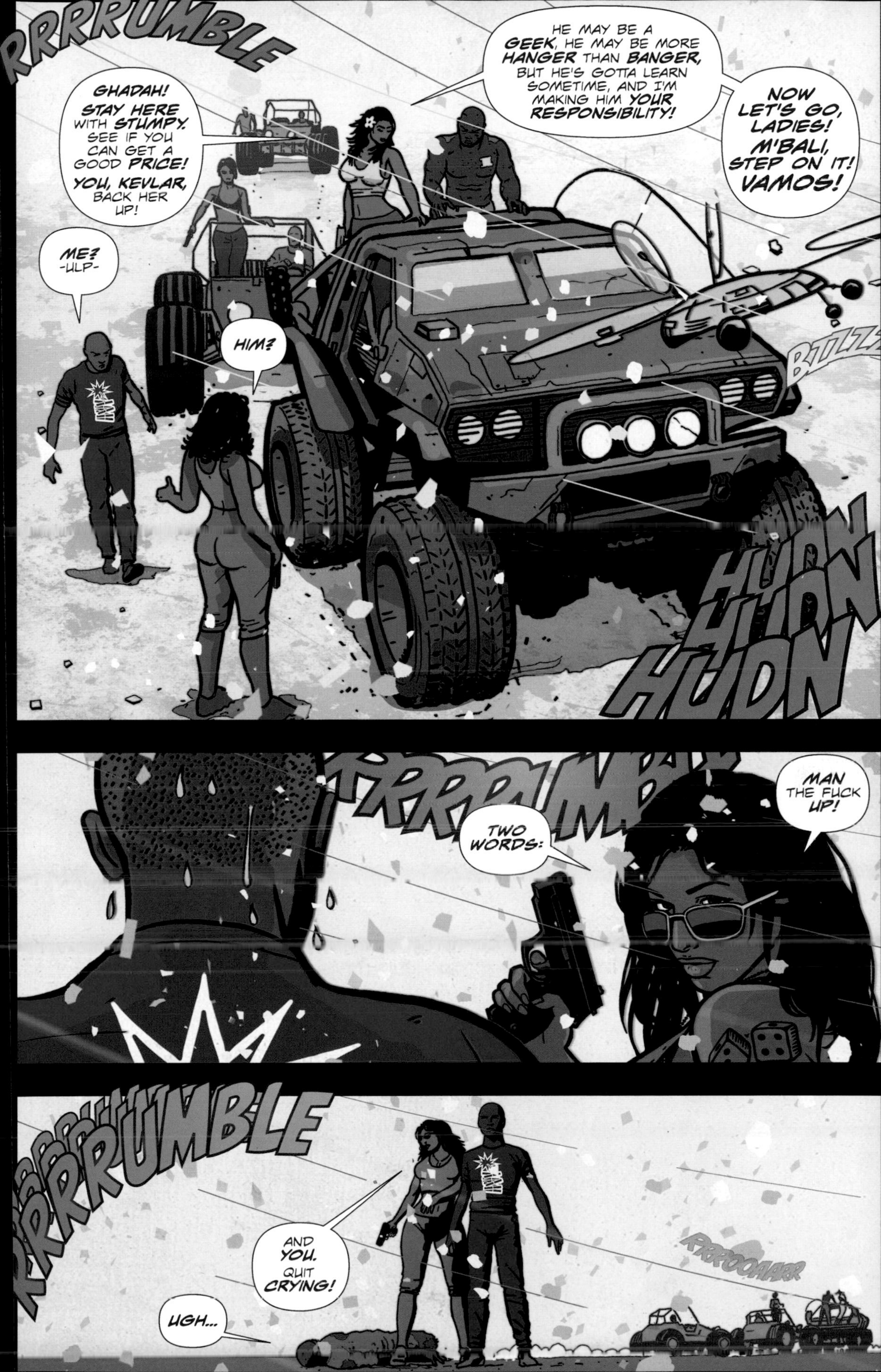
RRRRUMBLE
GHADAH! STAY HERE WITH STUMPY. SEE IF YOU CAN GET A GOOD PRICE! YOU, KEVLAR, BACK HER UP!
HE MAY BE A GEEK, HE MAY BE MORE HANGER THAN BANGER, BUT HE'S GOTTA LEARN SOMETIME, AND I'M MAKING HIM YOUR RESPONSIBILITY!
NOW LET'S GO, LADIES! M'BALI, STEP ON IT! VAMOS!
ME? -ULP-
HIM?
HUDN HUDN HUDN
RRRRUMBLE
TWO WORDS:
MAN THE FUCK UP!
RRRRUMBLE
AND YOU. QUIT CRYING!
UGH...
RRROOAARR

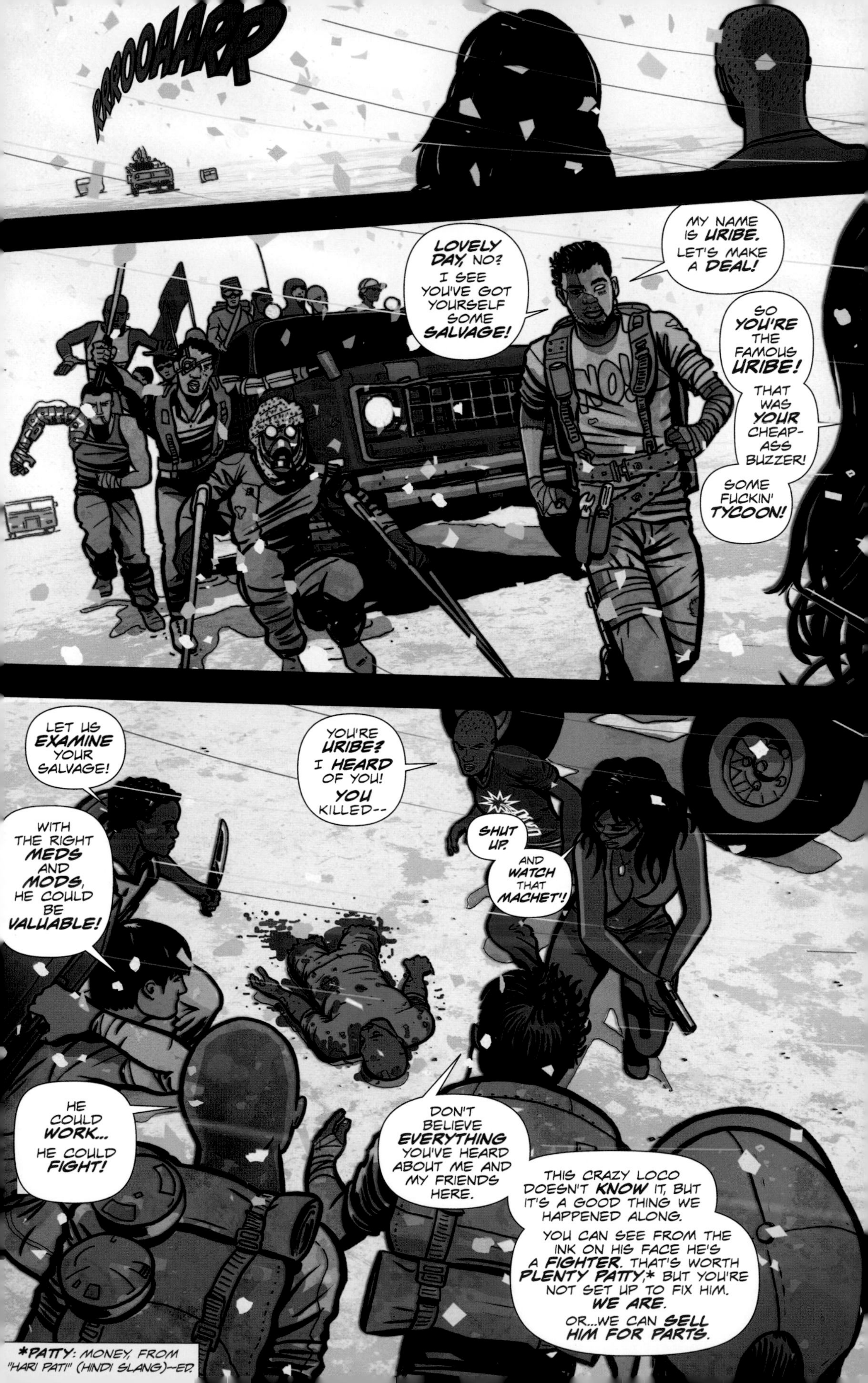
RRROOAARR
LOVELY DAY, NO? I SEE YOU'VE GOT YOURSELF SOME SALVAGE!
MY NAME IS URIBE. LET'S MAKE A DEAL!
SO YOU'RE THE FAMOUS URIBE!
THAT WAS YOUR CHEAP-ASS BUZZER!
SOME FUCKIN' TYCOON!
LET US EXAMINE YOUR SALVAGE!
WITH THE RIGHT MEDS AND MODS, HE COULD BE VALUABLE!
YOU'RE URIBE? I HEARD OF YOU! YOU KILLED--
SHUT UP.
AND WATCH THAT MACHET'!
HE COULD WORK... HE COULD FIGHT!
DON'T BELIEVE EVERYTHING YOU'VE HEARD ABOUT ME AND MY FRIENDS HERE.
THIS CRAZY LOCO DOESN'T KNOW IT, BUT IT'S A GOOD THING WE HAPPENED ALONG.
YOU CAN SEE FROM THE INK ON HIS FACE HE'S A FIGHTER. THAT'S WORTH PLENTY PATTY,* BUT YOU'RE NOT SET UP TO FIX HIM. WE ARE.
OR...WE CAN SELL HIM FOR PARTS.
*PATTY: MONEY, FROM "HARI PATI" (HINDI SLANG)--ED.

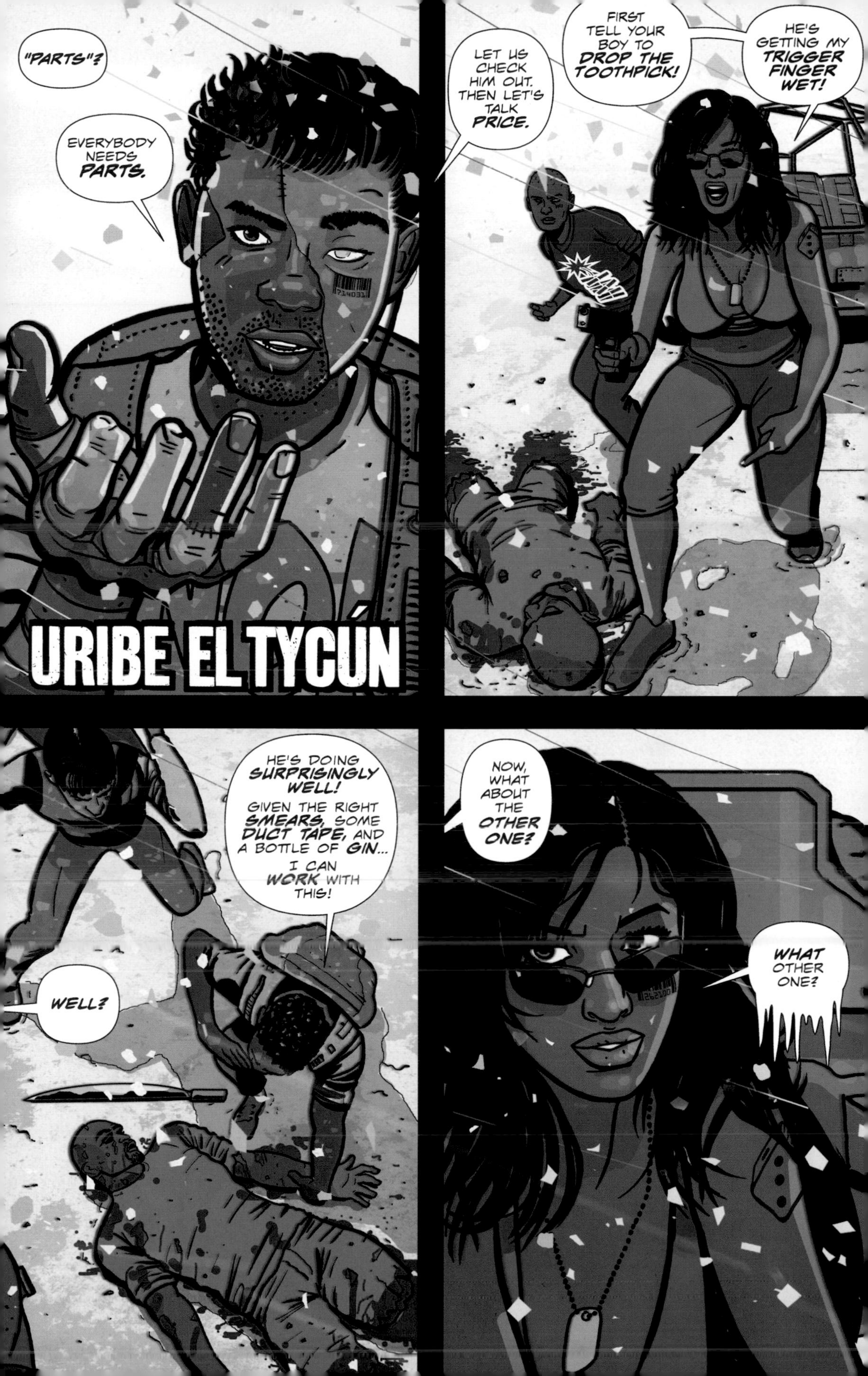
"PARTS"?
EVERYBODY NEEDS PARTS.
URIBE EL TYCÚN
LET US CHECK HIM OUT. THEN LET'S TALK PRICE.
FIRST TELL YOUR BOY TO DROP THE TOOTHPICK!
HE'S GETTING MY TRIGGER FINGER WET!
WELL?
HE'S DOING SURPRISINGLY WELL!
GIVEN THE RIGHT SMEARS, SOME DUCT TAPE, AND A BOTTLE OF GIN...
I CAN WORK WITH THIS!
NOW, WHAT ABOUT THE OTHER ONE?
WHAT OTHER ONE?

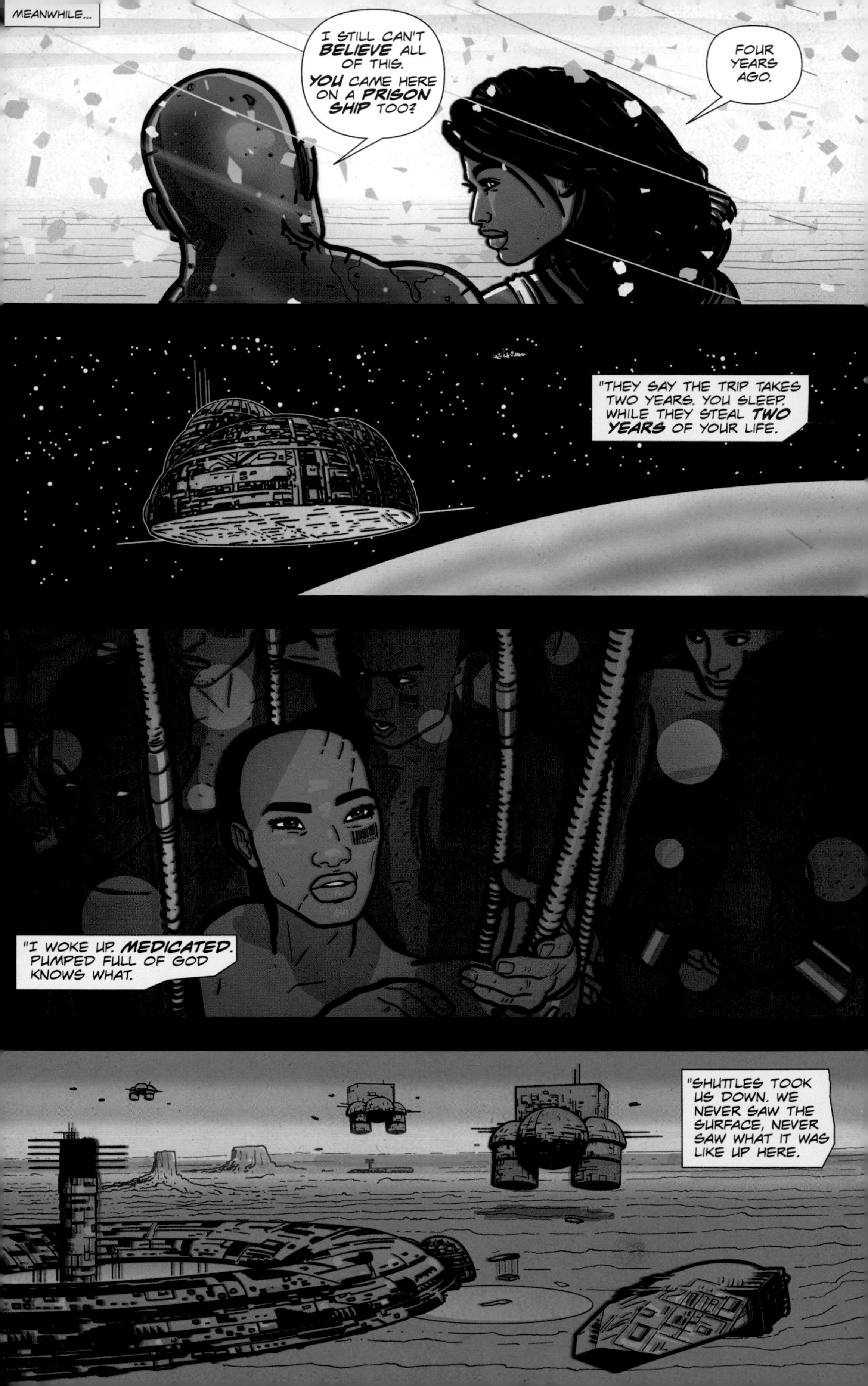
MEANWHILE...
I STILL CAN'T BELIEVE ALL OF THIS. YOU CAME HERE ON A PRISON SHIP TOO?
FOUR YEARS AGO.
"THEY SAY THE TRIP TAKES TWO YEARS. YOU SLEEP. WHILE THEY STEAL TWO YEARS OF YOUR LIFE.
"I WOKE UP. MEDICATED. PUMPED FULL OF GOD KNOWS WHAT.
"SHUTTLES TOOK US DOWN. WE NEVER SAW THE SURFACE, NEVER SAW WHAT IT WAS LIKE UP HERE.

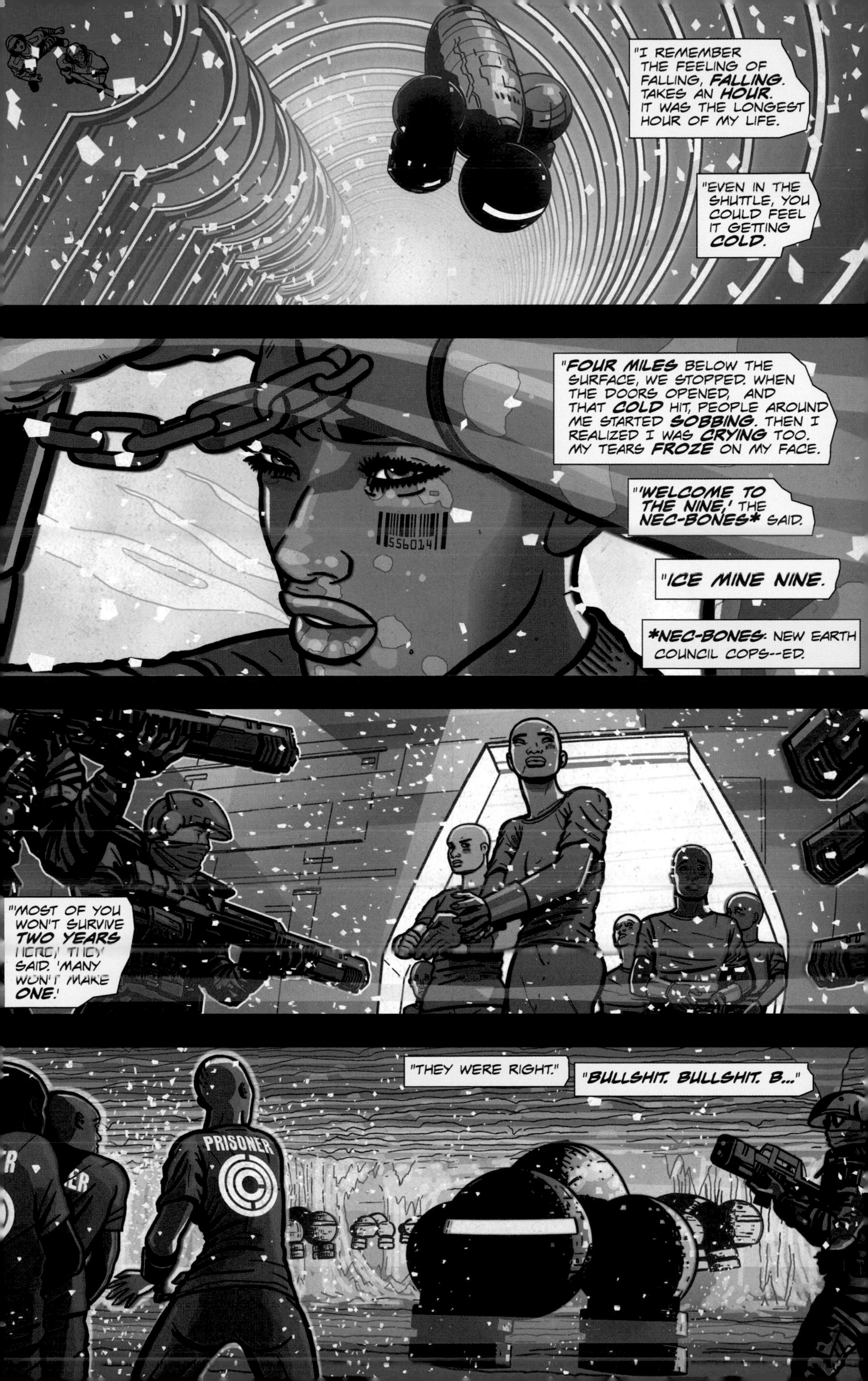
"I REMEMBER THE FEELING OF FALLING, **FALLING**. TAKES AN **HOUR**. IT WAS THE LONGEST HOUR OF MY LIFE.
"EVEN IN THE SHUTTLE, YOU COULD FEEL IT GETTING **COLD**.
"**FOUR MILES** BELOW THE SURFACE, WE STOPPED. WHEN THE DOORS OPENED, AND THAT **COLD** HIT, PEOPLE AROUND ME STARTED **SOBBING**. THEN I REALIZED I WAS **CRYING** TOO. MY TEARS **FROZE** ON MY FACE.
"**'WELCOME TO THE NINE,'** THE **NEC-BONES*** SAID.
"**ICE MINE NINE.**
***NEC-BONES**: NEW EARTH COUNCIL COPS--ED.
556014
"'MOST OF YOU WON'T SURVIVE **TWO YEARS**
SAID. 'MANY WON'T MAKE **ONE**.'
"THEY WERE RIGHT."
"**BULLSHIT. BULLSHIT. B...**"
PRISONER

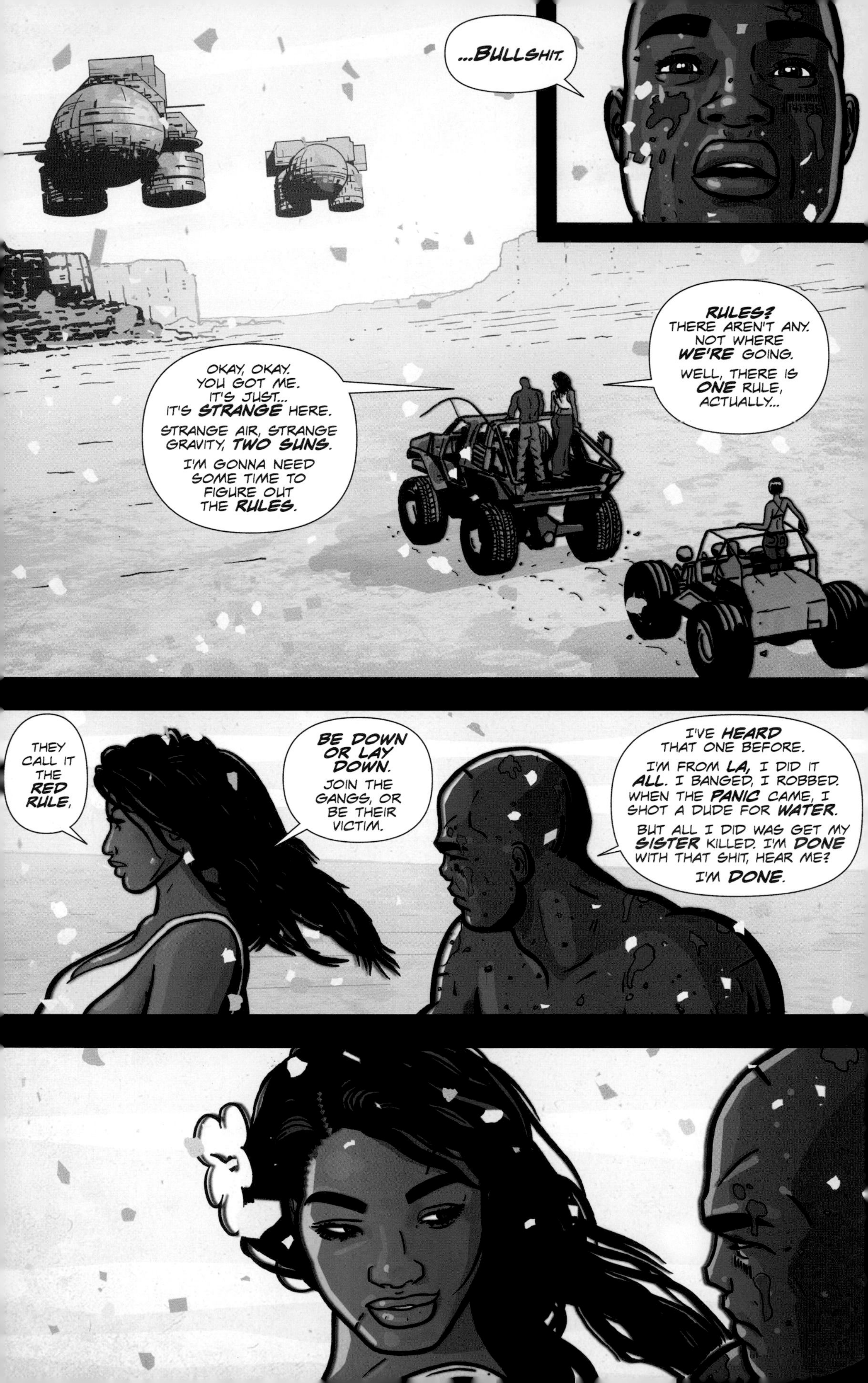
...BULLSHIT.
OKAY, OKAY. YOU GOT ME. IT'S JUST... IT'S STRANGE HERE. STRANGE AIR, STRANGE GRAVITY, TWO SUNS. I'M GONNA NEED SOME TIME TO FIGURE OUT THE RULES.
RULES? THERE AREN'T ANY. NOT WHERE WE'RE GOING. WELL, THERE IS ONE RULE, ACTUALLY...
THEY CALL IT THE RED RULE,
BE DOWN OR LAY DOWN. JOIN THE GANGS, OR BE THEIR VICTIM.
I'VE HEARD THAT ONE BEFORE. I'M FROM LA, I DID IT ALL. I BANGED, I ROBBED. WHEN THE PANIC CAME, I SHOT A DUDE FOR WATER. BUT ALL I DID WAS GET MY SISTER KILLED. I'M DONE WITH THAT SHIT, HEAR ME? I'M DONE.

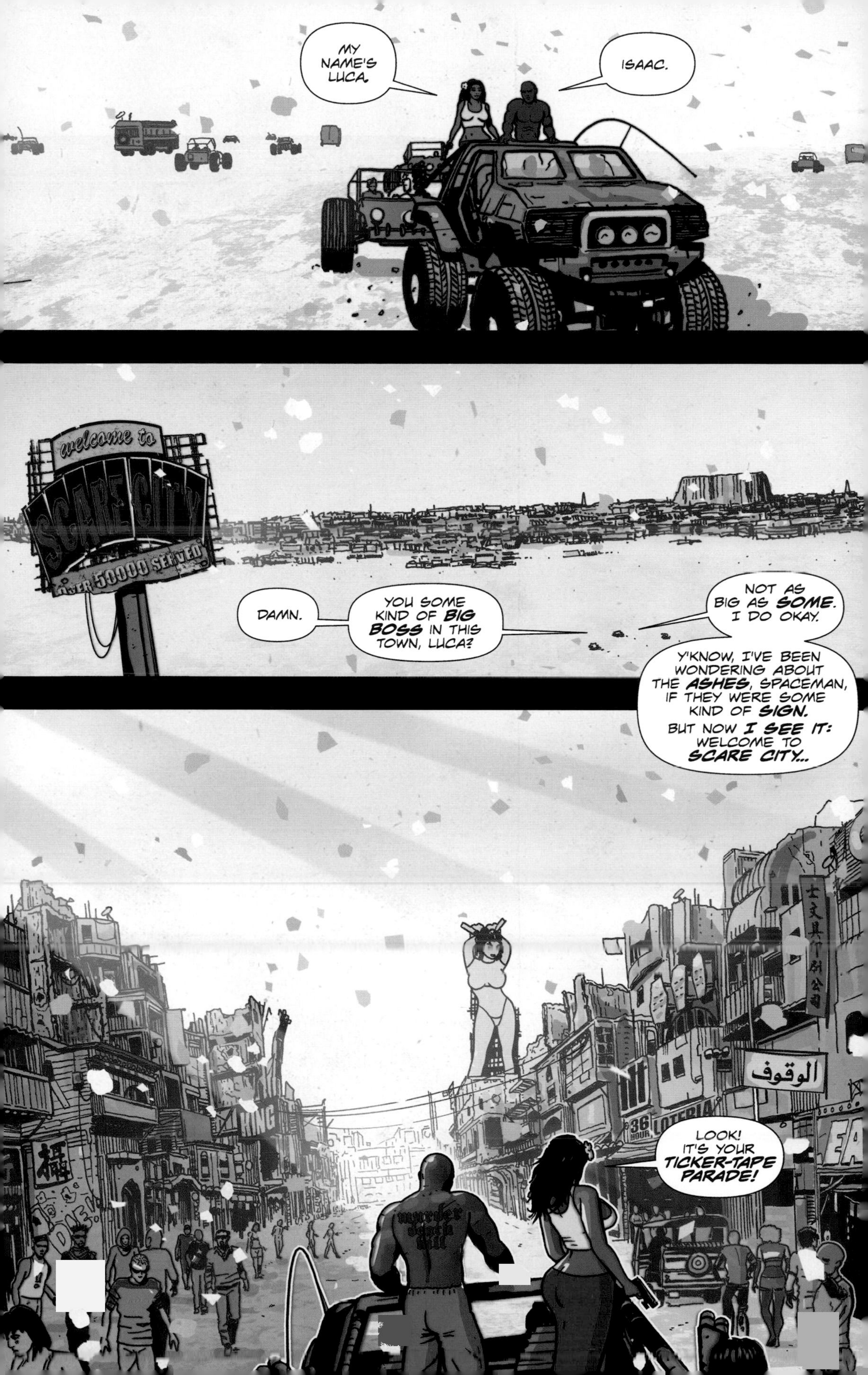
MY NAME'S LUCA.
ISAAC.
welcome to
SCARE CITY
OVER 50000 SERVED
DAMN.
YOU SOME KIND OF **BIG BOSS** IN THIS TOWN, LUCA?
NOT AS BIG AS **SOME**. I DO OKAY.
Y'KNOW, I'VE BEEN WONDERING ABOUT THE **ASHES**, SPACEMAN, IF THEY WERE SOME KIND OF **SIGN.**
BUT NOW **I SEE IT:** WELCOME TO **SCARE CITY...**
الوقوف
KING
36 HOUR
LOTERIA
LOOK! IT'S YOUR ***TICKER-TAPE PARADE!***

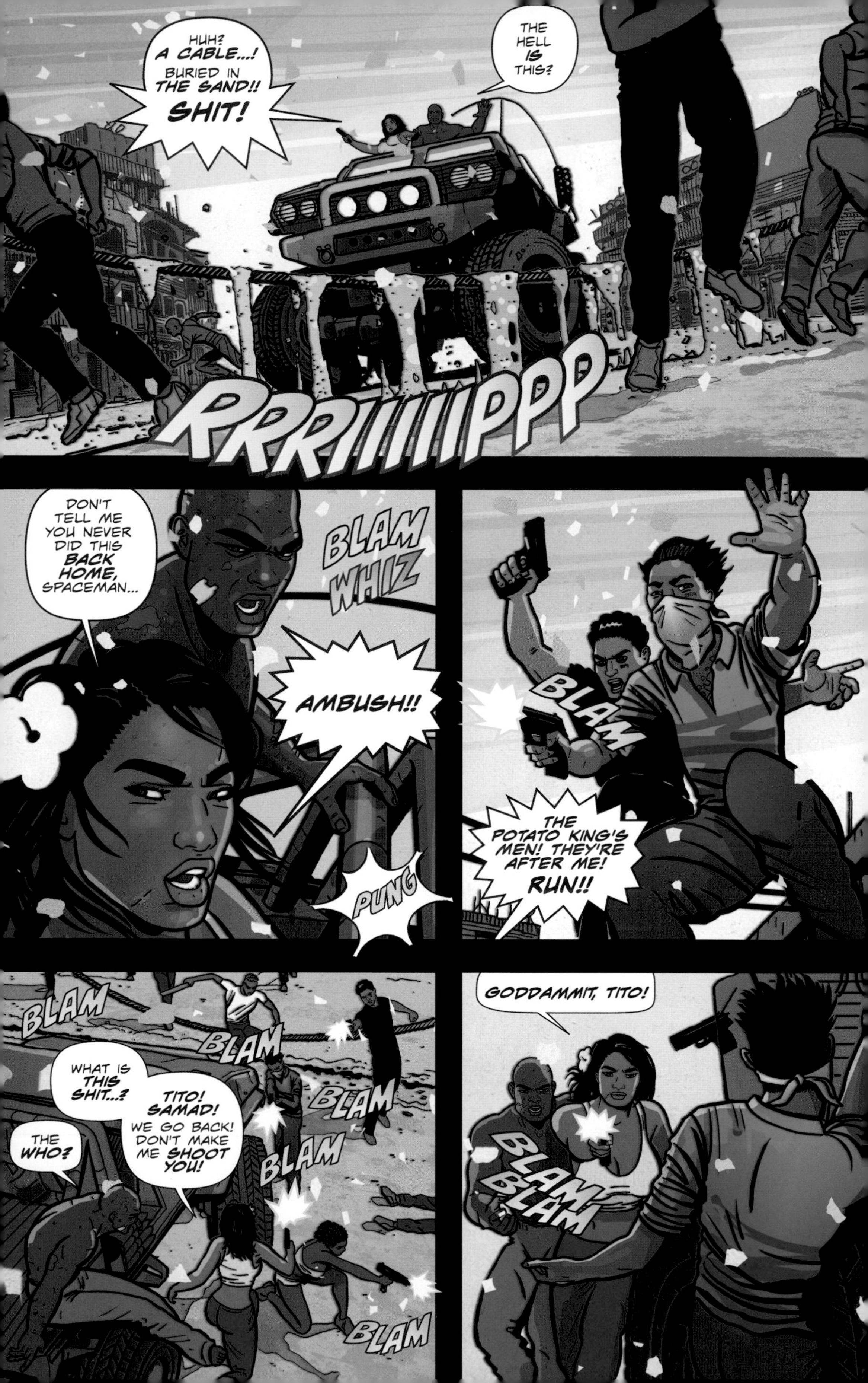
HUH? A CABLE...! BURIED IN THE SAND!! SHIT!
THE HELL IS THIS?
RRRIIIIIPPP
DON'T TELL ME YOU NEVER DID THIS BACK HOME, SPACEMAN...
BLAM
WHIZ
AMBUSH!!
PUNG
BLAM
THE POTATO KING'S MEN! THEY'RE AFTER ME! RUN!!
BLAM
BLAM
WHAT IS THIS SHIT...?
TITO! SAMAD! WE GO BACK! DON'T MAKE ME SHOOT YOU!
THE WHO?
BLAM
BLAM
BLAM
GODDAMMIT, TITO!
BLAM BLAM

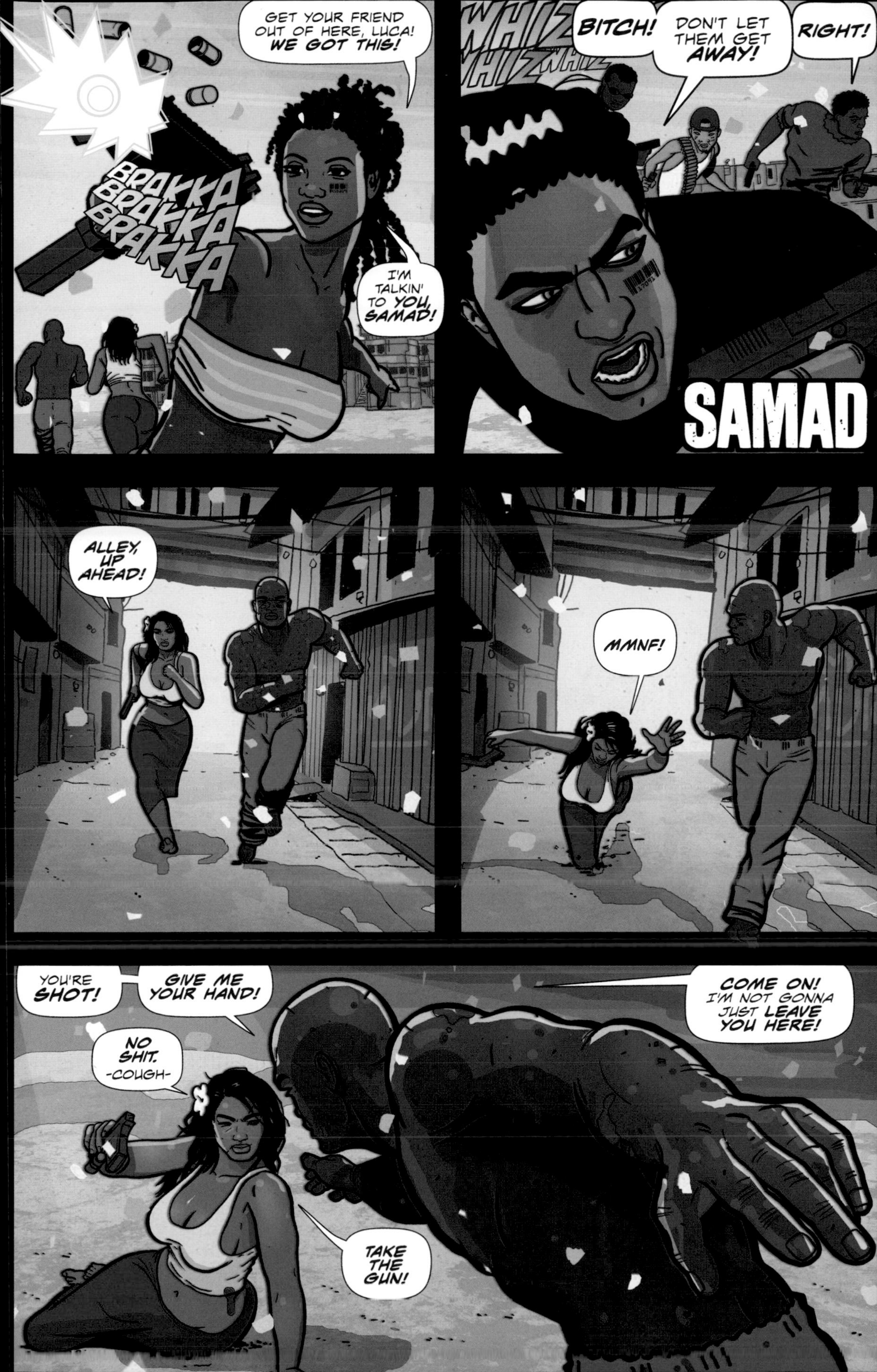
GET YOUR FRIEND OUT OF HERE, LUCA! WE GOT THIS!
BRAKKA BRAKKA BRAKKA
I'M TALKIN' TO YOU, SAMAD!
WHIZ WHIZ WHIZ
BITCH!
DON'T LET THEM GET AWAY!
RIGHT!
SAMAD
ALLEY, UP AHEAD!
MMNF!
YOU'RE SHOT!
GIVE ME YOUR HAND!
NO SHIT. -COUGH-
COME ON! I'M NOT GONNA JUST LEAVE YOU HERE!
TAKE THE GUN!

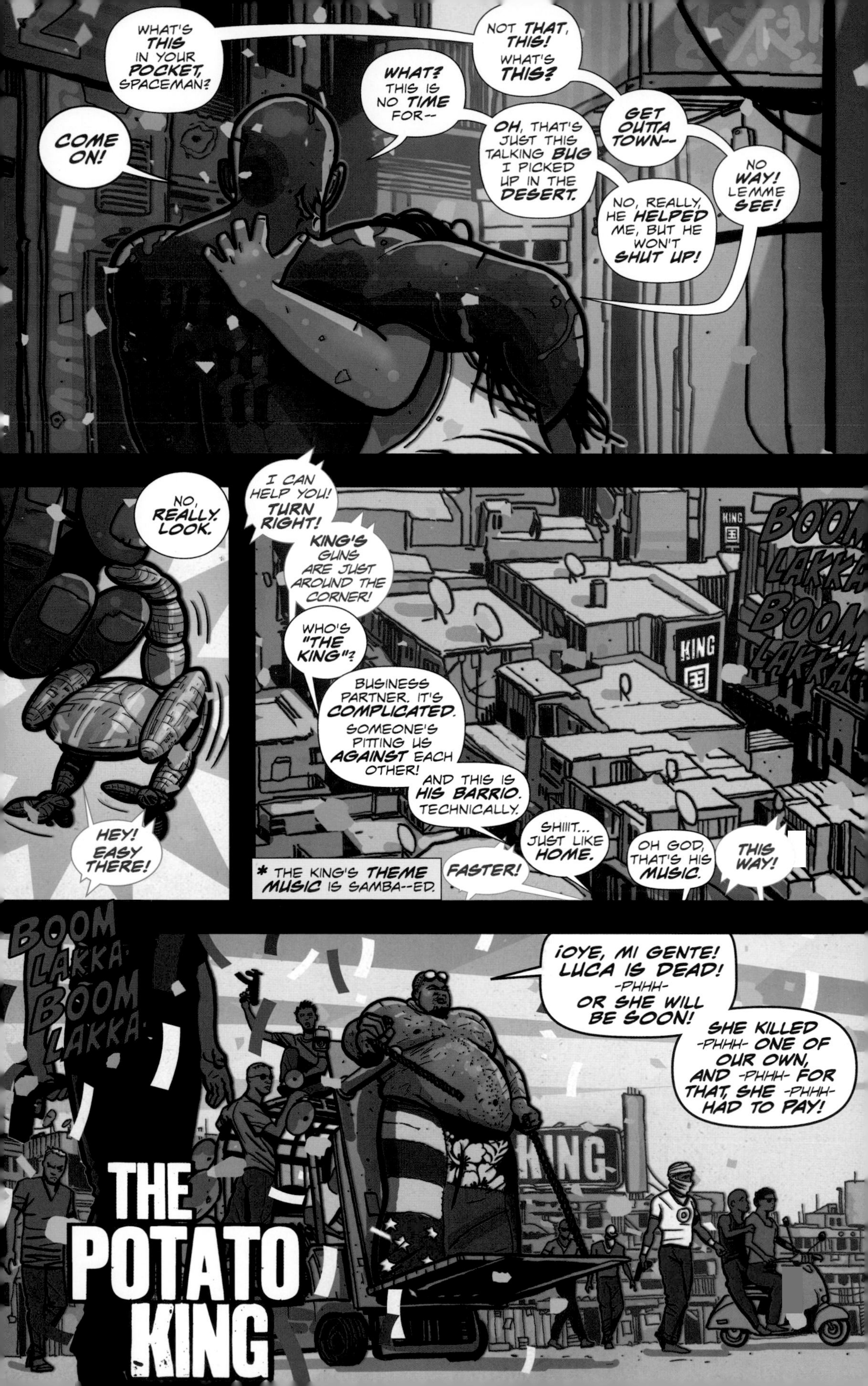

WHAT'S THIS IN YOUR POCKET, SPACEMAN?
COME ON!
WHAT? THIS IS NO TIME FOR--
NOT THAT, THIS! WHAT'S THIS?
OH, THAT'S JUST THIS TALKING BUG I PICKED UP IN THE DESERT.
GET OUTTA TOWN--
NO, REALLY, HE HELPED ME, BUT HE WON'T SHUT UP!
NO WAY! LEMME SEE!
NO, REALLY. LOOK.
HEY! EASY THERE!
I CAN HELP YOU! TURN RIGHT!
KING'S GUNS ARE JUST AROUND THE CORNER!
WHO'S "THE KING"?
BUSINESS PARTNER. IT'S COMPLICATED. SOMEONE'S PITTING US AGAINST EACH OTHER!
AND THIS IS HIS BARRIO. TECHNICALLY.
KING
KING
BOOM LAKKA BOOM LAKKA
* THE KING'S THEME MUSIC IS SAMBA--ED.
FASTER!
SHIIIT... JUST LIKE HOME.
OH GOD, THAT'S HIS MUSIC.
THIS WAY!
BOOM LAKKA BOOM LAKKA
¡OYE, MI GENTE! LUCA IS DEAD! -PHHH- OR SHE WILL BE SOON!
SHE KILLED -PHHH- ONE OF OUR OWN, AND -PHHH- FOR THAT, SHE -PHHH- HAD TO PAY!
KING
THE POTATO KING

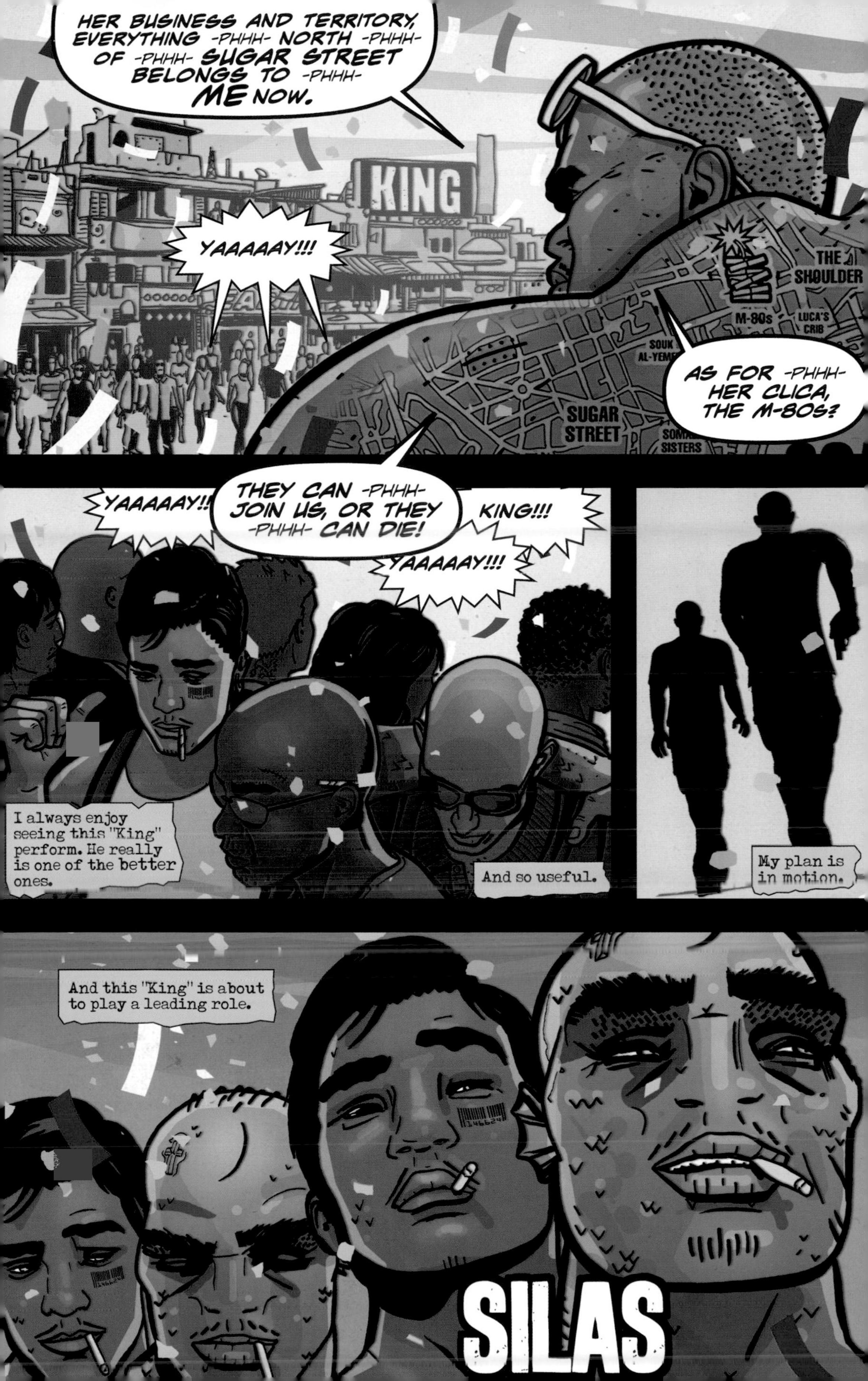
HER BUSINESS AND TERRITORY, EVERYTHING -PHHH- NORTH -PHHH- OF -PHHH- SUGAR STREET BELONGS TO -PHHH- ME NOW.
KING
YAAAAAY!!!
THE SHOULDER
M-80s
LUCA'S CRIB
SOUK AL-YEME
SUGAR STREET
SOMA SISTERS
AS FOR -PHHH- HER CLICA, THE M-80s?
YAAAAAY!!!
THEY CAN -PHHH- JOIN US, OR THEY -PHHH- CAN DIE!
KING!!!
YAAAAAY!!!
I always enjoy seeing this "King" perform. He really is one of the better ones.
And so useful.
My plan is in motion.
And this "King" is about to play a leading role.
SILAS

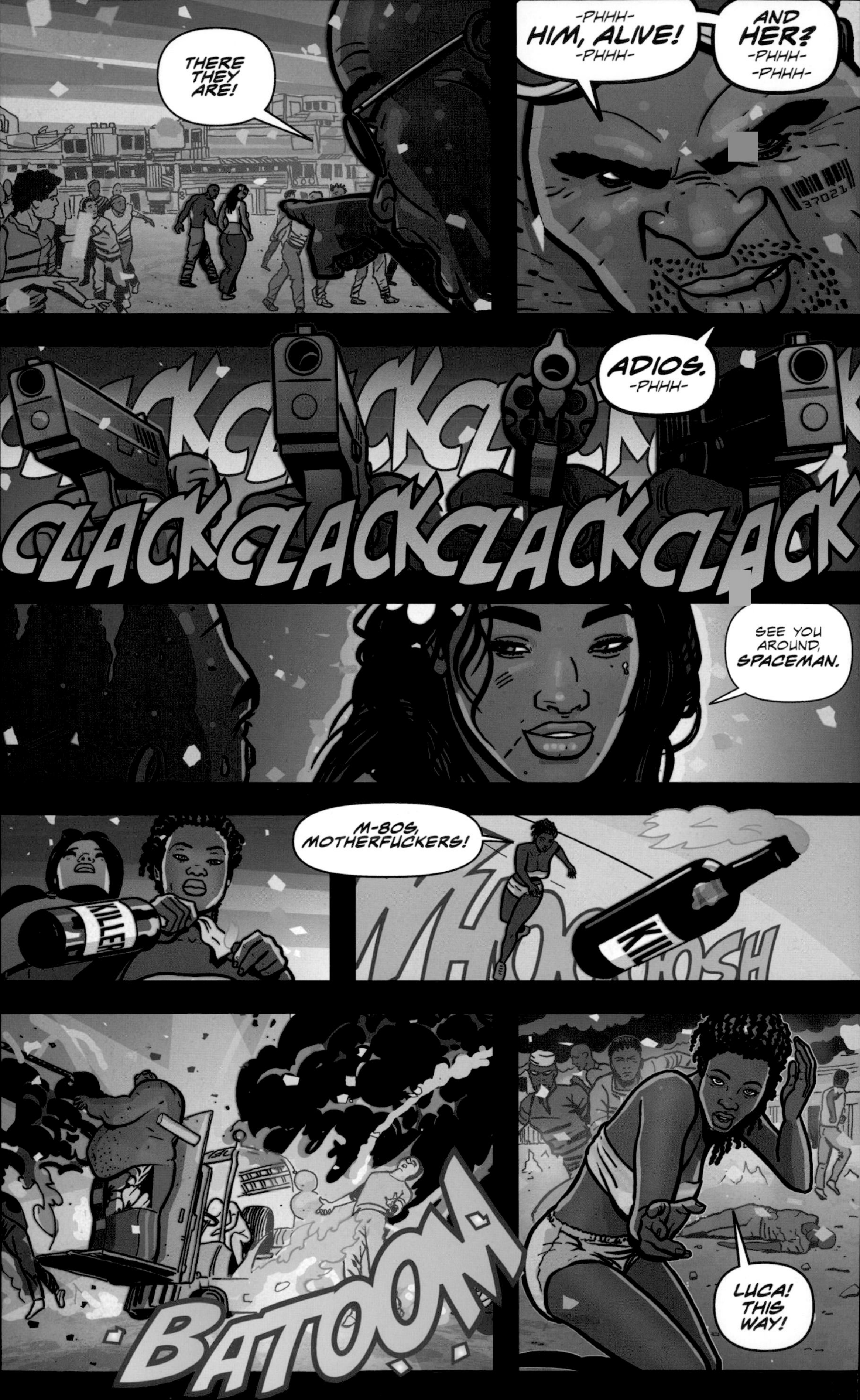
THERE THEY ARE!
-PHHH- HIM, ALIVE! -PHHH-
AND HER? -PHHH- -PHHH-
ADIOS. -PHHH-
CLACKCLACKCLACKCLACK
SEE YOU AROUND, SPACEMAN.
M-80S, MOTHERFUCKERS!
BATOOM
LUCA! THIS WAY!

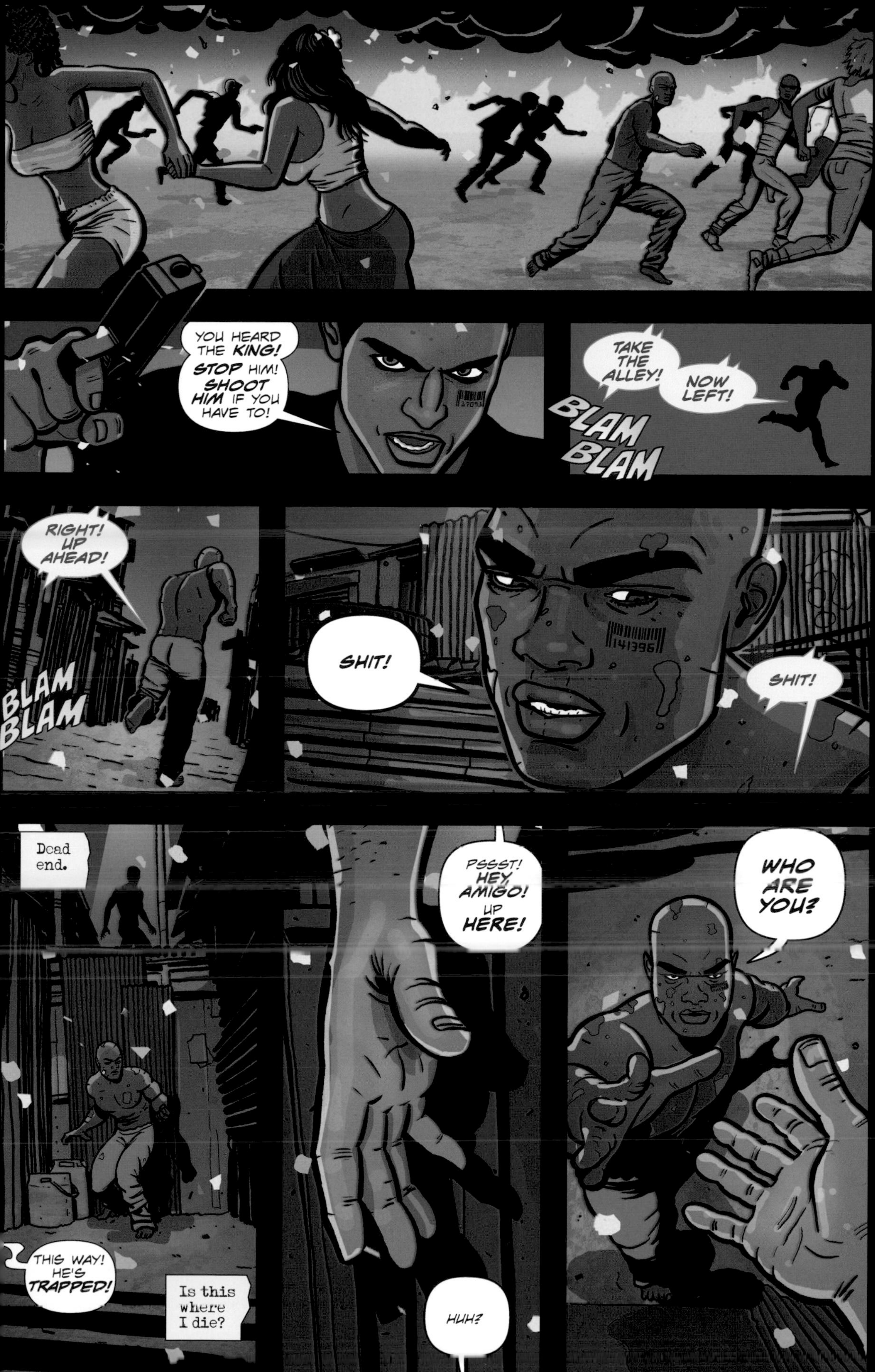
YOU HEARD THE KING! STOP HIM! SHOOT HIM IF YOU HAVE TO!
BLAM BLAM
TAKE THE ALLEY!
NOW LEFT!
RIGHT! UP AHEAD!
BLAM BLAM
SHIT!
SHIT!
Dead end.
THIS WAY! HE'S TRAPPED!
Is this where I die?
PSSST! HEY, AMIGO! UP HERE!
HUH?
WHO ARE YOU?

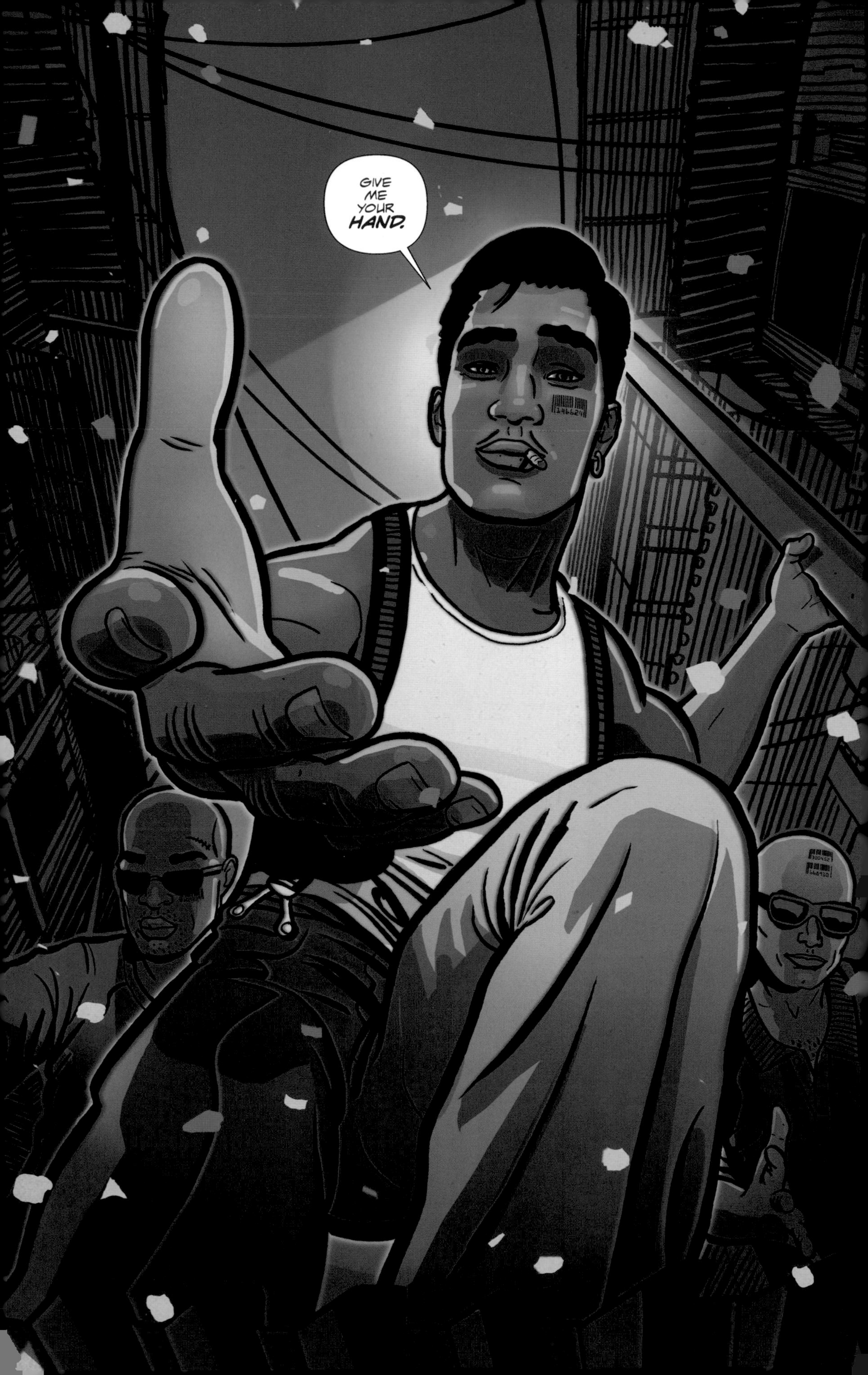
GIVE ME YOUR HAND.

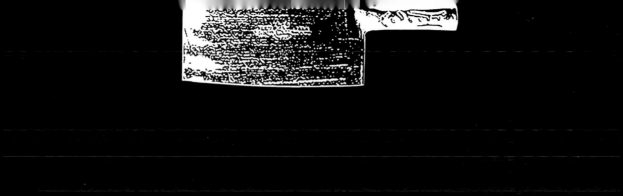

"We thought we were alone
on this planet. We're not."
—Talladega

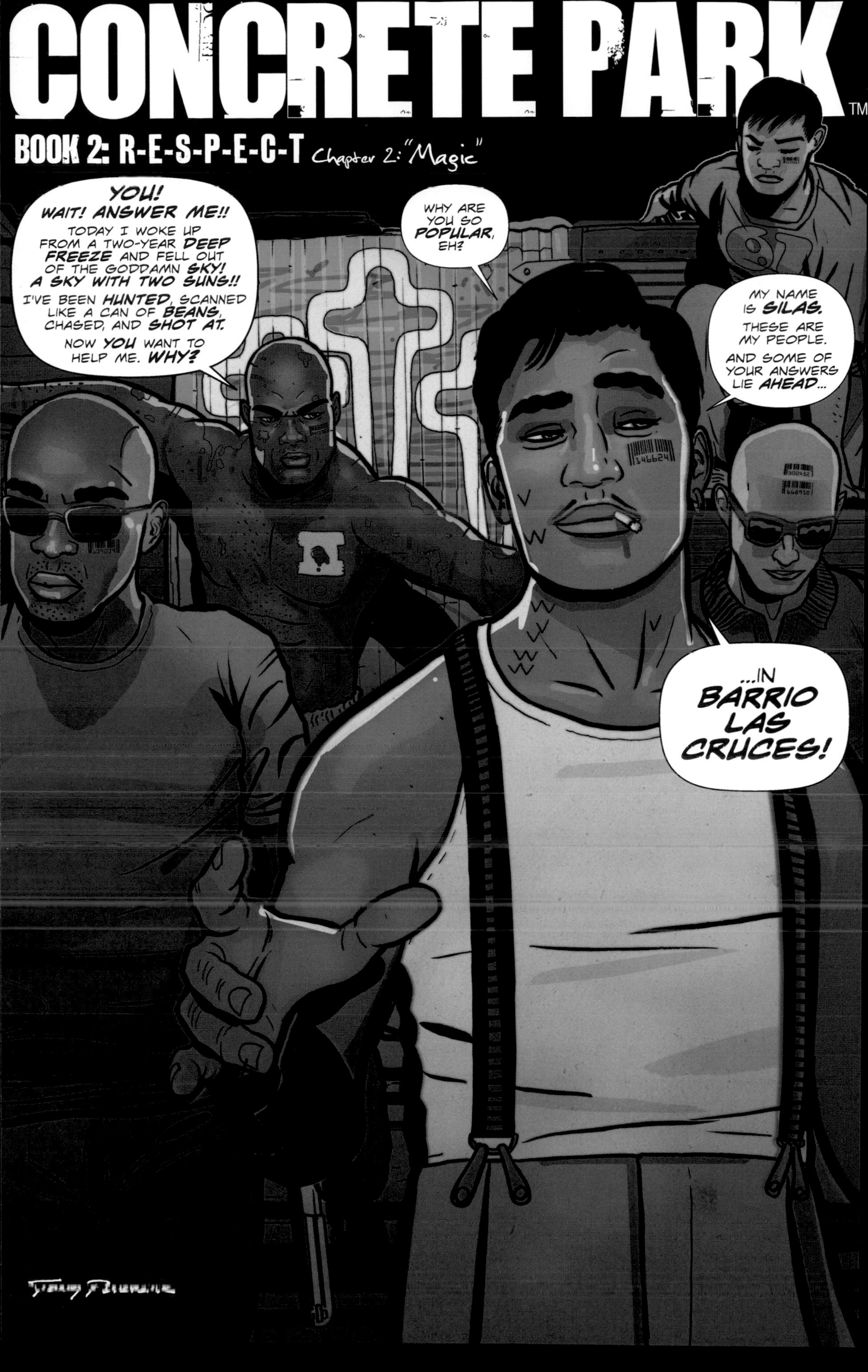
CONCRETE PARK™
BOOK 2: R-E-S-P-E-C-T Chapter 2: "Magic"
YOU! WAIT! ANSWER ME!! TODAY I WOKE UP FROM A TWO-YEAR DEEP FREEZE AND FELL OUT OF THE GODDAMN SKY! A SKY WITH TWO SUNS!! I'VE BEEN HUNTED, SCANNED LIKE A CAN OF BEANS, CHASED, AND SHOT AT. NOW YOU WANT TO HELP ME. WHY?
WHY ARE YOU SO POPULAR, EH?
MY NAME IS SILAS. THESE ARE MY PEOPLE. AND SOME OF YOUR ANSWERS LIE AHEAD...
...IN BARRIO LAS CRUCES!

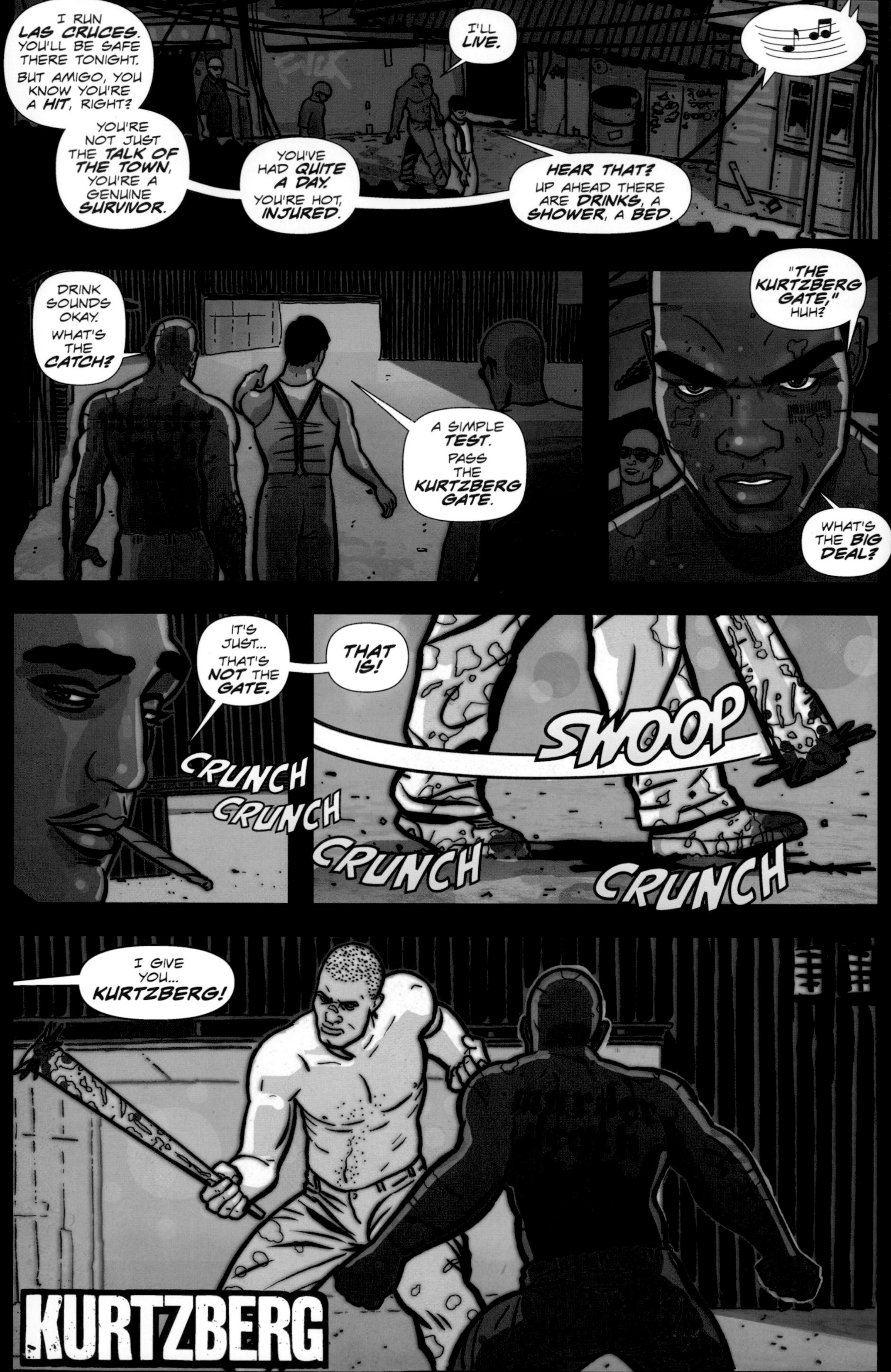
I RUN LAS CRUCES. YOU'LL BE SAFE THERE TONIGHT.
BUT AMIGO, YOU KNOW YOU'RE A HIT, RIGHT?
YOU'RE NOT JUST THE TALK OF THE TOWN, YOU'RE A GENUINE SURVIVOR.
I'LL LIVE.
YOU'VE HAD QUITE A DAY. YOU'RE HOT, INJURED.
HEAR THAT? UP AHEAD THERE ARE DRINKS, A SHOWER, A BED.
DRINK SOUNDS OKAY. WHAT'S THE CATCH?
A SIMPLE TEST. PASS THE KURTZBERG GATE.
"THE KURTZBERG GATE," HUH?
WHAT'S THE BIG DEAL?
IT'S JUST... THAT'S NOT THE GATE.
THAT IS!
CRUNCH
CRUNCH
CRUNCH
SWOOP
CRUNCH
I GIVE YOU... KURTZBERG!
KURTZBERG

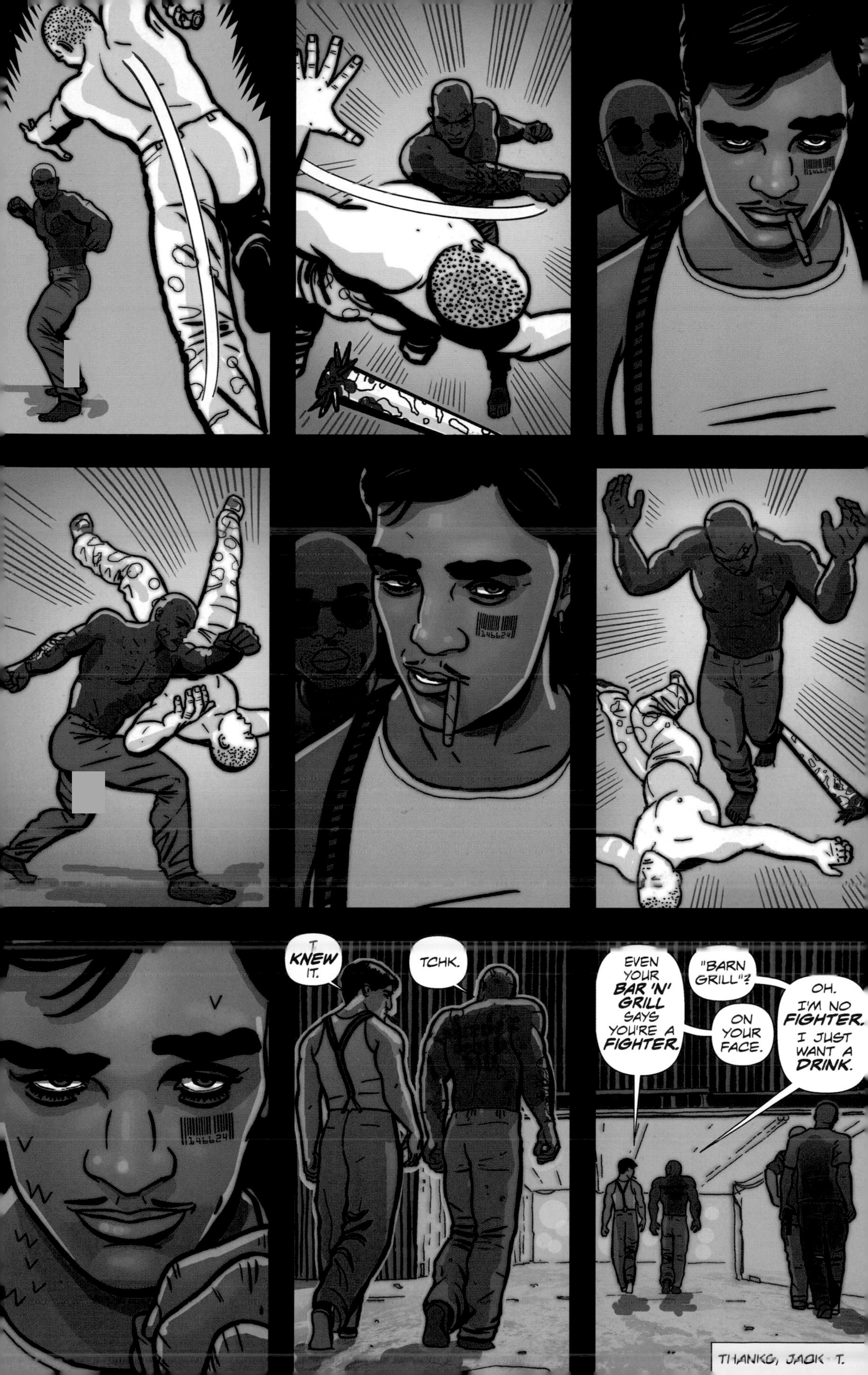
I KNEW IT.
TCHK.
EVEN YOUR BAR 'N' GRILL SAYS YOU'RE A FIGHTER.
"BARN GRILL"?
ON YOUR FACE.
OH. I'M NO FIGHTER. I JUST WANT A DRINK.
THANKS, JACK T.

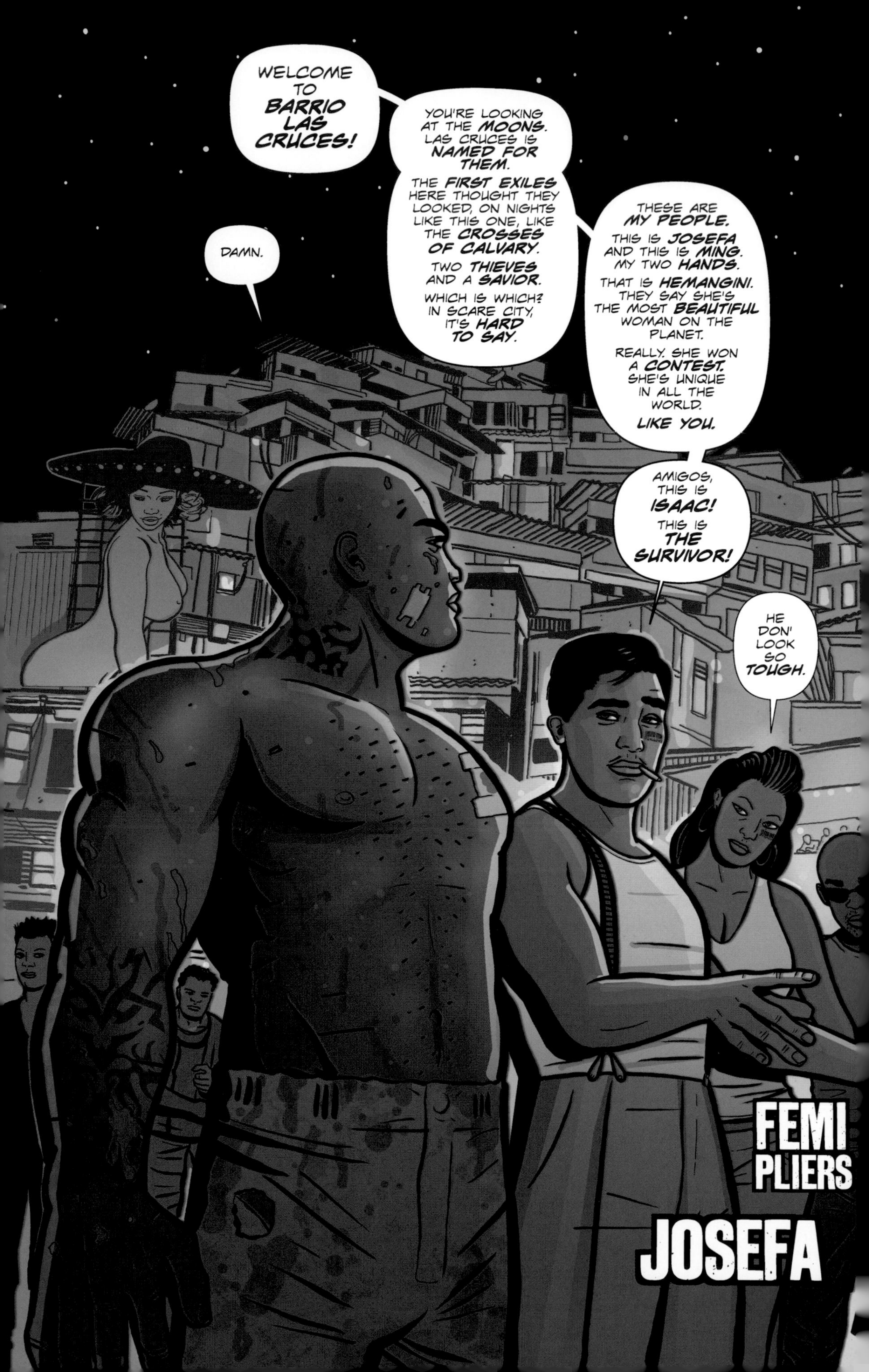
WELCOME TO BARRIO LAS CRUCES!
YOU'RE LOOKING AT THE MOONS. LAS CRUCES IS NAMED FOR THEM.
THE FIRST EXILES HERE THOUGHT THEY LOOKED, ON NIGHTS LIKE THIS ONE, LIKE THE CROSSES OF CALVARY.
TWO THIEVES AND A SAVIOR.
WHICH IS WHICH? IN SCARE CITY, IT'S HARD TO SAY.
DAMN.
THESE ARE MY PEOPLE.
THIS IS JOSEFA AND THIS IS MING. MY TWO HANDS.
THAT IS HEMANGINI. THEY SAY SHE'S THE MOST BEAUTIFUL WOMAN ON THE PLANET.
REALLY. SHE WON A CONTEST. SHE'S UNIQUE IN ALL THE WORLD.
LIKE YOU.
AMIGOS, THIS IS ISAAC! THIS IS THE SURVIVOR!
HE DON' LOOK SO TOUGH.
FEMI PLIERS
JOSEFA

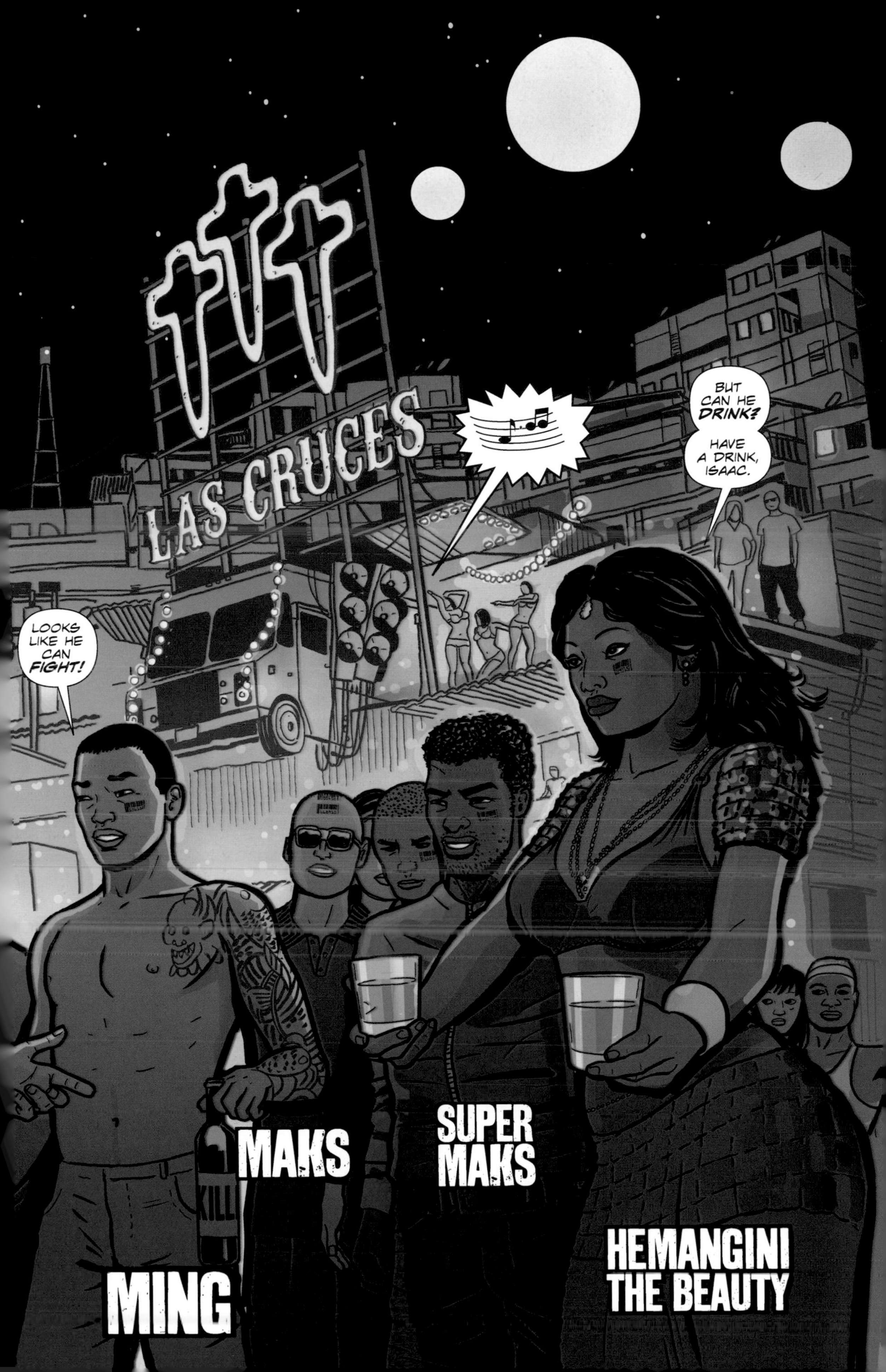
LAS CRUCES
LOOKS LIKE HE CAN FIGHT!
BUT CAN HE DRINK?
HAVE A DRINK, ISAAC.
KILL
MAKS
SUPER MAKS
MING
HEMANGINI THE BEAUTY

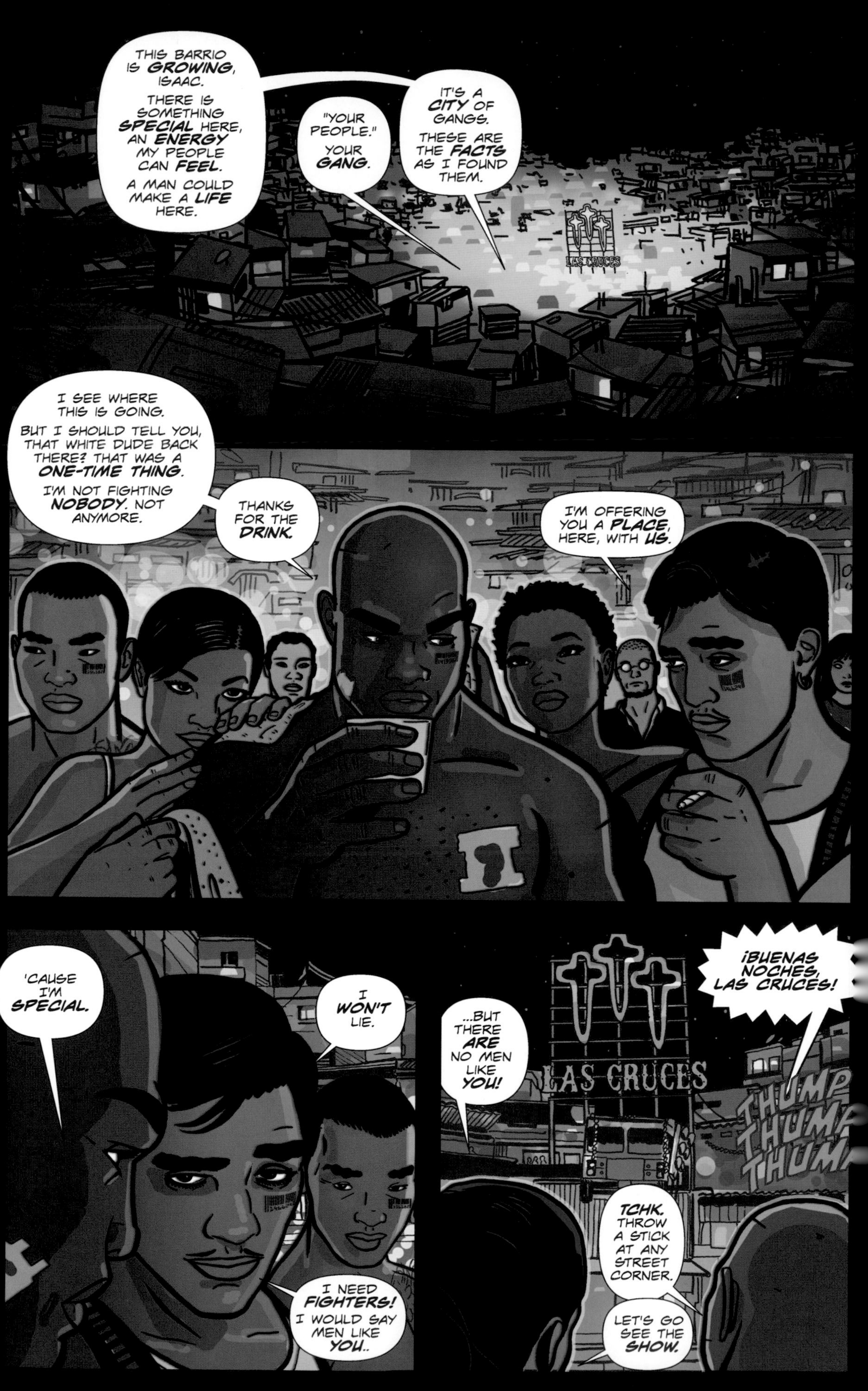

THIS BARRIO IS GROWING, ISAAC.
THERE IS SOMETHING SPECIAL HERE, AN ENERGY MY PEOPLE CAN FEEL.
A MAN COULD MAKE A LIFE HERE.
"YOUR PEOPLE." YOUR GANG.
IT'S A CITY OF GANGS.
THESE ARE THE FACTS AS I FOUND THEM.
LAS CRUCES
I SEE WHERE THIS IS GOING.
BUT I SHOULD TELL YOU, THAT WHITE DUDE BACK THERE? THAT WAS A ONE-TIME THING.
I'M NOT FIGHTING NOBODY. NOT ANYMORE.
THANKS FOR THE DRINK.
I'M OFFERING YOU A PLACE, HERE, WITH US.
'CAUSE I'M SPECIAL.
I WON'T LIE.
I NEED FIGHTERS! I WOULD SAY MEN LIKE YOU..
...BUT THERE ARE NO MEN LIKE YOU!
LAS CRUCES
¡BUENAS NOCHES, LAS CRUCES!
TCHK. THROW A STICK AT ANY STREET CORNER.
LET'S GO SEE THE SHOW.

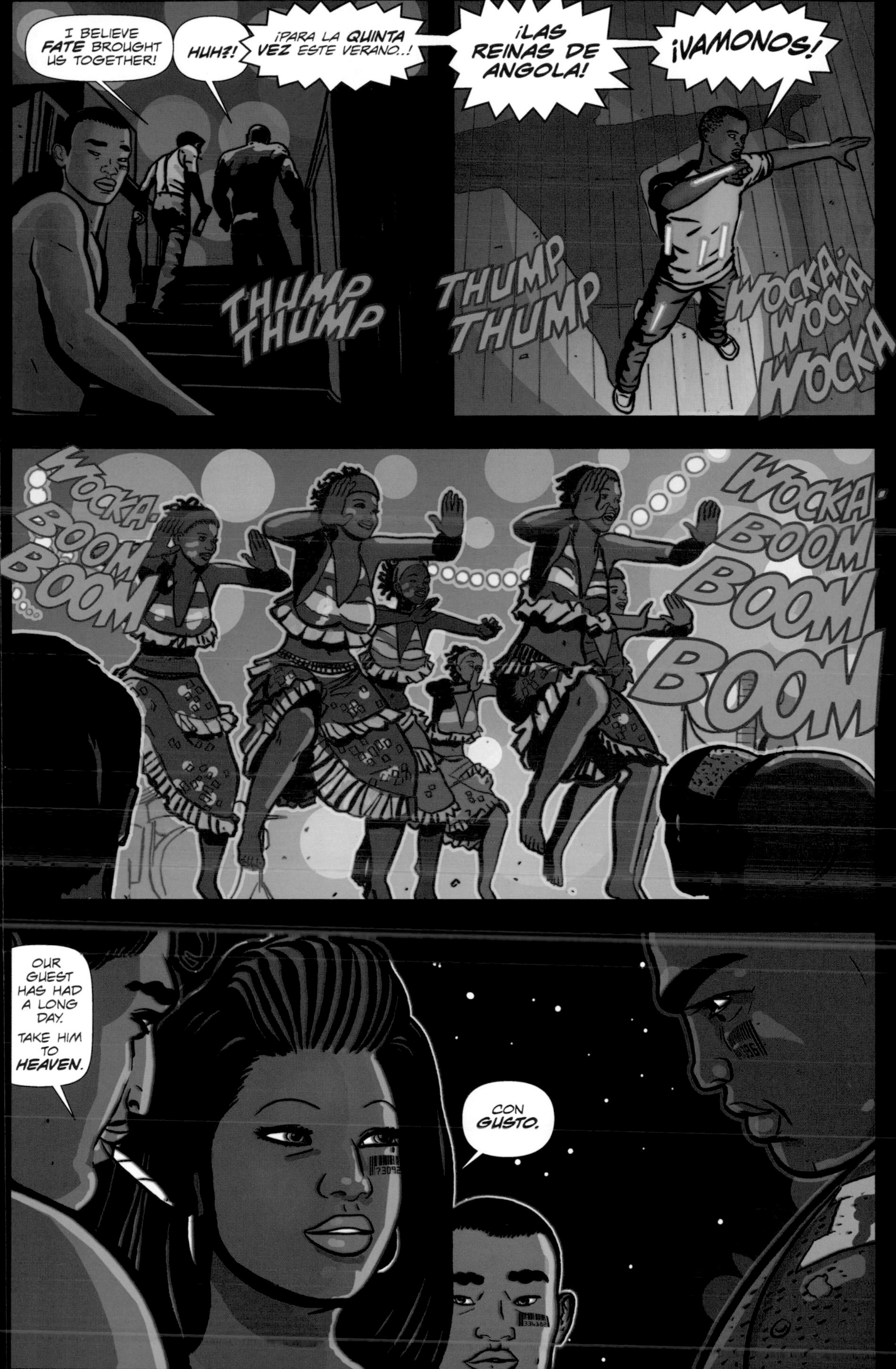
I BELIEVE FATE BROUGHT US TOGETHER!
HUH?!
¡PARA LA QUINTA VEZ ESTE VERANO..!
¡LAS REINAS DE ANGOLA!
¡VAMONOS!
THUMP THUMP
THUMP THUMP
WOCKA-A WOCKA WOCKA
WOCKA-BOOM BOOM
WOCKA-BOOM BOOM BOOM
OUR GUEST HAS HAD A LONG DAY.
TAKE HIM TO HEAVEN.
CON GUSTO.

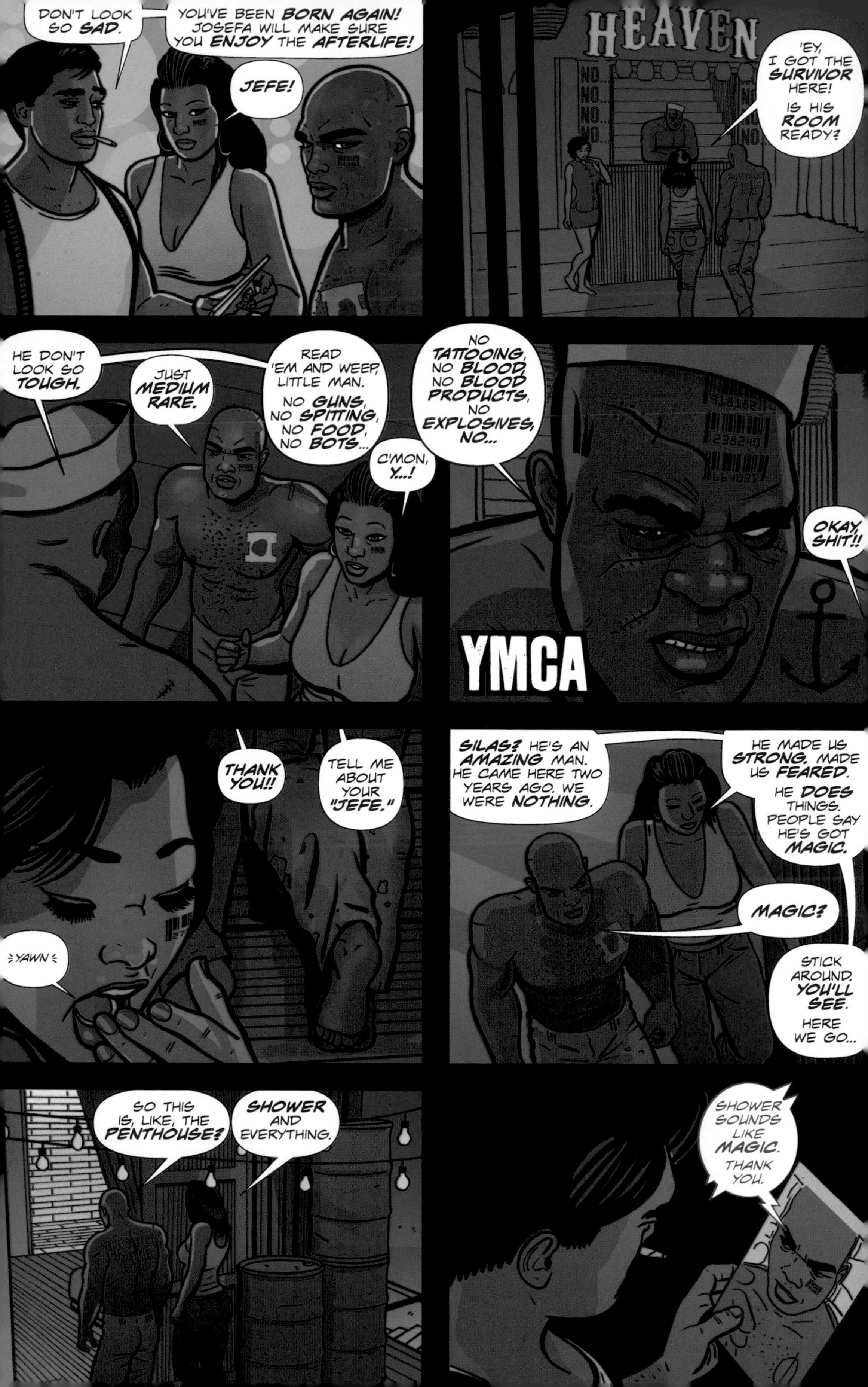
DON'T LOOK SO SAD.
YOU'VE BEEN BORN AGAIN! JOSEFA WILL MAKE SURE YOU ENJOY THE AFTERLIFE!
JEFE!
HEAVEN
NO... NO... NO... NO... NO...
'EY, I GOT THE SURVIVOR HERE! IS HIS ROOM READY?
HE DON'T LOOK SO TOUGH.
JUST MEDIUM RARE.
READ 'EM AND WEEP, LITTLE MAN. NO GUNS, NO SPITTING, NO FOOD, NO BOTS...
C'MON, Y...!
NO TATTOOING, NO BLOOD, NO BLOOD PRODUCTS, NO EXPLOSIVES, NO...
OKAY, SHIT!!
YMCA
THANK YOU!!
TELL ME ABOUT YOUR "JEFE."
YAWN
SILAS? HE'S AN AMAZING MAN. HE CAME HERE TWO YEARS AGO. WE WERE NOTHING.
HE MADE US STRONG. MADE US FEARED. HE DOES THINGS. PEOPLE SAY HE'S GOT MAGIC.
MAGIC?
STICK AROUND. YOU'LL SEE. HERE WE GO...
SO THIS IS, LIKE, THE PENTHOUSE?
SHOWER AND EVERYTHING.
SHOWER SOUNDS LIKE MAGIC. THANK YOU.

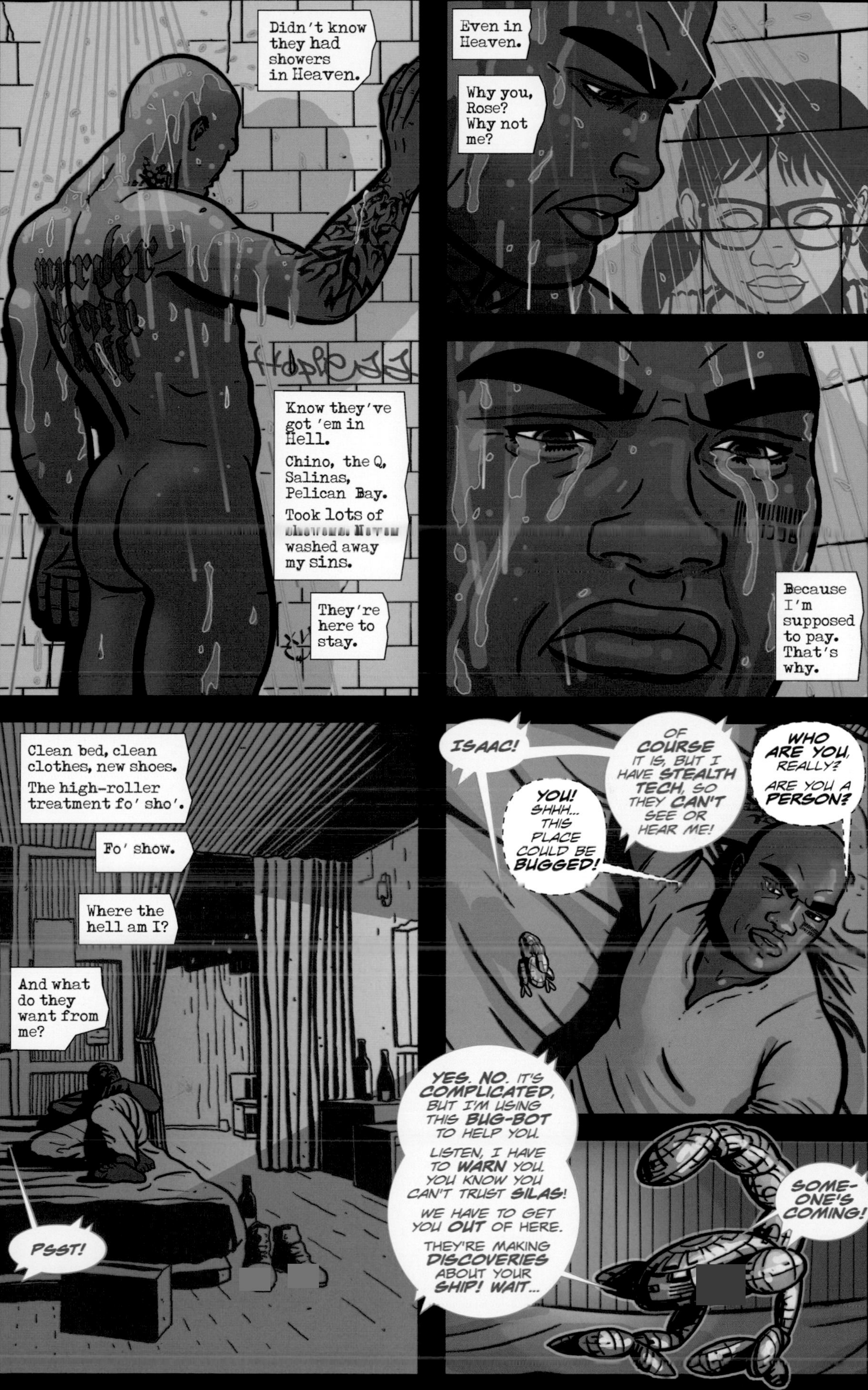
Didn't know they had showers in Heaven.
Know they've got 'em in Hell.
Chino, the Q, Salinas, Pelican Bay.
Took lots of
washed away my sins.
They're here to stay.
Even in Heaven.
Why you, Rose? Why not me?
Because I'm supposed to pay. That's why.
Clean bed, clean clothes, new shoes.
The high-roller treatment fo' sho'.
Fo' show.
Where the hell am I?
And what do they want from me?
PSST!
ISAAC!
YOU! SHHH... THIS PLACE COULD BE BUGGED!
OF COURSE IT IS, BUT I HAVE STEALTH TECH, SO THEY CAN'T SEE OR HEAR ME!
WHO ARE YOU, REALLY? ARE YOU A PERSON?
YES. NO. IT'S COMPLICATED, BUT I'M USING THIS BUG-BOT TO HELP YOU.
LISTEN, I HAVE TO WARN YOU. YOU KNOW YOU CAN'T TRUST SILAS!
WE HAVE TO GET YOU OUT OF HERE.
THEY'RE MAKING DISCOVERIES ABOUT YOUR SHIP! WAIT...
SOME-ONE'S COMING!

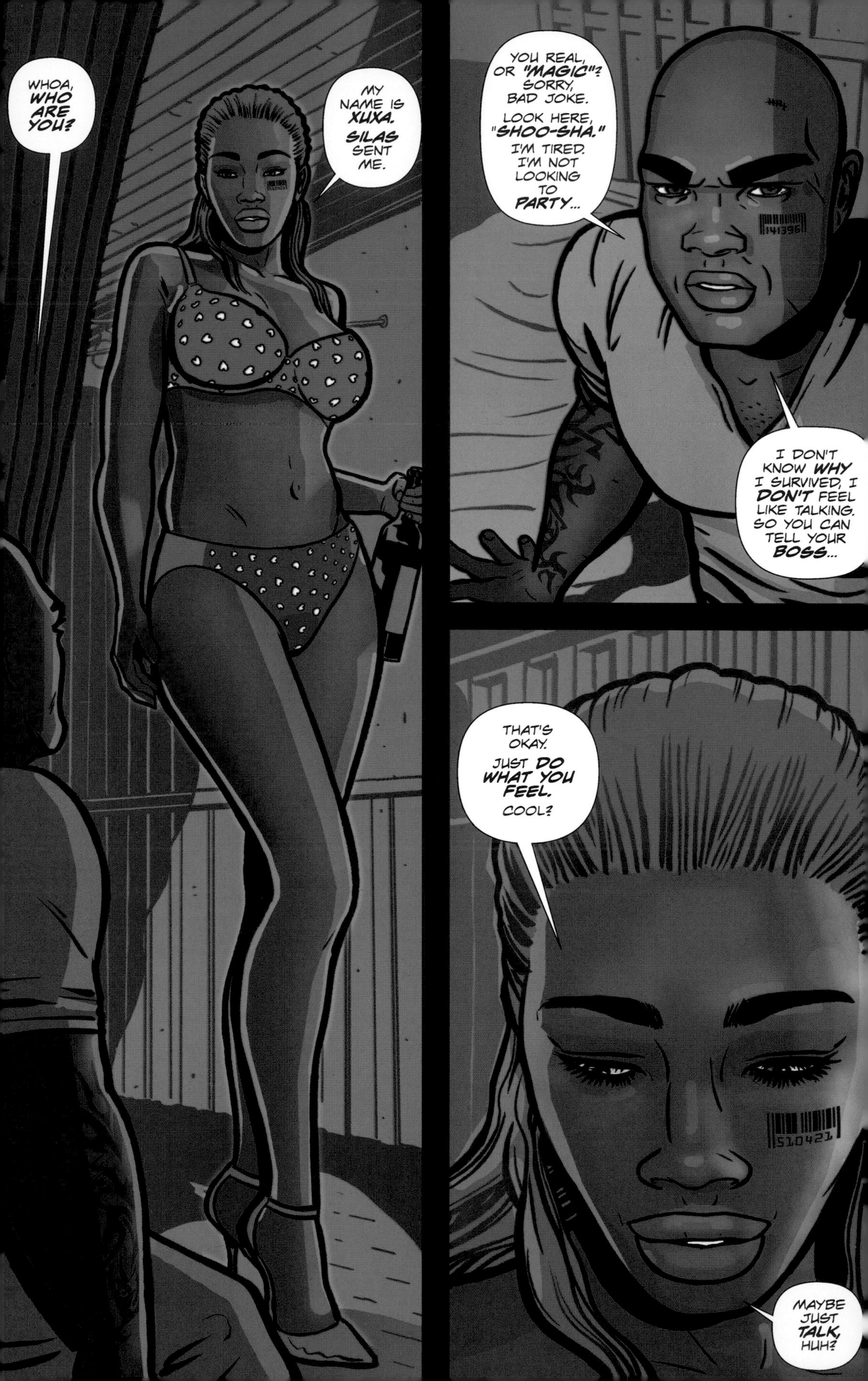
WHOA, WHO ARE YOU?
MY NAME IS XUXA. SILAS SENT ME.
YOU REAL, OR "MAGIC"? SORRY, BAD JOKE.
LOOK HERE, "SHOO-SHA." I'M TIRED. I'M NOT LOOKING TO PARTY...
I DON'T KNOW WHY I SURVIVED, I DON'T FEEL LIKE TALKING. SO YOU CAN TELL YOUR BOSS...
THAT'S OKAY.
JUST DO WHAT YOU FEEL.
COOL?
MAYBE JUST TALK, HUH?

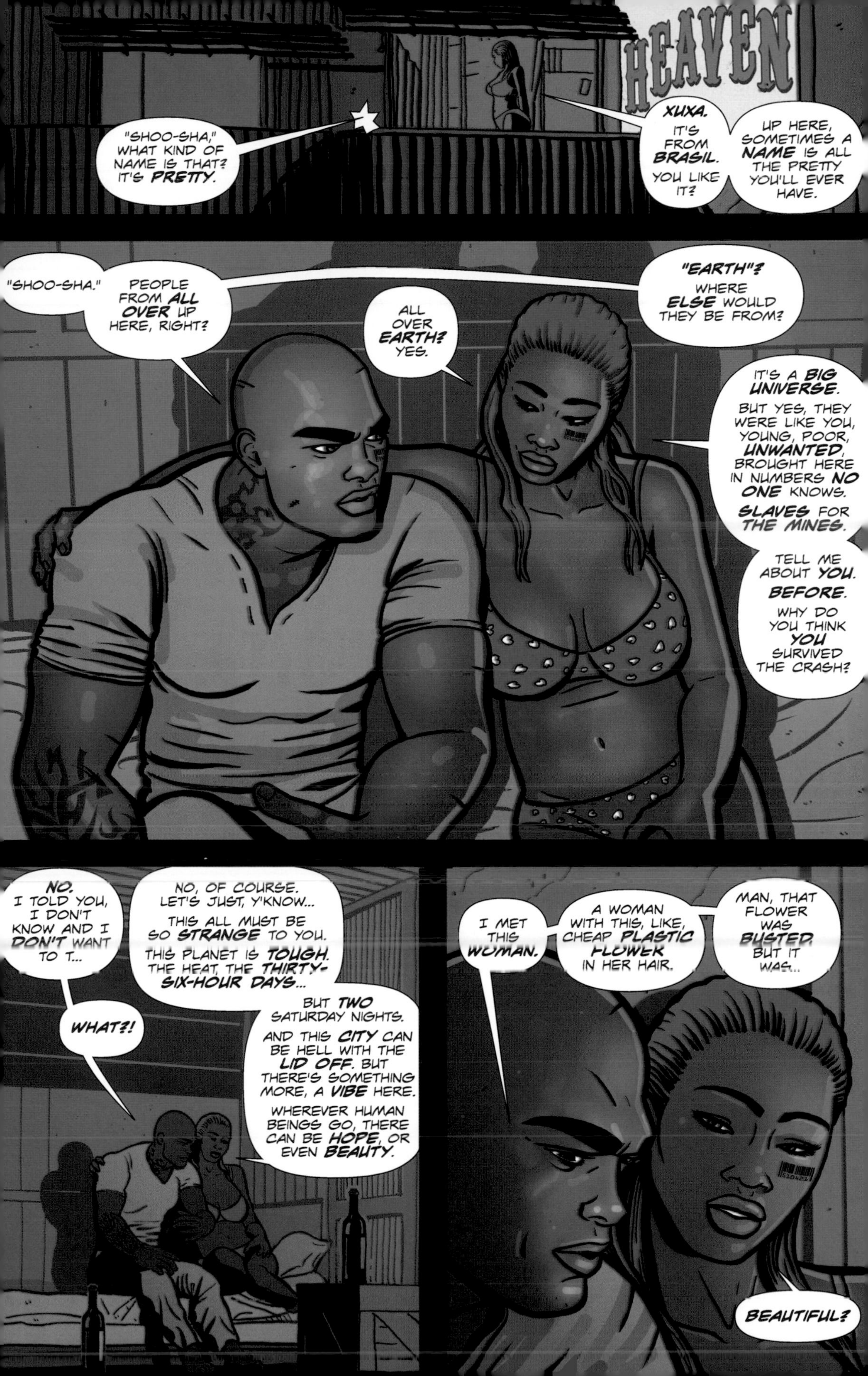
HEAVEN
"SHOO-SHA," WHAT KIND OF NAME IS THAT? IT'S PRETTY.
XUXA. IT'S FROM BRASIL. YOU LIKE IT?
UP HERE, SOMETIMES A NAME IS ALL THE PRETTY YOU'LL EVER HAVE.
"SHOO-SHA."
PEOPLE FROM ALL OVER UP HERE, RIGHT?
ALL OVER EARTH? YES.
"EARTH"? WHERE ELSE WOULD THEY BE FROM?
IT'S A BIG UNIVERSE.
BUT YES, THEY WERE LIKE YOU, YOUNG, POOR, UNWANTED, BROUGHT HERE IN NUMBERS NO ONE KNOWS.
SLAVES FOR THE MINES.
TELL ME ABOUT YOU. BEFORE.
WHY DO YOU THINK YOU SURVIVED THE CRASH?
NO. I TOLD YOU, I DON'T KNOW AND I DON'T WANT TO T...
NO, OF COURSE. LET'S JUST, Y'KNOW...
THIS ALL MUST BE SO STRANGE TO YOU.
THIS PLANET IS TOUGH. THE HEAT, THE THIRTY-SIX-HOUR DAYS...
WHAT?!
BUT TWO SATURDAY NIGHTS.
AND THIS CITY CAN BE HELL WITH THE LID OFF. BUT THERE'S SOMETHING MORE, A VIBE HERE.
WHEREVER HUMAN BEINGS GO, THERE CAN BE HOPE, OR EVEN BEAUTY.
I MET THIS WOMAN.
A WOMAN WITH THIS, LIKE, CHEAP PLASTIC FLOWER IN HER HAIR.
MAN, THAT FLOWER WAS BUSTED. BUT IT WAS...
BEAUTIFUL?

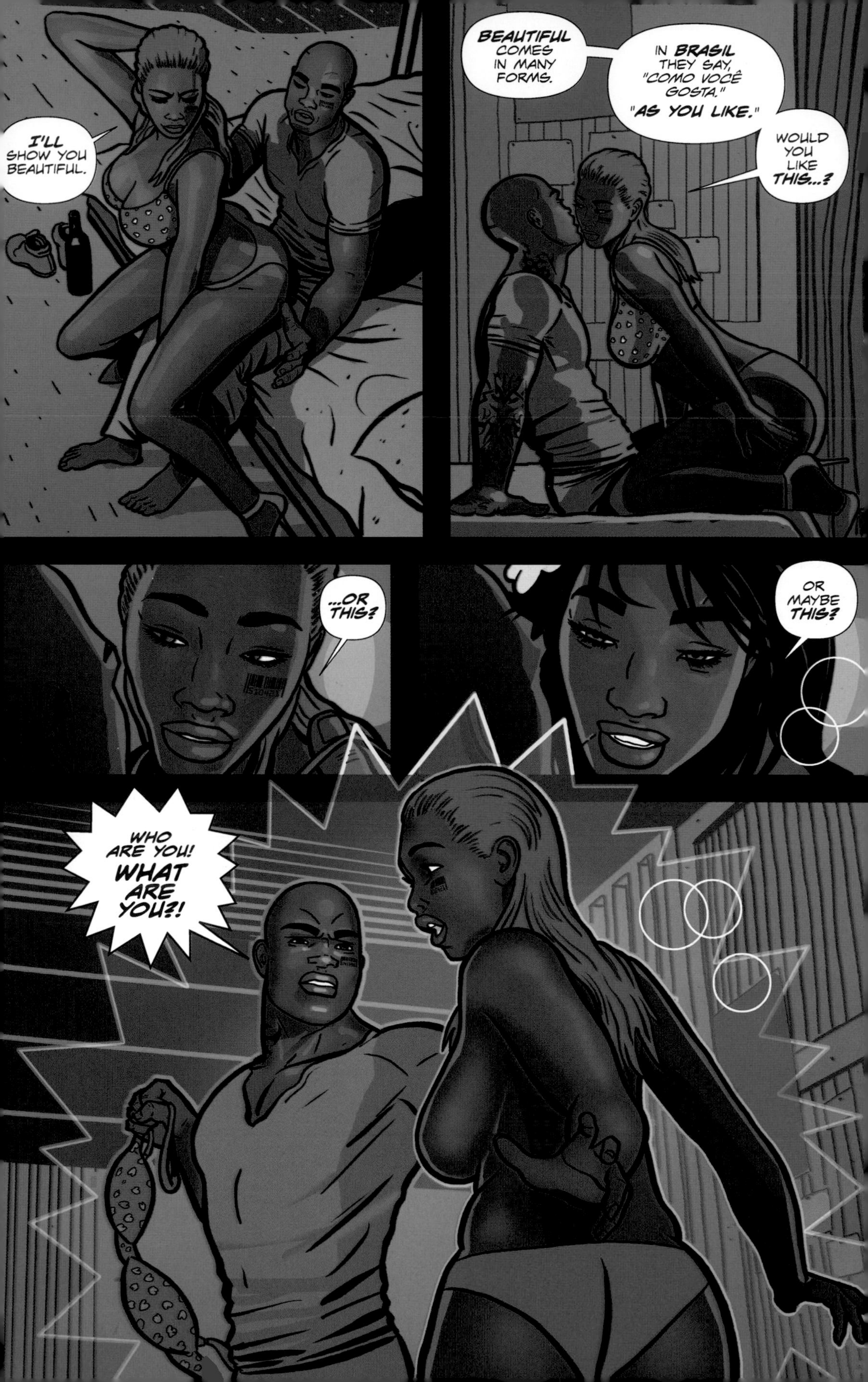
I'LL SHOW YOU BEAUTIFUL.
BEAUTIFUL COMES IN MANY FORMS.
IN BRASIL THEY SAY, "COMO VOCÊ GOSTA." "AS YOU LIKE."
WOULD YOU LIKE THIS...?
...OR THIS?
OR MAYBE THIS?
WHO ARE YOU! WHAT ARE YOU?!

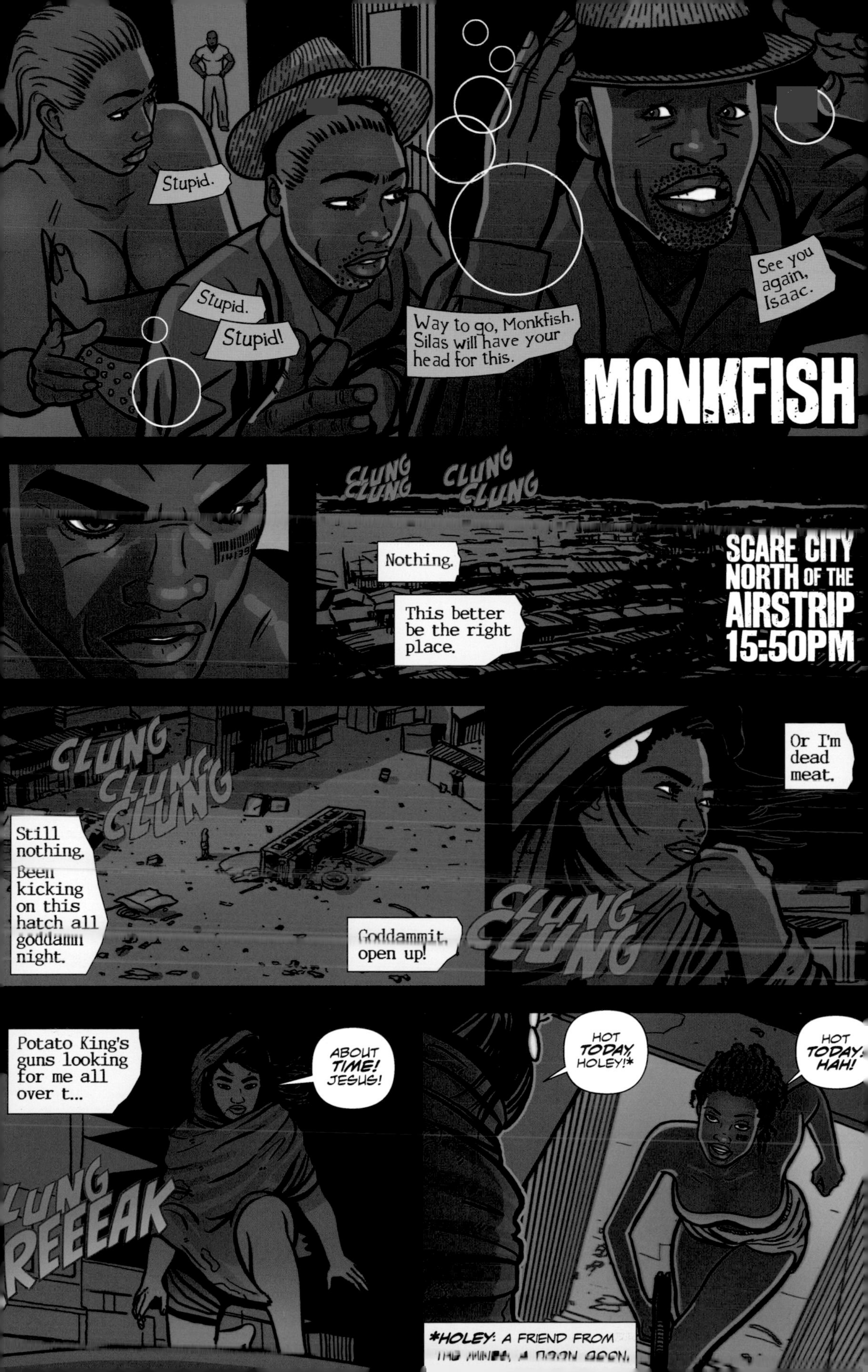

Stupid.
Stupid.
Stupid!
Way to go, Monkfish. Silas will have your head for this.
See you again, Isaac.
MONKFISH
CLUNG CLUNG CLUNG CLUNG
SCARE CITY NORTH OF THE AIRSTRIP 15:50PM
Nothing.
This better be the right place.
Or I'm dead meat.
CLUNG CLUNG CLUNG
Still nothing. Been kicking on this hatch all goddamn night.
Goddammit, open up!
CLUNG CLUNG
Potato King's guns looking for me all over t...
ABOUT TIME! JESUS!
CLUNG REEEAK
HOT TODAY, HOLEY!*
HOT TODAY. HAH!
*HOLEY: A FRIEND FROM

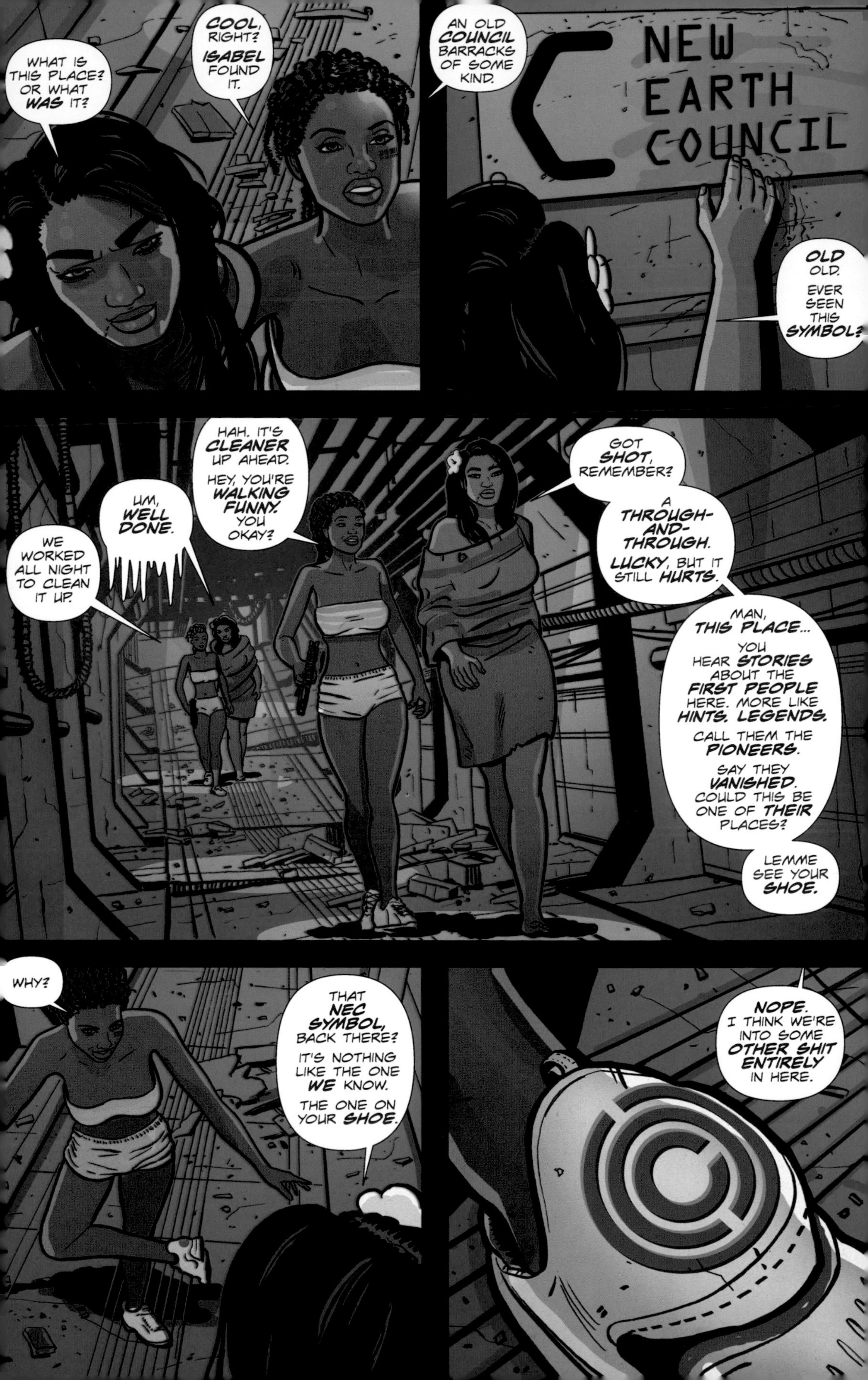
WHAT IS THIS PLACE? OR WHAT WAS IT?
COOL, RIGHT? ISABEL FOUND IT.
AN OLD COUNCIL BARRACKS OF SOME KIND.
NEW EARTH COUNCIL
OLD OLD. EVER SEEN THIS SYMBOL?
WE WORKED ALL NIGHT TO CLEAN IT UP.
UM, WELL DONE.
HAH. IT'S CLEANER UP AHEAD. HEY, YOU'RE WALKING FUNNY. YOU OKAY?
GOT SHOT, REMEMBER?
A THROUGH-AND-THROUGH. LUCKY, BUT IT STILL HURTS.
MAN, THIS PLACE... YOU HEAR STORIES ABOUT THE FIRST PEOPLE HERE. MORE LIKE HINTS. LEGENDS. CALL THEM THE PIONEERS. SAY THEY VANISHED. COULD THIS BE ONE OF THEIR PLACES?
LEMME SEE YOUR SHOE.
WHY?
THAT NEC SYMBOL, BACK THERE? IT'S NOTHING LIKE THE ONE WE KNOW. THE ONE ON YOUR SHOE.
NOPE. I THINK WE'RE INTO SOME OTHER SHIT ENTIRELY IN HERE.

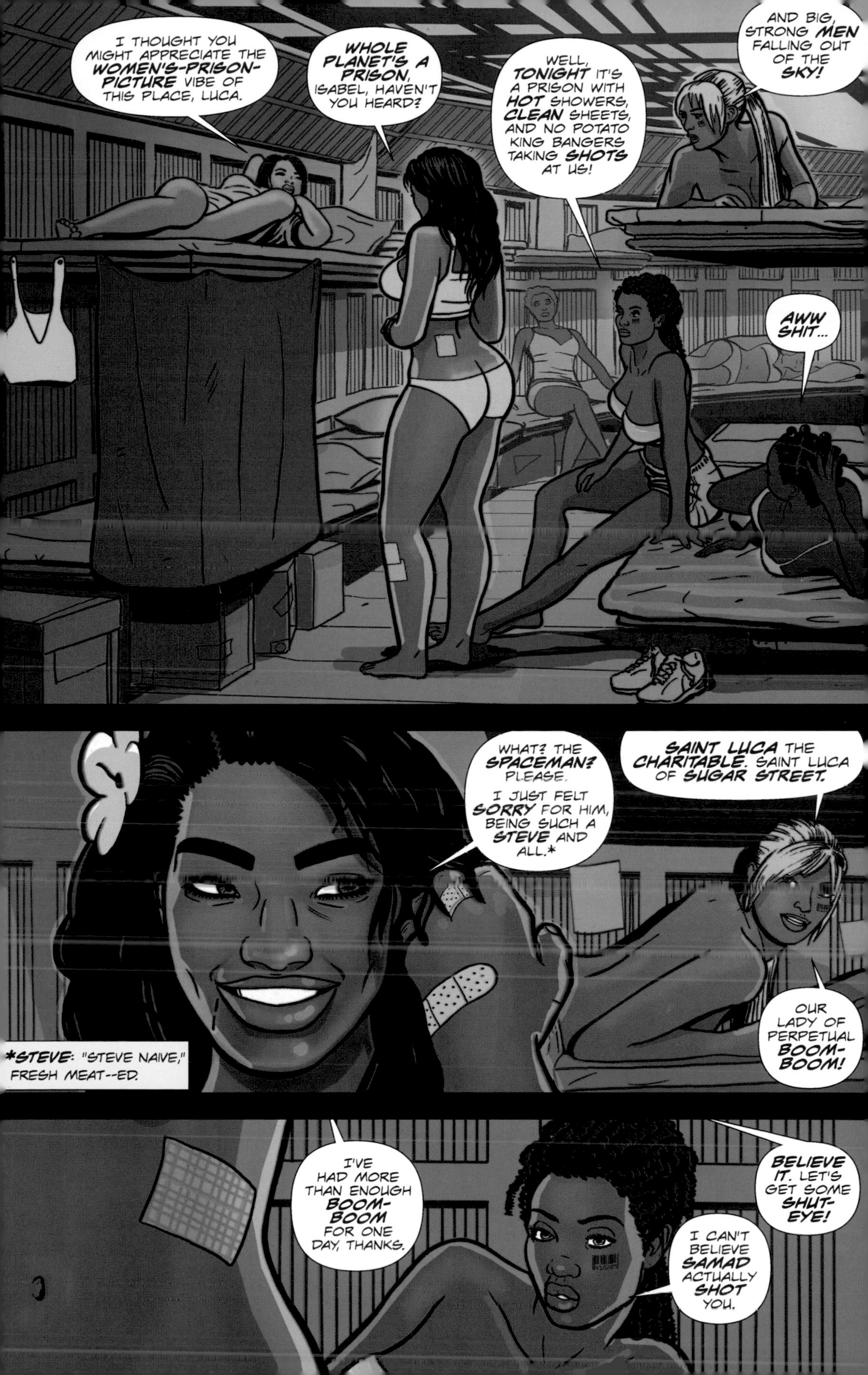
I THOUGHT YOU MIGHT APPRECIATE THE WOMEN'S-PRISON-PICTURE VIBE OF THIS PLACE, LUCA.
WHOLE PLANET'S A PRISON, ISABEL, HAVEN'T YOU HEARD?
WELL, TONIGHT IT'S A PRISON WITH HOT SHOWERS, CLEAN SHEETS, AND NO POTATO KING BANGERS TAKING SHOTS AT US!
AND BIG, STRONG MEN FALLING OUT OF THE SKY!
AWW SHIT...
WHAT? THE SPACEMAN? PLEASE.
I JUST FELT SORRY FOR HIM, BEING SUCH A STEVE AND ALL.*
SAINT LUCA THE CHARITABLE. SAINT LUCA OF SUGAR STREET.
OUR LADY OF PERPETUAL BOOM-BOOM!
*STEVE: "STEVE NAIVE," FRESH MEAT--ED.
I'VE HAD MORE THAN ENOUGH BOOM-BOOM FOR ONE DAY, THANKS.
BELIEVE IT. LET'S GET SOME SHUT-EYE!
I CAN'T BELIEVE SAMAD ACTUALLY SHOT YOU.

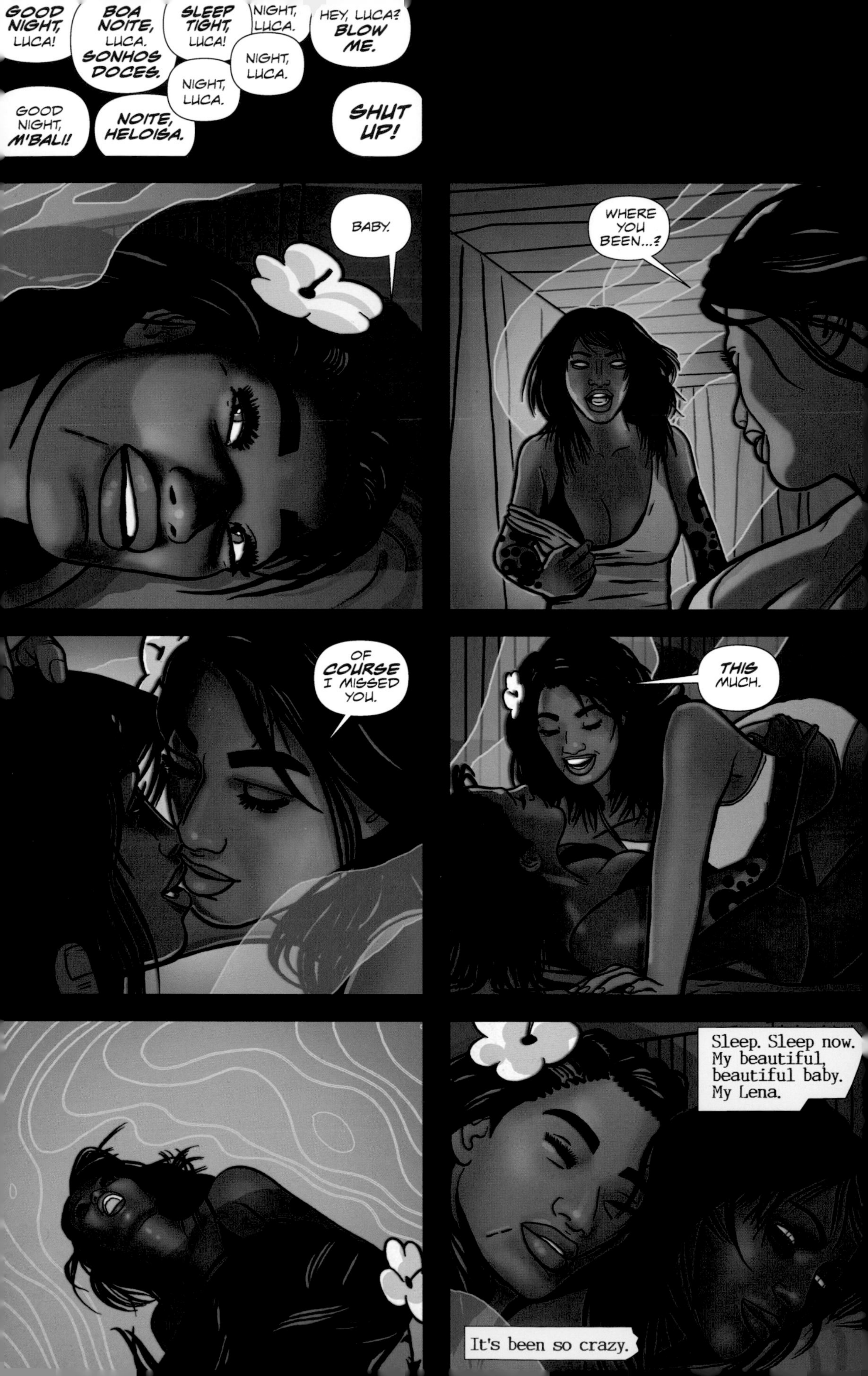
GOOD NIGHT, LUCA!
BOA NOITE, LUCA. SONHOS DOCES.
SLEEP TIGHT, LUCA!
NIGHT, LUCA.
HEY, LUCA? BLOW ME.
NIGHT, LUCA.
NIGHT, LUCA.
GOOD NIGHT, M'BALI!
NOITE, HELOISA.
SHUT UP!
BABY.
WHERE YOU BEEN...?
OF COURSE I MISSED YOU.
THIS MUCH.
Sleep. Sleep now. My beautiful, beautiful baby. My Lena.
It's been so crazy.

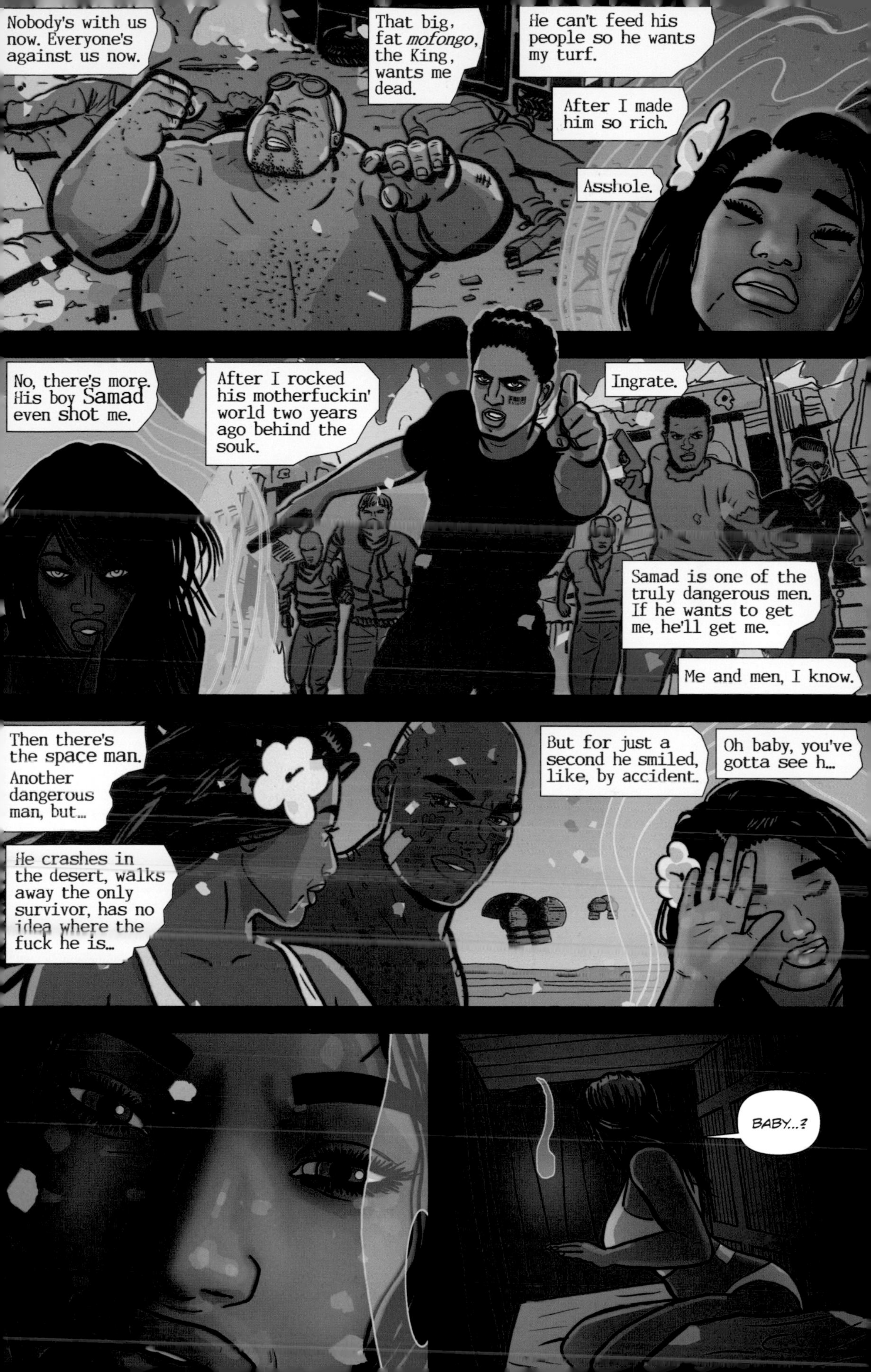
Nobody's with us now. Everyone's against us now.
That big, fat *mofongo*, the King, wants me dead.
He can't feed his people so he wants my turf.
After I made him so rich.
Asshole.
No, there's more. His boy Samad even shot me.
After I rocked his motherfuckin' world two years ago behind the souk.
Ingrate.
Samad is one of the truly dangerous men. If he wants to get me, he'll get me.
Me and men, I know.
Then there's the space man.
Another dangerous man, but...
He crashes in the desert, walks away the only survivor, has no idea where the fuck he is...
But for just a second he smiled, like, by accident.
Oh baby, you've gotta see h...
BABY...?

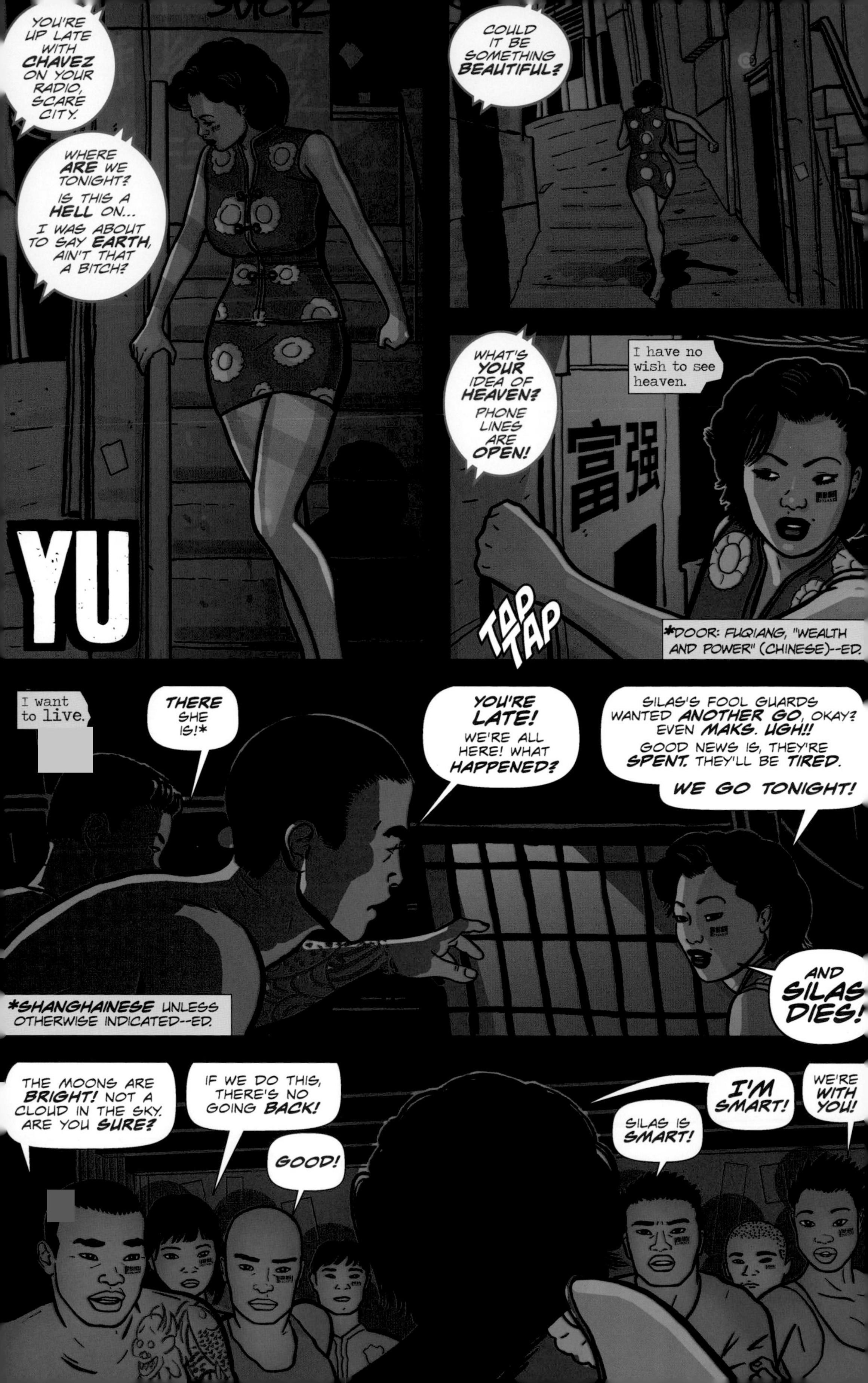

YOU'RE UP LATE WITH CHAVEZ ON YOUR RADIO, SCARE CITY.
WHERE ARE WE TONIGHT? IS THIS A HELL ON... I WAS ABOUT TO SAY EARTH, AIN'T THAT A BITCH?
YU
COULD IT BE SOMETHING BEAUTIFUL?
WHAT'S YOUR IDEA OF HEAVEN? PHONE LINES ARE OPEN!
I have no wish to see heaven.
富强
TAP TAP
*DOOR: FUQIANG, "WEALTH AND POWER" (CHINESE)--ED.
I want to live.
THERE SHE IS!*
YOU'RE LATE! WE'RE ALL HERE! WHAT HAPPENED?
SILAS'S FOOL GUARDS WANTED ANOTHER GO, OKAY? EVEN MAKS. UGH!! GOOD NEWS IS, THEY'RE SPENT. THEY'LL BE TIRED.
WE GO TONIGHT!
AND SILAS DIES!
*SHANGHAINESE UNLESS OTHERWISE INDICATED--ED.
THE MOONS ARE BRIGHT! NOT A CLOUD IN THE SKY. ARE YOU SURE?
IF WE DO THIS, THERE'S NO GOING BACK!
GOOD!
SILAS IS SMART!
I'M SMART!
WE'RE WITH YOU!

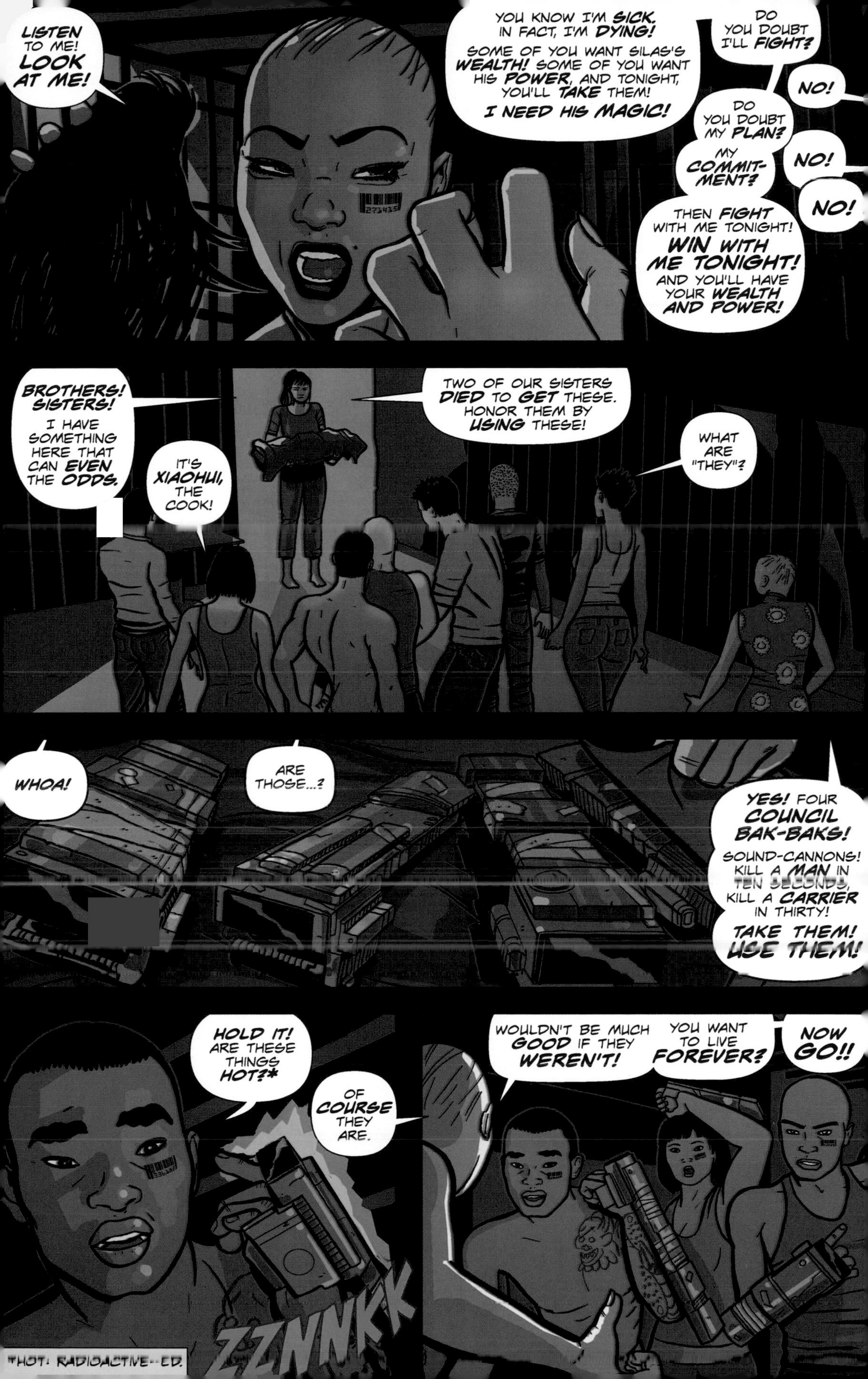
LISTEN TO ME! LOOK AT ME!
YOU KNOW I'M SICK. IN FACT, I'M DYING!
SOME OF YOU WANT SILAS'S WEALTH! SOME OF YOU WANT HIS POWER, AND TONIGHT, YOU'LL TAKE THEM!
I NEED HIS MAGIC!
DO YOU DOUBT I'LL FIGHT?
NO!
DO YOU DOUBT MY PLAN?
NO!
MY COMMIT-MENT?
NO!
THEN FIGHT WITH ME TONIGHT! WIN WITH ME TONIGHT!
AND YOU'LL HAVE YOUR WEALTH AND POWER!
BROTHERS! SISTERS!
I HAVE SOMETHING HERE THAT CAN EVEN THE ODDS.
IT'S XIAOHUI, THE COOK!
TWO OF OUR SISTERS DIED TO GET THESE. HONOR THEM BY USING THESE!
WHAT ARE "THEY"?
WHOA!
ARE THOSE...?
YES! FOUR COUNCIL BAK-BAKS!
SOUND-CANNONS! KILL A MAN IN TEN SECONDS, KILL A CARRIER IN THIRTY!
TAKE THEM! USE THEM!
HOLD IT! ARE THESE THINGS HOT?*
OF COURSE THEY ARE.
ZZNNKK
THOT: RADIOACTIVE--ED.
WOULDN'T BE MUCH GOOD IF THEY WEREN'T!
YOU WANT TO LIVE FOREVER?
NOW GO!!

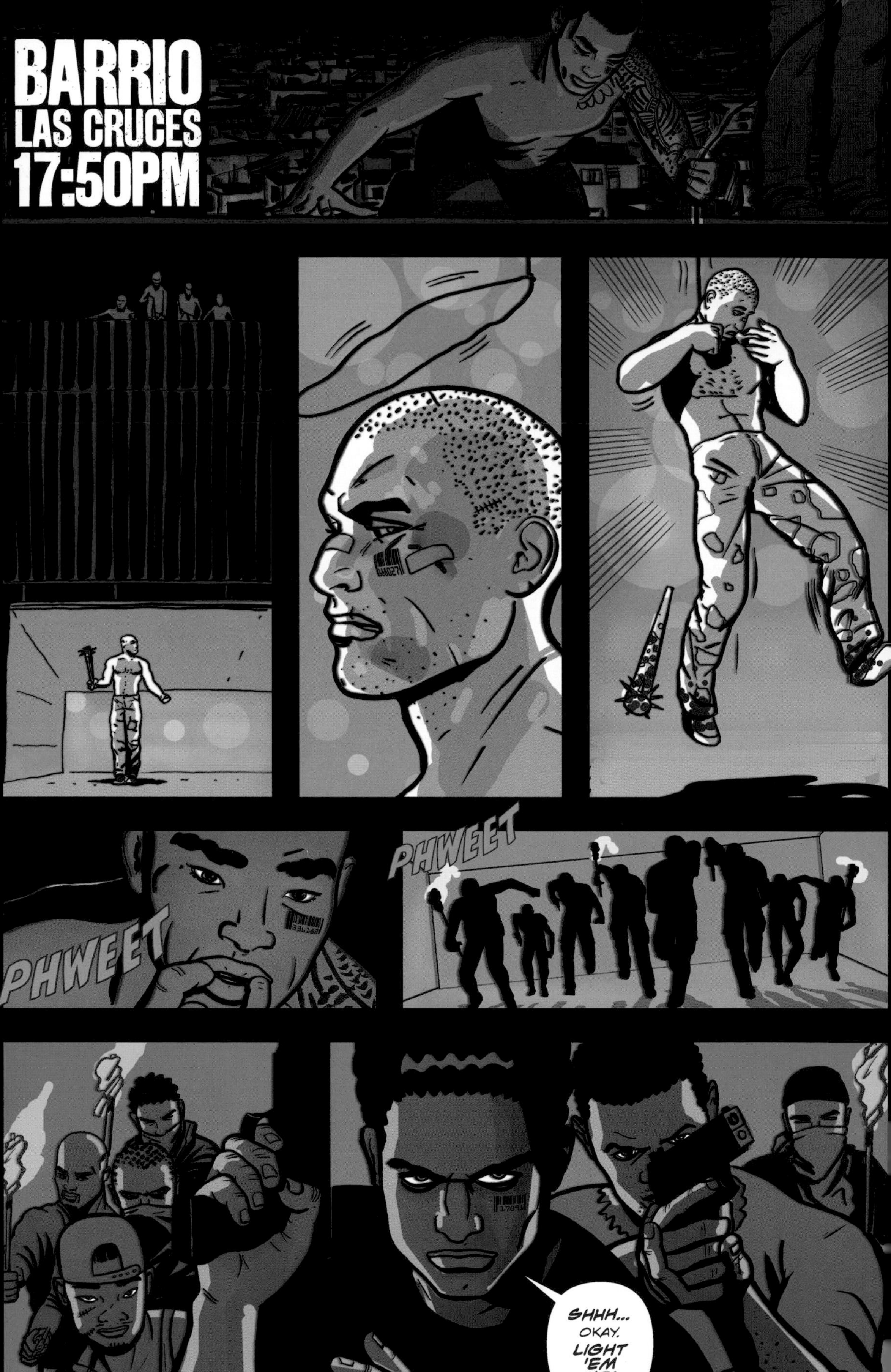
BARRIO LAS CRUCES 17:50PM
PHWEET
PHWEET
SHHH... OKAY. LIGHT 'EM UP!

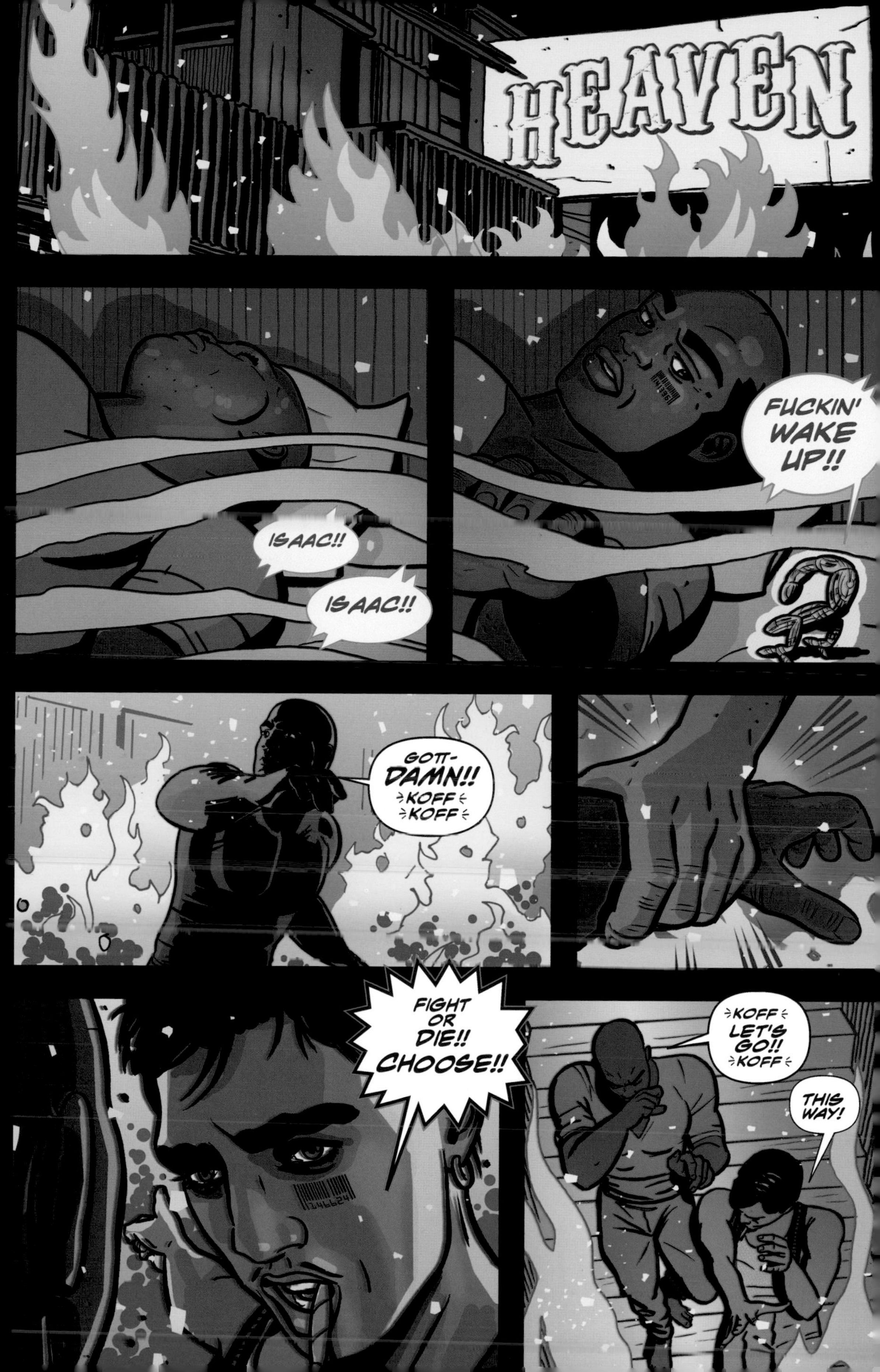
HEAVEN
ISAAC!!
ISAAC!!
FUCKIN' WAKE UP!!
GOTT-DAMN!! KOFF KOFF
FIGHT OR DIE!! CHOOSE!!
KOFF LET'S GO!! KOFF
THIS WAY!

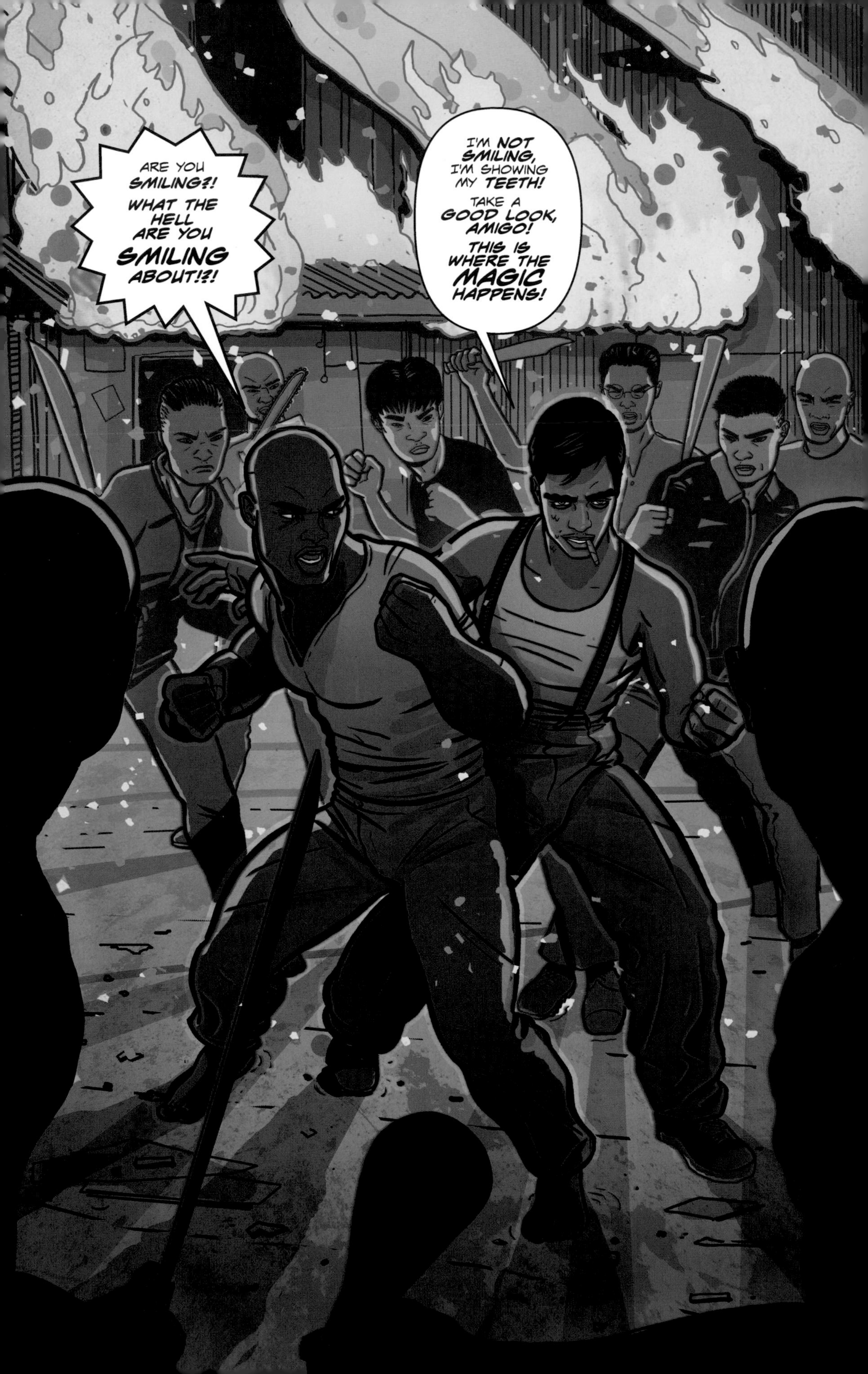
ARE YOU SMILING?! WHAT THE HELL ARE YOU SMILING ABOUT!?!
I'M NOT SMILING, I'M SHOWING MY TEETH! TAKE A GOOD LOOK, AMIGO! THIS IS WHERE THE MAGIC HAPPENS!

"You wanted wealth and
power. I offered you magic . . .
I offered you destiny!
Here . . . Take your destiny!"
—Silas

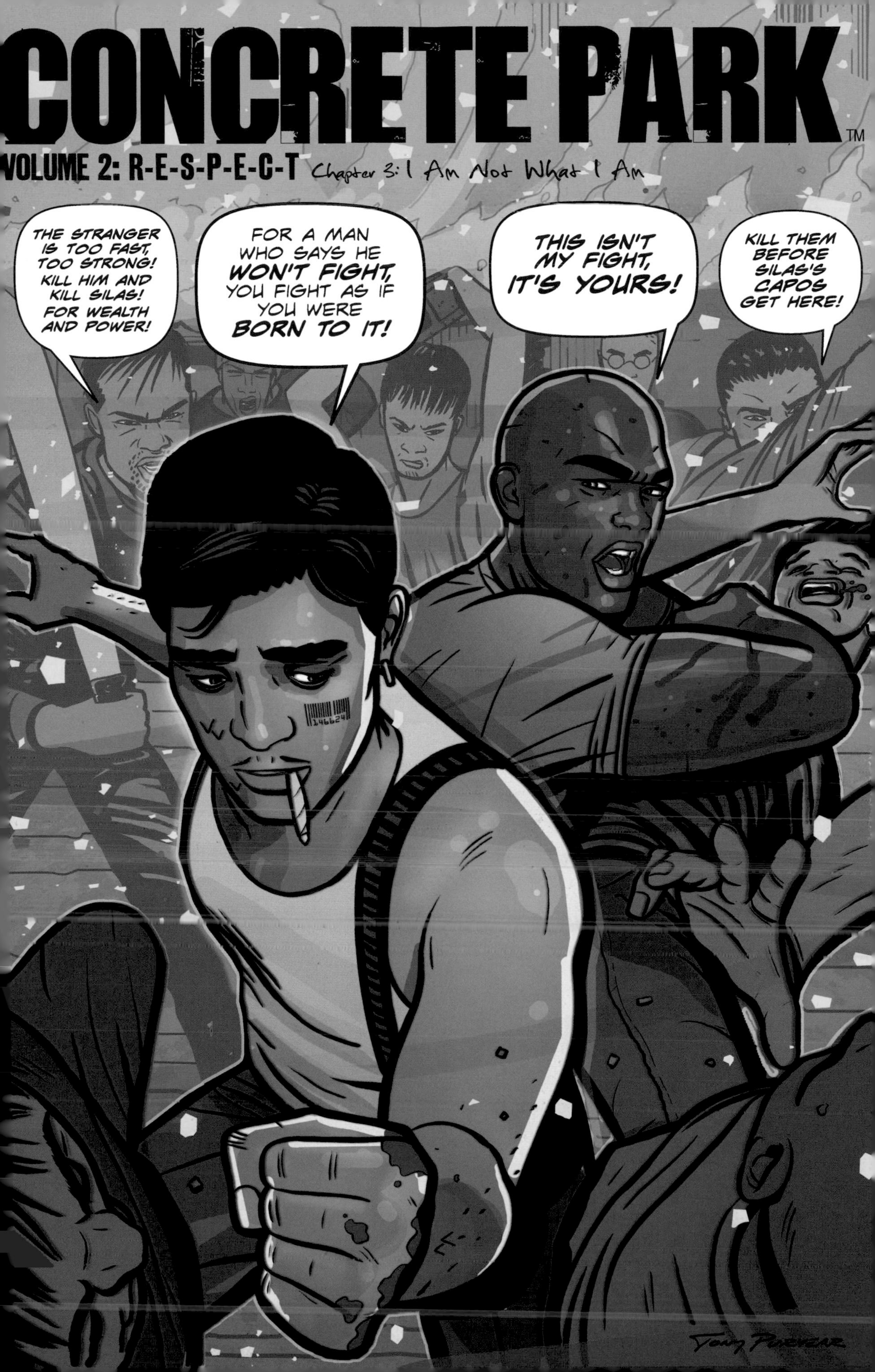
CONCRETE PARK™
VOLUME 2: R-E-S-P-E-C-T Chapter 3: I Am Not What I Am
THE STRANGER IS TOO FAST, TOO STRONG! KILL HIM AND KILL SILAS! FOR WEALTH AND POWER!
FOR A MAN WHO SAYS HE WON'T FIGHT, YOU FIGHT AS IF YOU WERE BORN TO IT!
THIS ISN'T MY FIGHT, IT'S YOURS!
KILL THEM BEFORE SILAS'S CAPOS GET HERE!
146624

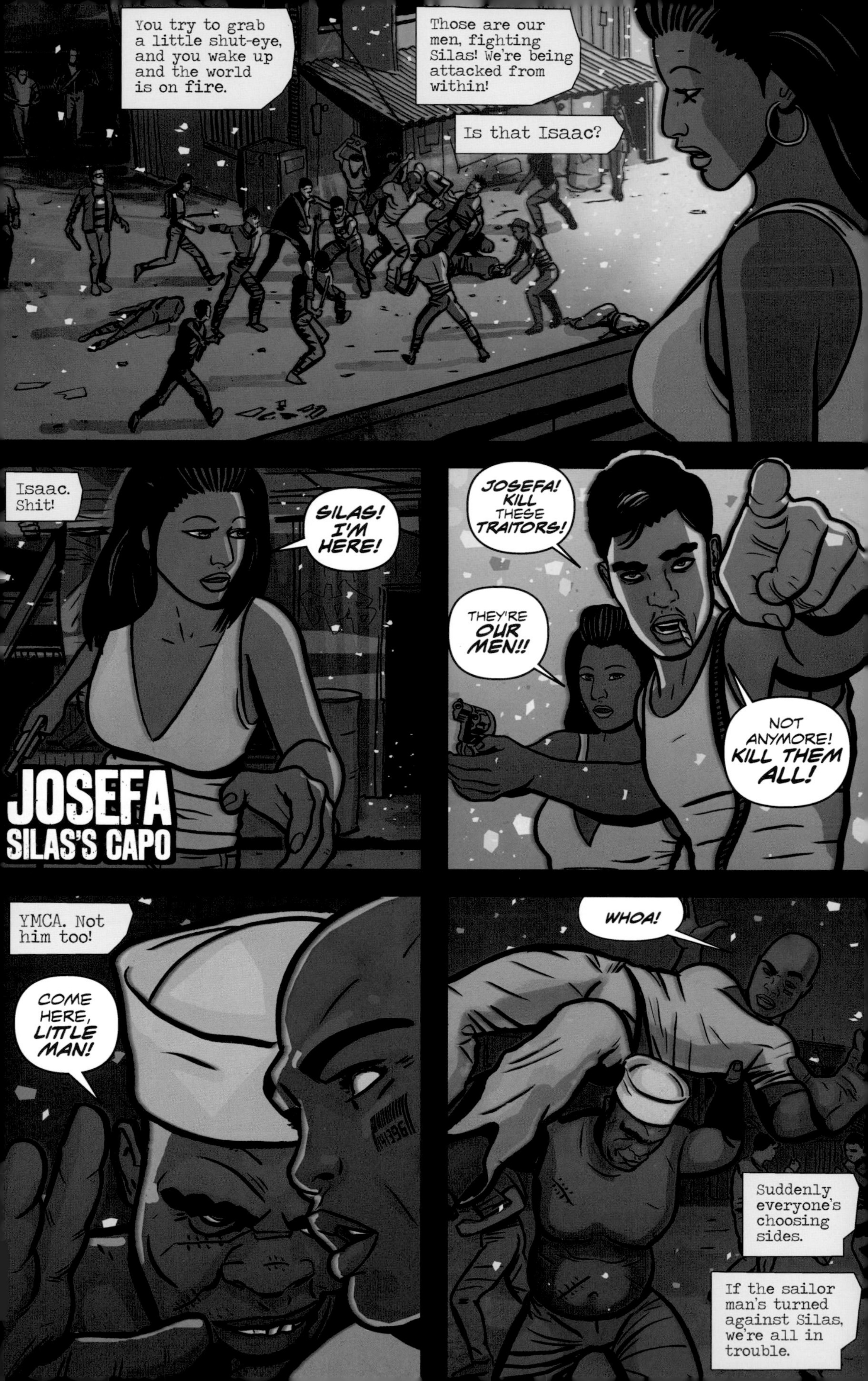

You try to grab a little shut-eye, and you wake up and the world is on fire.
Those are our men, fighting Silas! We're being attacked from within!
Is that Isaac?
Isaac. Shit!
SILAS! I'M HERE!
JOSEFA
SILAS'S CAPO
JOSEFA! KILL THESE TRAITORS!
THEY'RE OUR MEN!!
NOT ANYMORE! KILL THEM ALL!
YMCA. Not him too!
COME HERE, LITTLE MAN!
WHOA!
Suddenly everyone's choosing sides.
If the sailor man's turned against Silas, we're all in trouble.

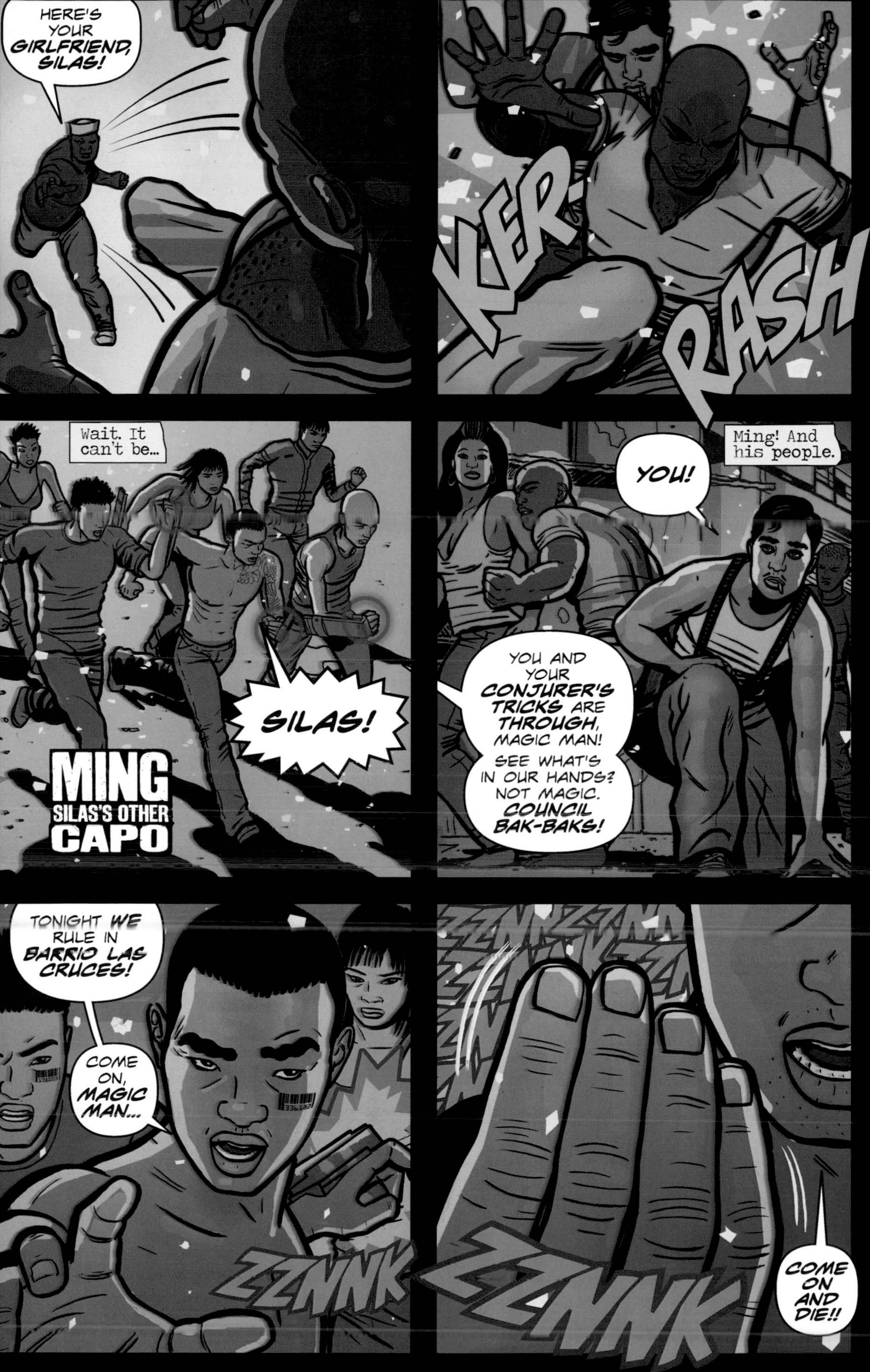
HERE'S YOUR GIRLFRIEND, SILAS!
KER-RASH
Wait. It can't be...
SILAS!
MING SILAS'S OTHER CAPO
Ming! And his people.
YOU!
YOU AND YOUR CONJURER'S TRICKS ARE THROUGH, MAGIC MAN!
SEE WHAT'S IN OUR HANDS? NOT MAGIC. COUNCIL BAK-BAKS!
TONIGHT WE RULE IN BARRIO LAS CRUCES!
COME ON, MAGIC MAN...
ZZNNK
ZZNNK
COME ON AND DIE!!

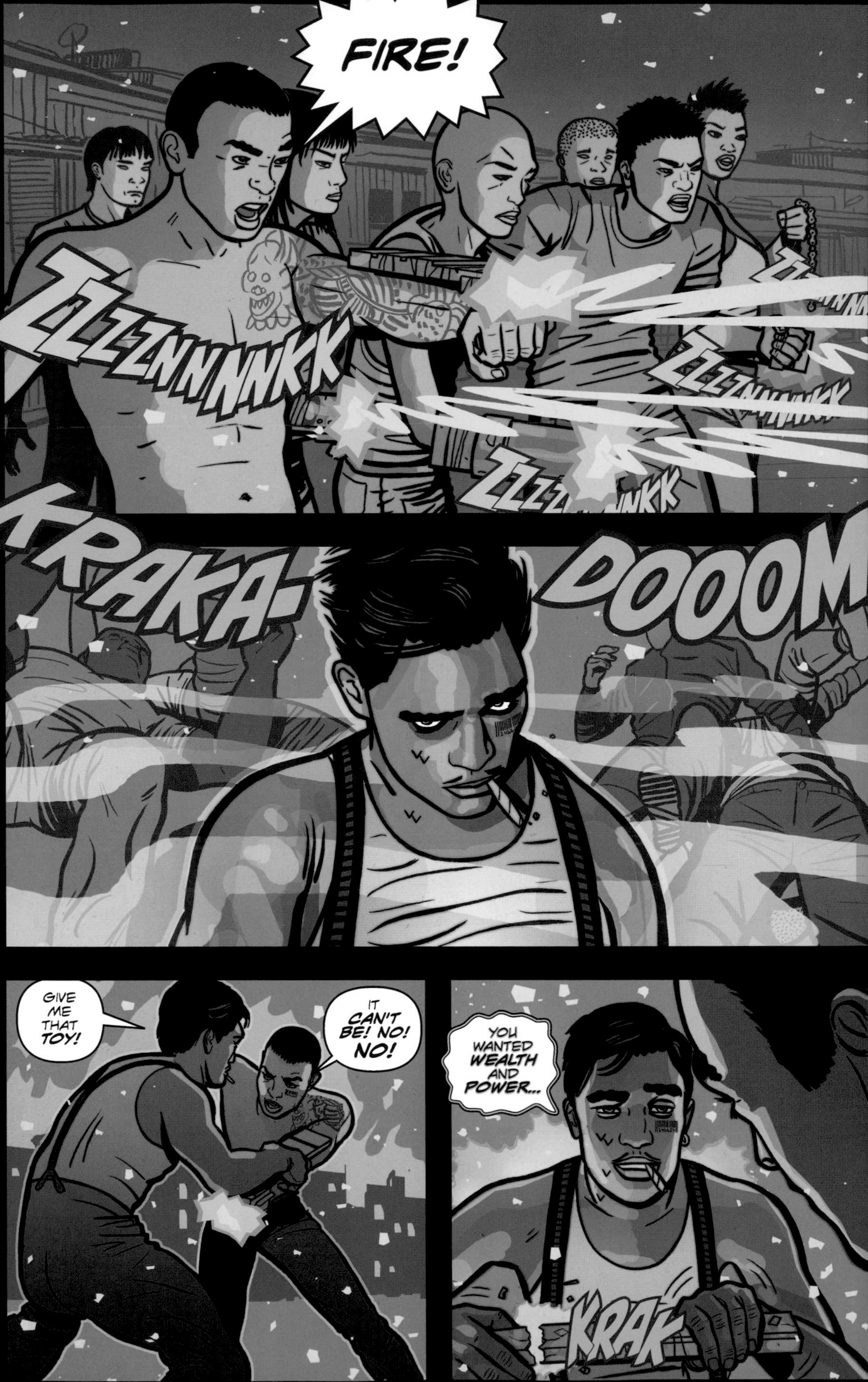
FIRE!
ZZZZNNNNNKK
ZZZZNNNNK
ZZZZNNNNKK
ZZZZ...NNKK
KRAKA-
DOOOM
GIVE ME THAT TOY!
IT CAN'T BE! NO! NO!
YOU WANTED WEALTH AND POWER...
KRAK

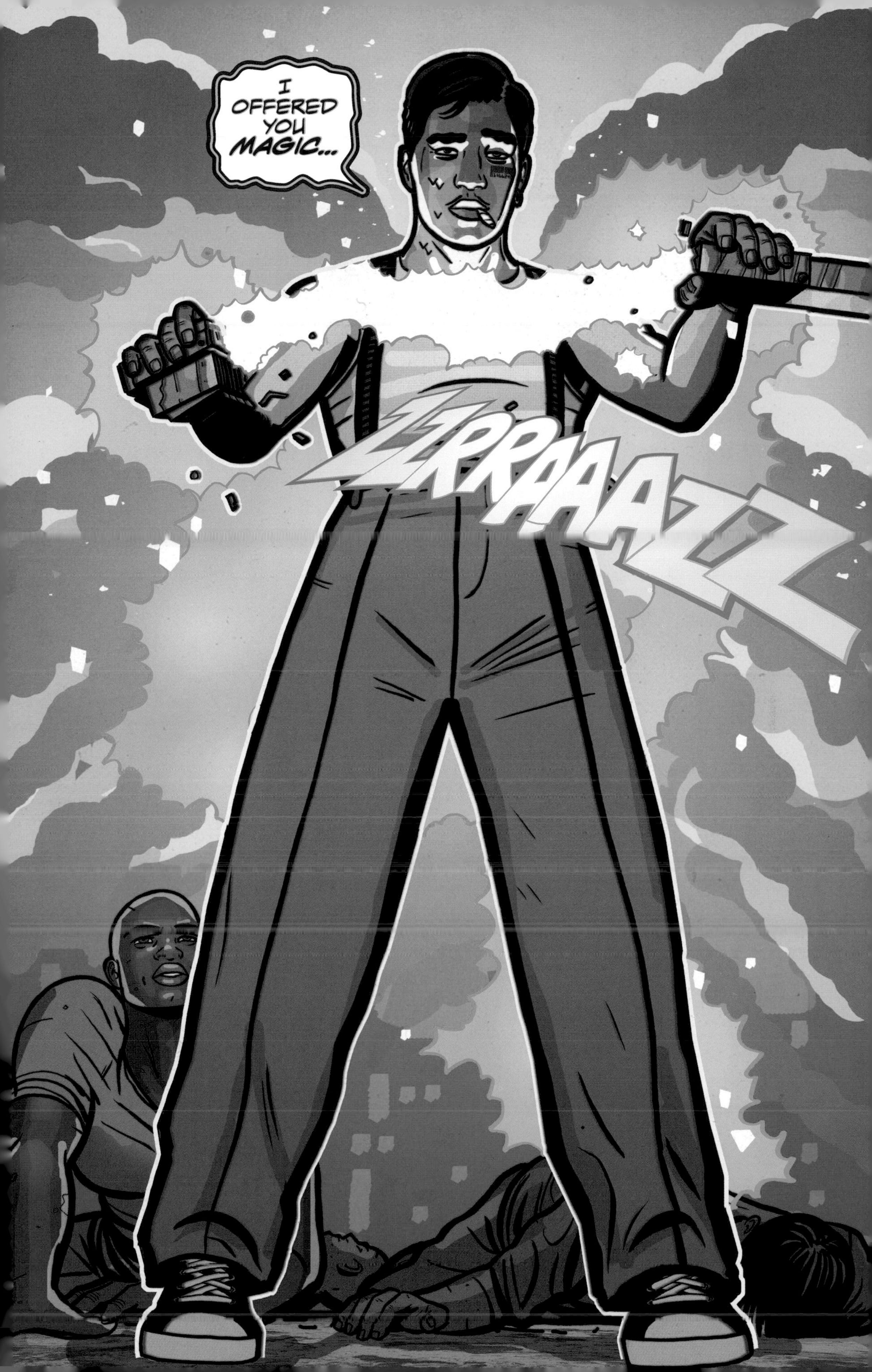
I OFFERED YOU MAGIC...
ZZRRAAAZZZ

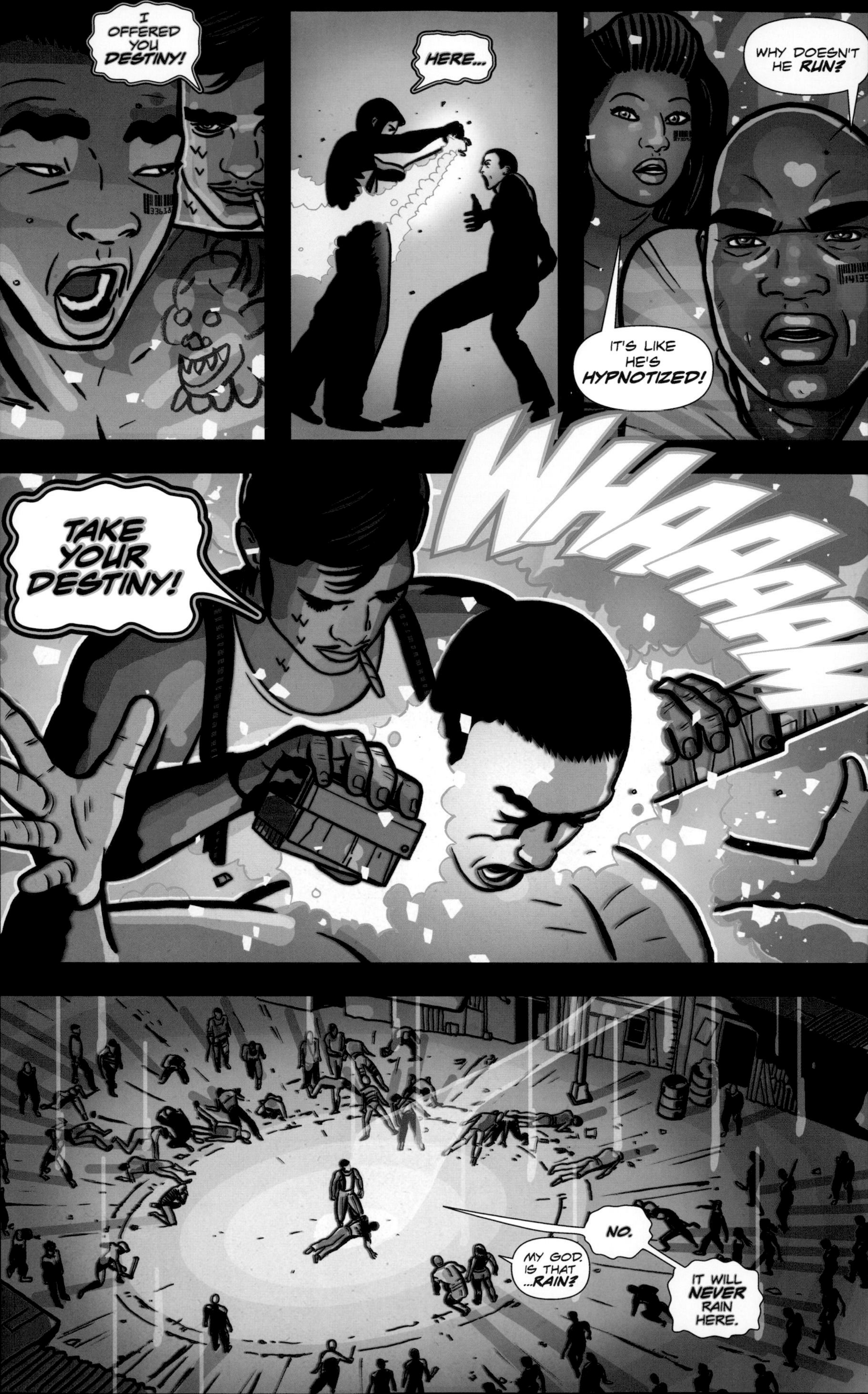
I OFFERED YOU DESTINY!
HERE...
WHY DOESN'T HE RUN?
IT'S LIKE HE'S HYPNOTIZED!
TAKE YOUR DESTINY!
WHAAAAM
MY GOD. IS THAT ...RAIN?
NO.
IT WILL NEVER RAIN HERE.

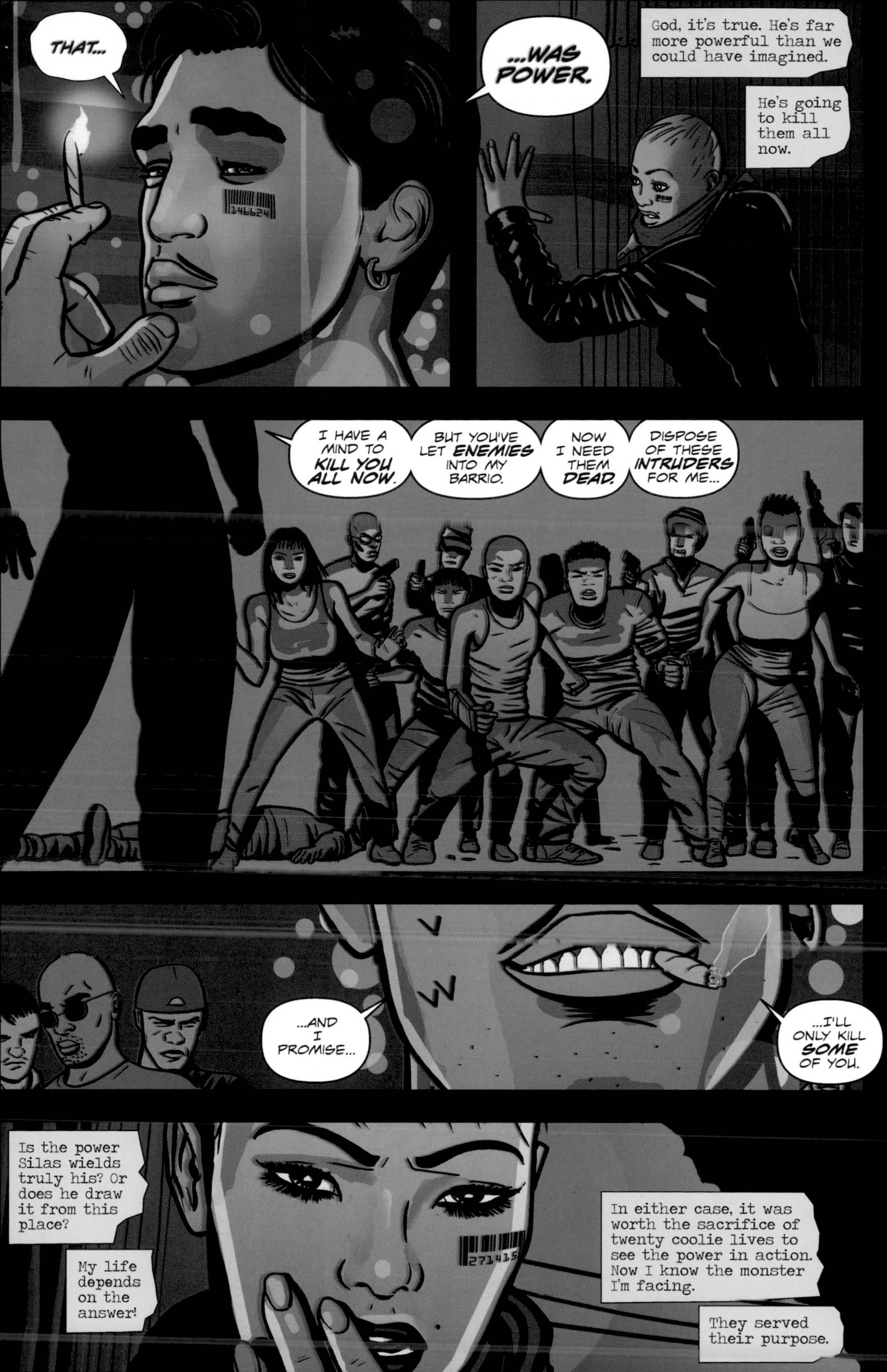
THAT...
...WAS POWER.
God, it's true. He's far more powerful than we could have imagined.
He's going to kill them all now.
I HAVE A MIND TO KILL YOU ALL NOW.
BUT YOU'VE LET ENEMIES INTO MY BARRIO.
NOW I NEED THEM DEAD.
DISPOSE OF THESE INTRUDERS FOR ME...
...AND I PROMISE...
...I'LL ONLY KILL SOME OF YOU.
Is the power Silas wields truly his? Or does he draw it from this place?
My life depends on the answer!
In either case, it was worth the sacrifice of twenty coolie lives to see the power in action. Now I know the monster I'm facing.
They served their purpose.

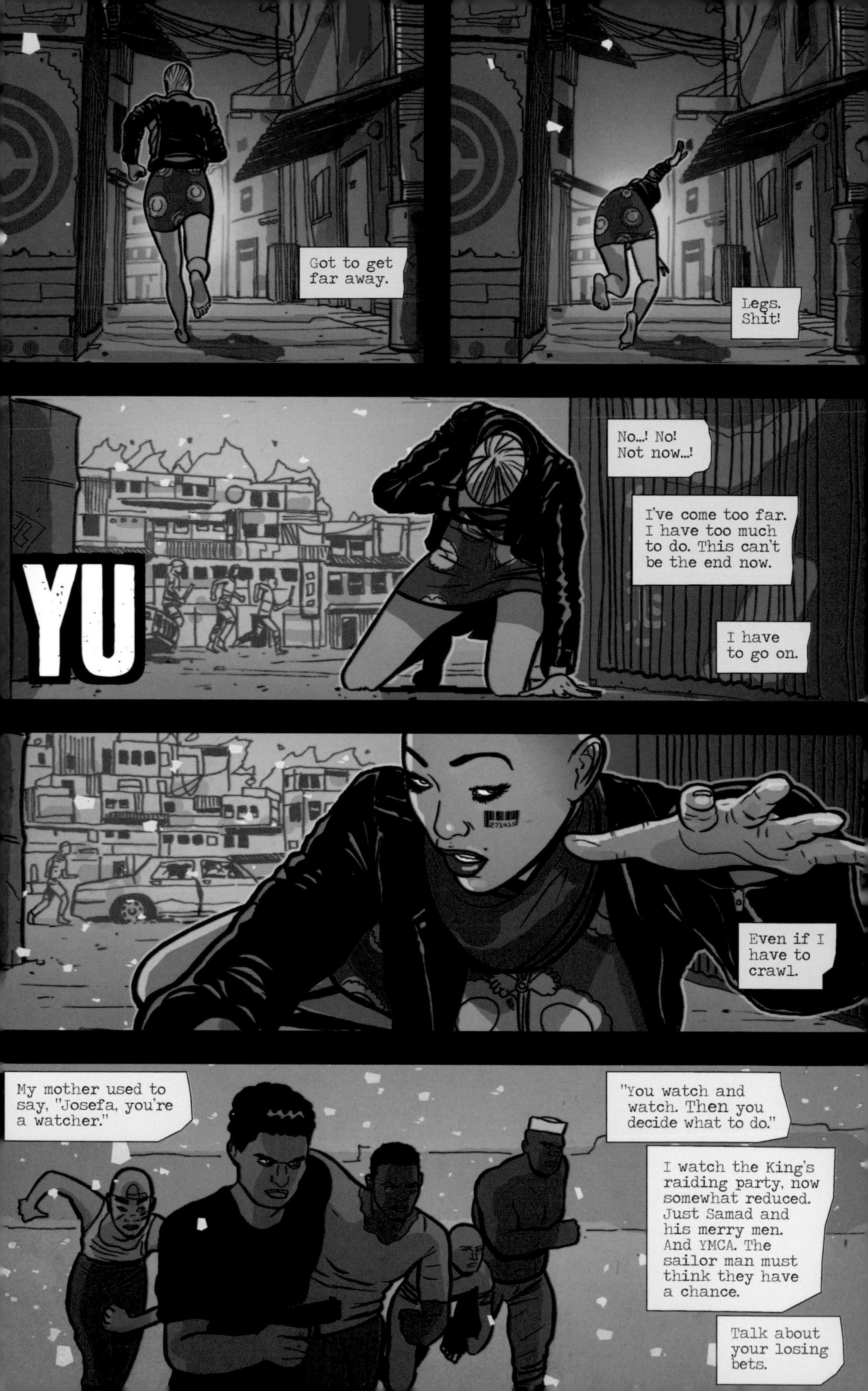

Got to get far away.
Legs. Shit!
No...! No! Not now...!
I've come too far. I have too much to do. This can't be the end now.
I have to go on.
YU
Even if I have to crawl.
My mother used to say, "Josefa, you're a watcher."
"You watch and watch. Then you decide what to do."
I watch the King's raiding party, now somewhat reduced. Just Samad and his merry men. And YMCA. The sailor man must think they have a chance.
Talk about your losing bets.

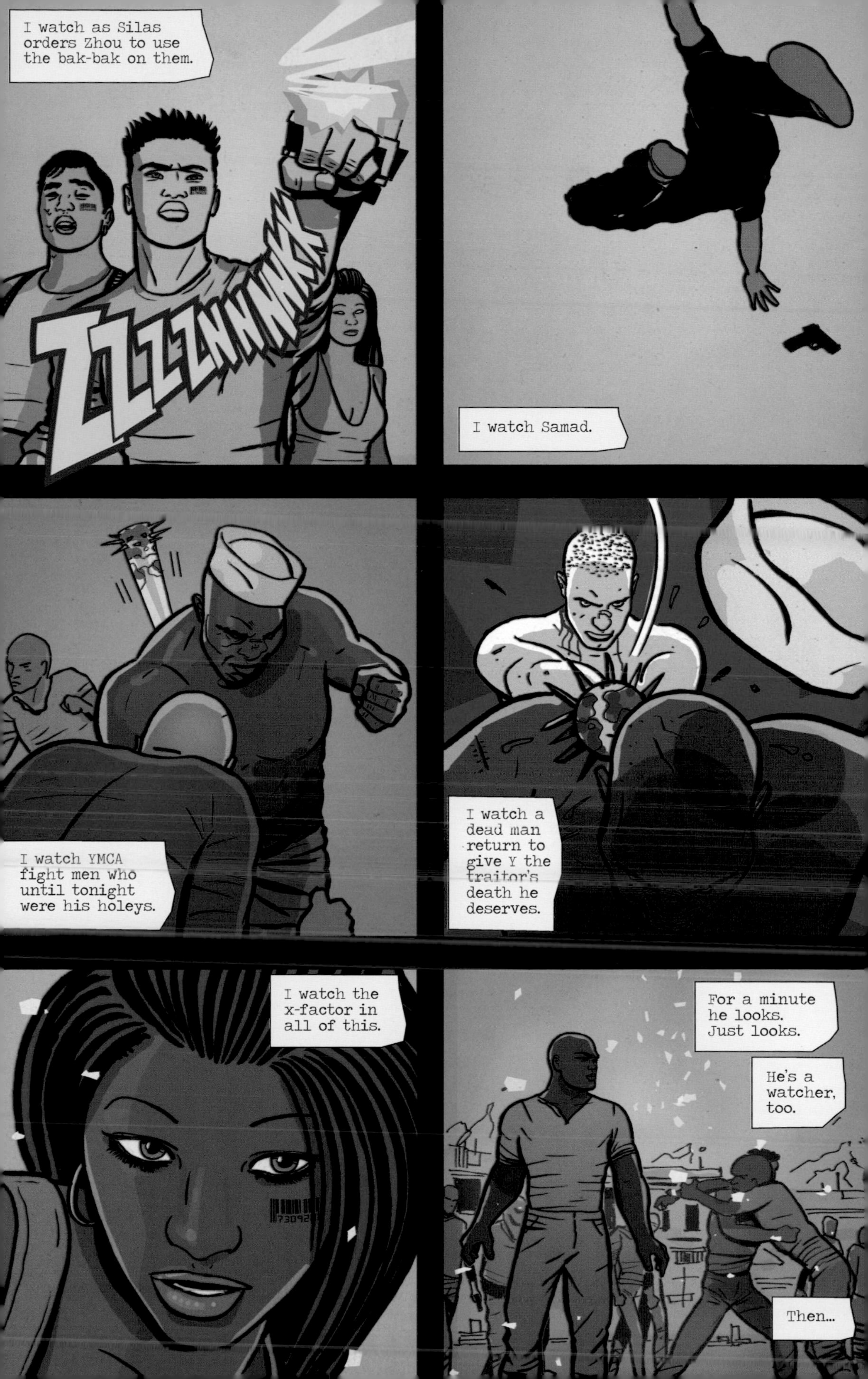
I watch as Silas orders Zhou to use the bak-bak on them.
ZZZZNNNNKK
I watch Samad.
I watch YMCA fight men who until tonight were his holeys.
I watch a dead man return to give Y the traitor's death he deserves.
I watch the x-factor in all of this.
For a minute he looks. Just looks.
He's a watcher, too.
Then...

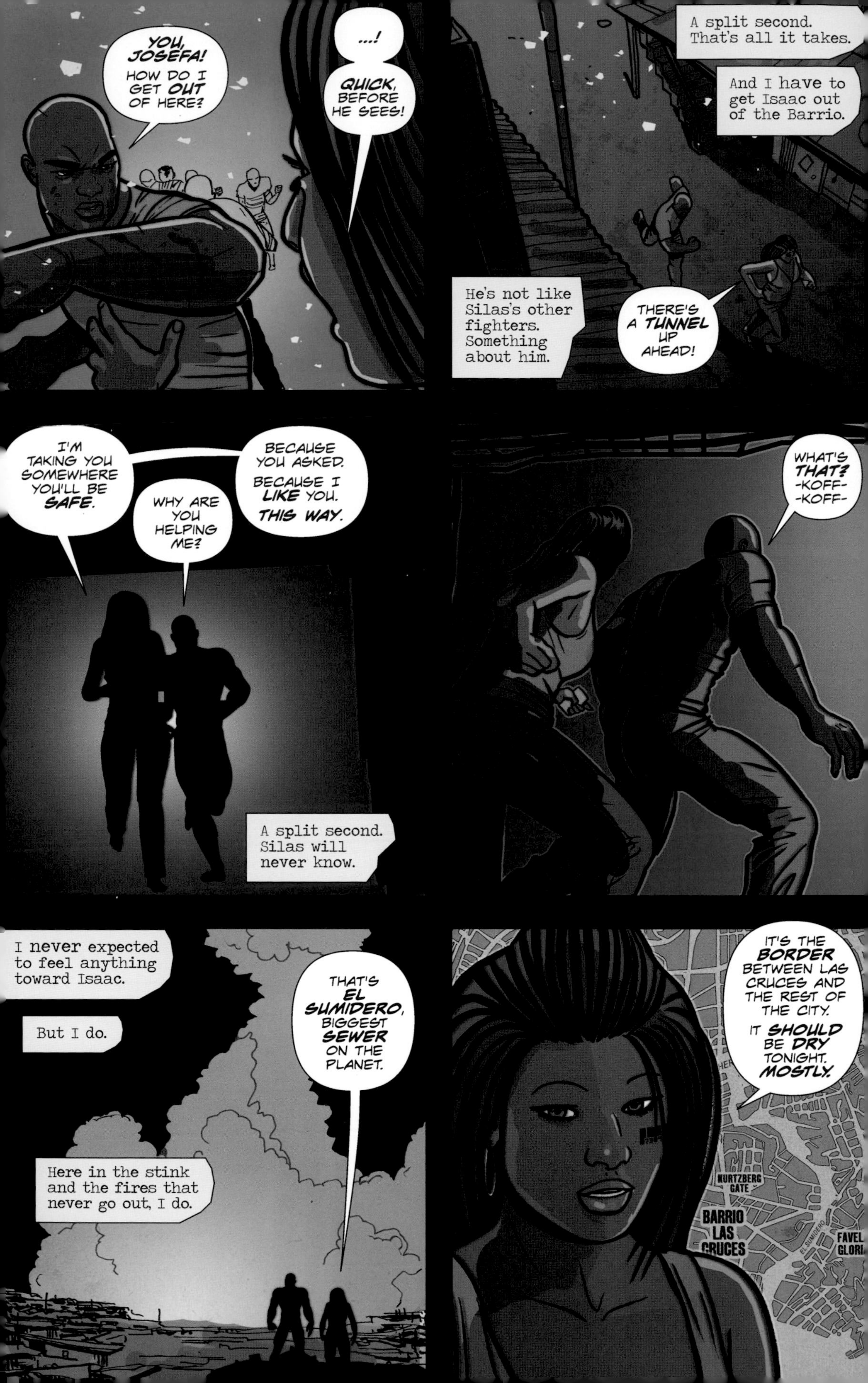

YOU, JOSEFA! HOW DO I GET OUT OF HERE?
...!
QUICK, BEFORE HE SEES!
A split second. That's all it takes.
And I have to get Isaac out of the Barrio.
He's not like Silas's other fighters. Something about him.
THERE'S A TUNNEL UP AHEAD!
I'M TAKING YOU SOMEWHERE YOU'LL BE SAFE.
WHY ARE YOU HELPING ME?
BECAUSE YOU ASKED. BECAUSE I LIKE YOU. THIS WAY.
A split second. Silas will never know.
WHAT'S THAT? -KOFF- -KOFF-
I never expected to feel anything toward Isaac.
But I do.
Here in the stink and the fires that never go out, I do.
THAT'S EL SUMIDERO, BIGGEST SEWER ON THE PLANET.
IT'S THE BORDER BETWEEN LAS CRUCES AND THE REST OF THE CITY.
IT SHOULD BE DRY TONIGHT. MOSTLY.
KURTZBERG GATE
BARRIO LAS CRUCES
EL SUMIDERO

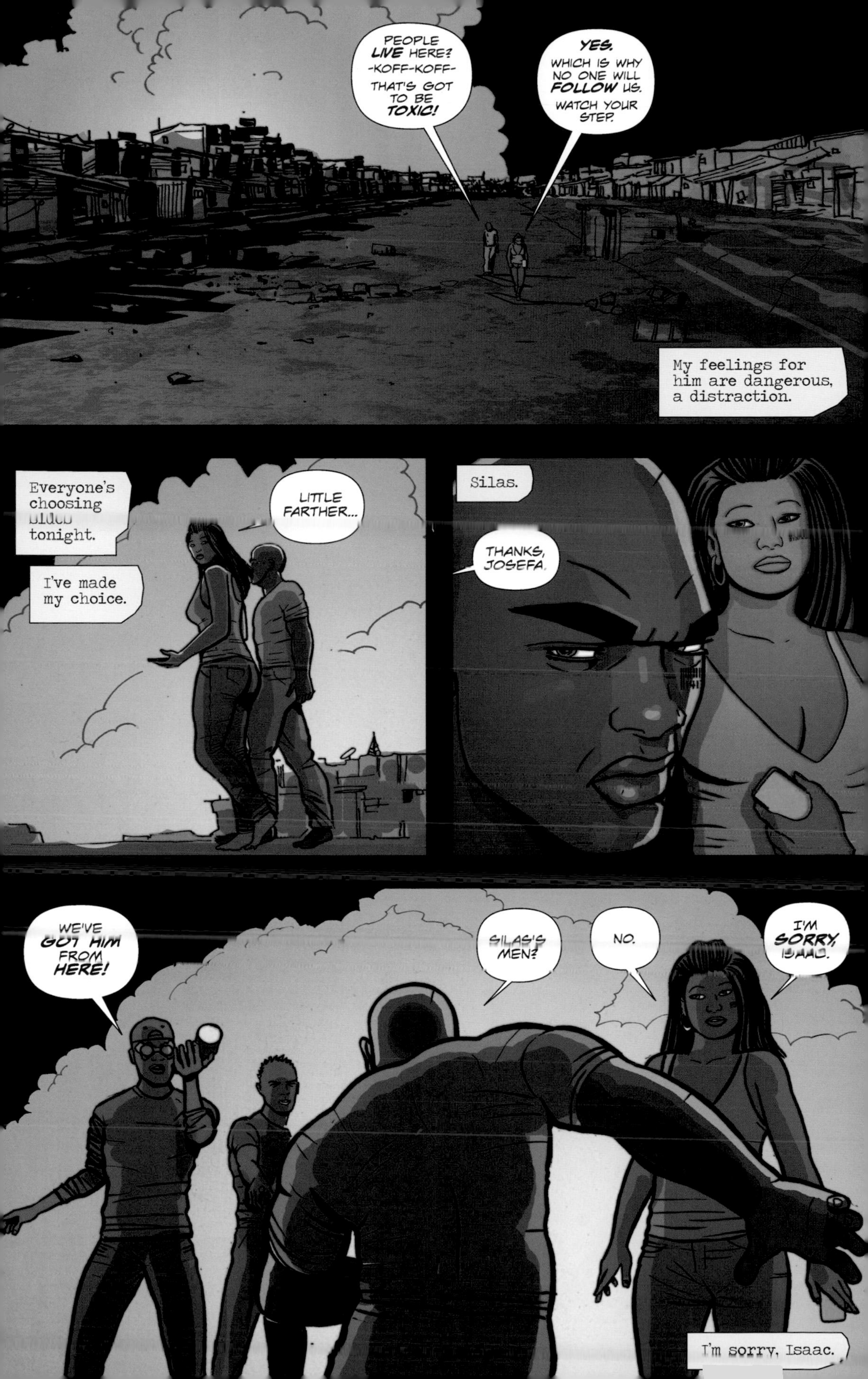
PEOPLE LIVE HERE? -KOFF-KOFF- THAT'S GOT TO BE TOXIC!
YES. WHICH IS WHY NO ONE WILL FOLLOW US. WATCH YOUR STEP.
My feelings for him are dangerous, a distraction.
Everyone's choosing blood tonight.
I've made my choice.
LITTLE FARTHER...
Silas.
THANKS, JOSEFA.
WE'VE GOT HIM FROM HERE!
SILAS'S MEN?
NO.
I'M SORRY, ISAAC.
I'm sorry, Isaac.

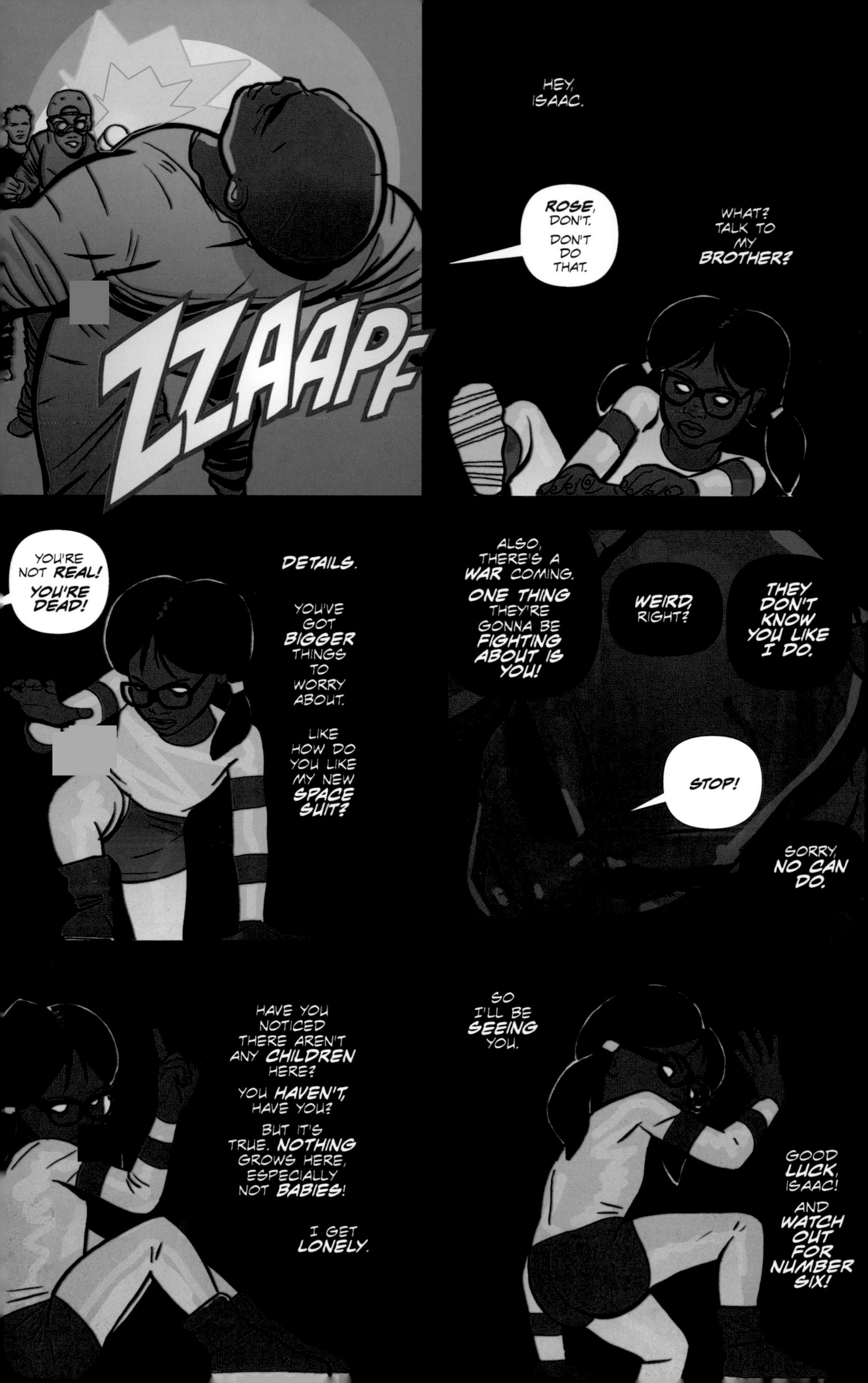
ZZAAPF
HEY, ISAAC.
ROSE, DON'T.
DON'T DO THAT.
WHAT? TALK TO MY BROTHER?
YOU'RE NOT REAL! YOU'RE DEAD!
DETAILS.
YOU'VE GOT BIGGER THINGS TO WORRY ABOUT.
LIKE HOW DO YOU LIKE MY NEW SPACE SUIT?
ALSO, THERE'S A WAR COMING. ONE THING THEY'RE GONNA BE FIGHTING ABOUT IS YOU!
WEIRD, RIGHT?
THEY DON'T KNOW YOU LIKE I DO.
STOP!
SORRY, NO CAN DO.
HAVE YOU NOTICED THERE AREN'T ANY CHILDREN HERE?
YOU HAVEN'T, HAVE YOU?
BUT IT'S TRUE. NOTHING GROWS HERE, ESPECIALLY NOT BABIES!
I GET LONELY.
SO I'LL BE SEEING YOU.
GOOD LUCK, ISAAC!
AND WATCH OUT FOR NUMBER SIX!

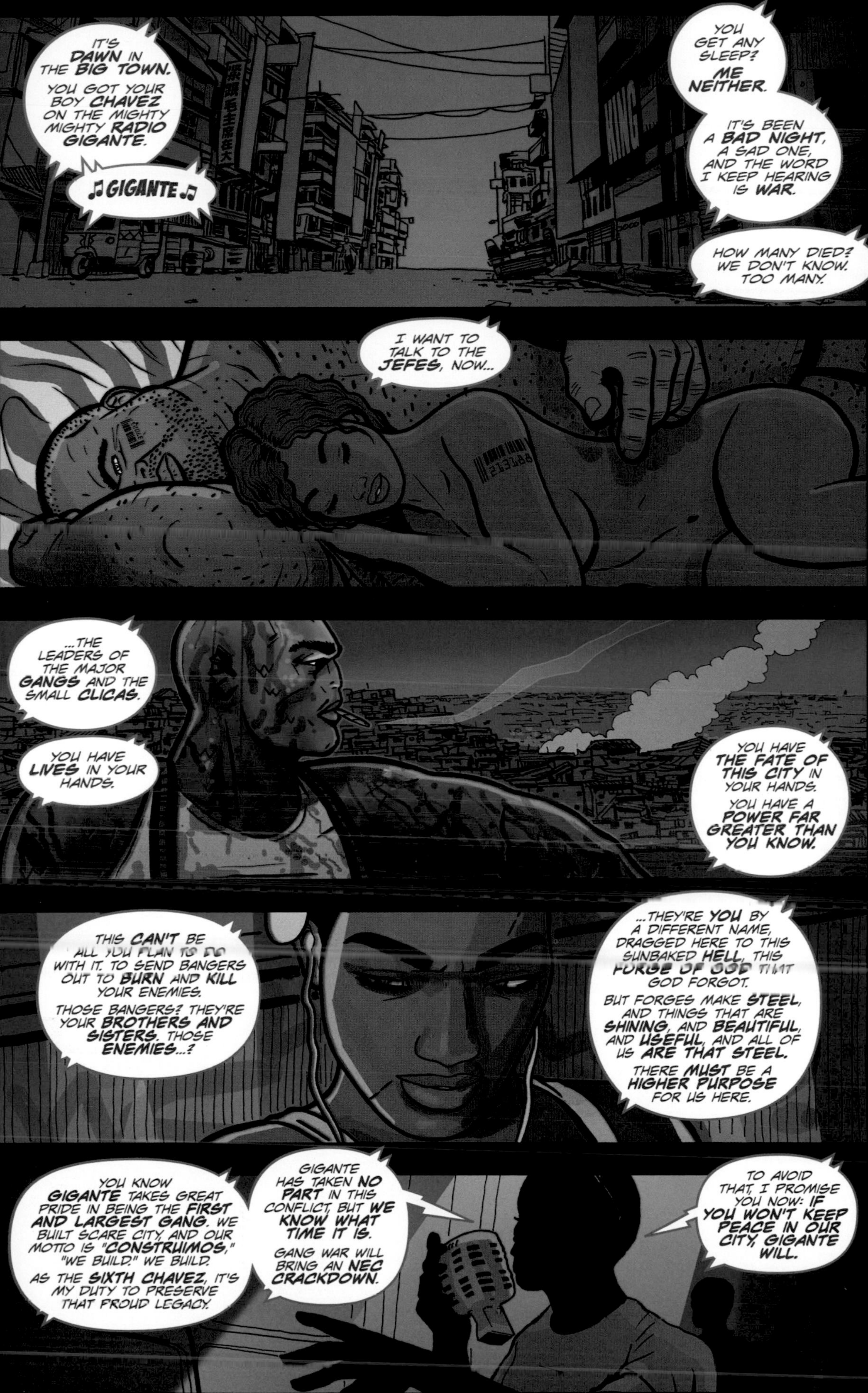

IT'S DAWN IN THE BIG TOWN.
YOU GOT YOUR BOY CHAVEZ ON THE MIGHTY MIGHTY RADIO GIGANTE.
♫GIGANTE♫
YOU GET ANY SLEEP? ME NEITHER.
IT'S BEEN A BAD NIGHT, A SAD ONE, AND THE WORD I KEEP HEARING IS WAR.
HOW MANY DIED? WE DON'T KNOW. TOO MANY.
I WANT TO TALK TO THE JEFES, NOW...
...THE LEADERS OF THE MAJOR GANGS AND THE SMALL CLICAS.
YOU HAVE LIVES IN YOUR HANDS.
YOU HAVE THE FATE OF THIS CITY IN YOUR HANDS.
YOU HAVE A POWER FAR GREATER THAN YOU KNOW.
THIS CAN'T BE ALL YOU PLAN TO DO WITH IT. TO SEND BANGERS OUT TO BURN AND KILL YOUR ENEMIES.
THOSE BANGERS? THEY'RE YOUR BROTHERS AND SISTERS. THOSE ENEMIES...?
...THEY'RE YOU BY A DIFFERENT NAME, DRAGGED HERE TO THIS SUNBAKED HELL, THIS FORGE OF GOD THAT GOD FORGOT.
BUT FORGES MAKE STEEL, AND THINGS THAT ARE SHINING, AND BEAUTIFUL, AND USEFUL, AND ALL OF US ARE THAT STEEL.
THERE MUST BE A HIGHER PURPOSE FOR US HERE.
YOU KNOW GIGANTE TAKES GREAT PRIDE IN BEING THE FIRST AND LARGEST GANG. WE BUILT SCARE CITY, AND OUR MOTTO IS "CONSTRUIMOS," "WE BUILD." WE BUILD.
AS THE SIXTH CHAVEZ, IT'S MY DUTY TO PRESERVE THAT PROUD LEGACY.
GIGANTE HAS TAKEN NO PART IN THIS CONFLICT, BUT WE KNOW WHAT TIME IT IS.
GANG WAR WILL BRING AN NEC CRACKDOWN.
TO AVOID THAT, I PROMISE YOU NOW: IF YOU WON'T KEEP PEACE IN OUR CITY, GIGANTE WILL.

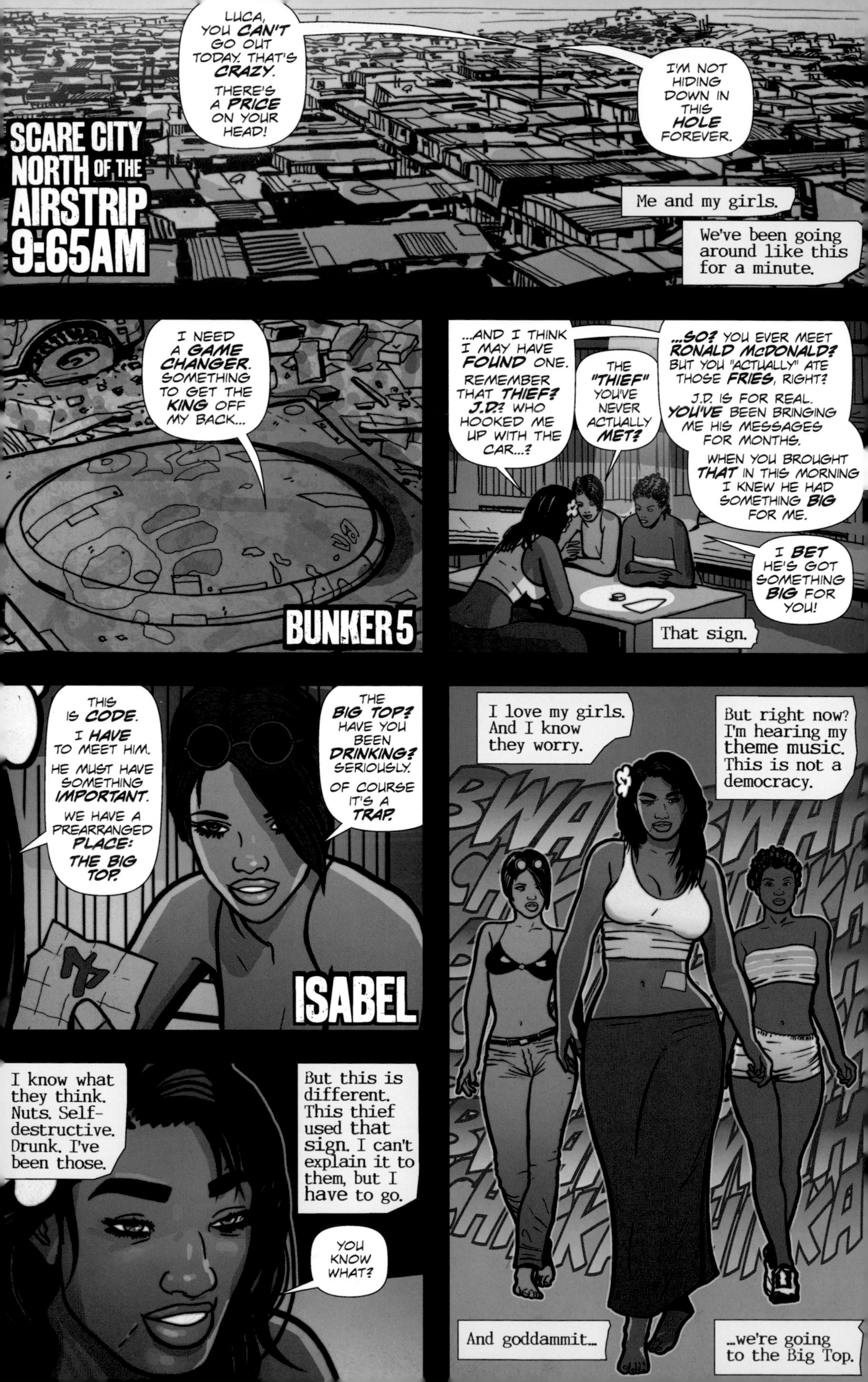

LUCA, YOU CAN'T GO OUT TODAY. THAT'S CRAZY.
THERE'S A PRICE ON YOUR HEAD!
I'M NOT HIDING DOWN IN THIS HOLE FOREVER.
SCARE CITY NORTH OF THE AIRSTRIP 9:65AM
Me and my girls.
We've been going around like this for a minute.
I NEED A GAME CHANGER. SOMETHING TO GET THE KING OFF MY BACK...
BUNKER 5
...AND I THINK I MAY HAVE FOUND ONE. REMEMBER THAT THIEF? J.D.? WHO HOOKED ME UP WITH THE CAR...?
THE "THIEF" YOU'VE NEVER ACTUALLY MET?
...SO? YOU EVER MEET RONALD McDONALD? BUT YOU "ACTUALLY" ATE THOSE FRIES, RIGHT?
J.D. IS FOR REAL. YOU'VE BEEN BRINGING ME HIS MESSAGES FOR MONTHS.
WHEN YOU BROUGHT THAT IN THIS MORNING I KNEW HE HAD SOMETHING BIG FOR ME.
I BET HE'S GOT SOMETHING BIG FOR YOU!
That sign.
THIS IS CODE.
I HAVE TO MEET HIM.
HE MUST HAVE SOMETHING IMPORTANT.
WE HAVE A PREARRANGED PLACE: THE BIG TOP.
THE BIG TOP? HAVE YOU BEEN DRINKING? SERIOUSLY.
OF COURSE IT'S A TRAP.
ISABEL
I know what they think. Nuts. Self-destructive. Drunk. I've been those.
But this is different. This thief used that sign. I can't explain it to them, but I have to go.
YOU KNOW WHAT?
I love my girls. And I know they worry.
But right now? I'm hearing my theme music. This is not a democracy.
And goddammit...
...we're going to the Big Top.

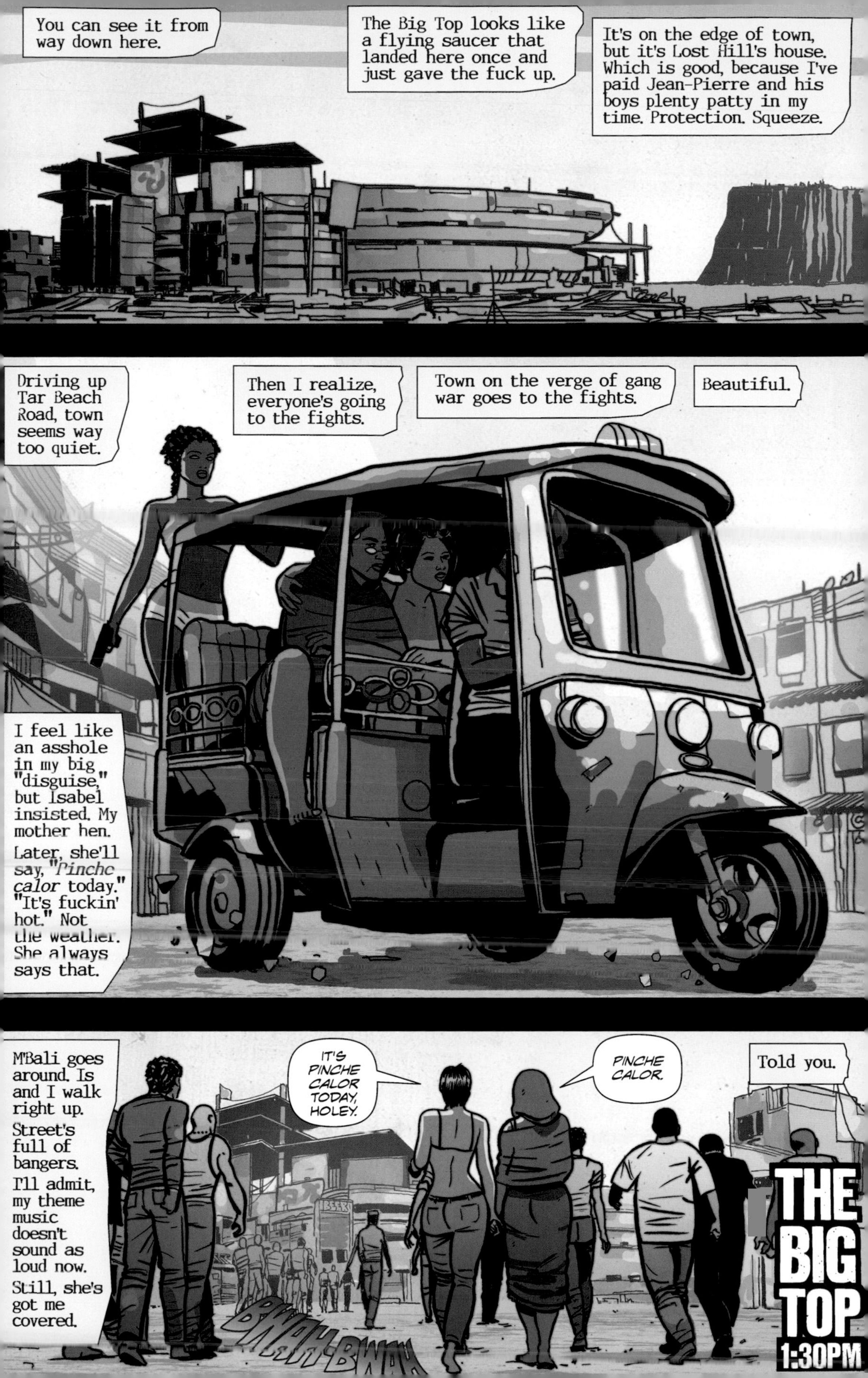
You can see it from way down here.
The Big Top looks like a flying saucer that landed here once and just gave the fuck up.
It's on the edge of town, but it's Lost Hill's house. Which is good, because I've paid Jean-Pierre and his boys plenty patty in my time. Protection. Squeeze.
Driving up Tar Beach Road, town seems way too quiet.
Then I realize, everyone's going to the fights.
Town on the verge of gang war goes to the fights.
Beautiful.
I feel like an asshole in my big "disguise," but Isabel insisted. My mother hen.
Later, she'll say, "*Pinche calor* today." "It's fuckin' hot." Not the weather. She always says that.
M'Bali goes around. Is and I walk right up.
Street's full of bangers.
I'll admit, my theme music doesn't sound as loud now.
Still, she's got me covered.
IT'S PINCHE CALOR TODAY, HOLEY.
PINCHE CALOR.
Told you.
BWAH-BWAH
THE BIG TOP 1:30PM

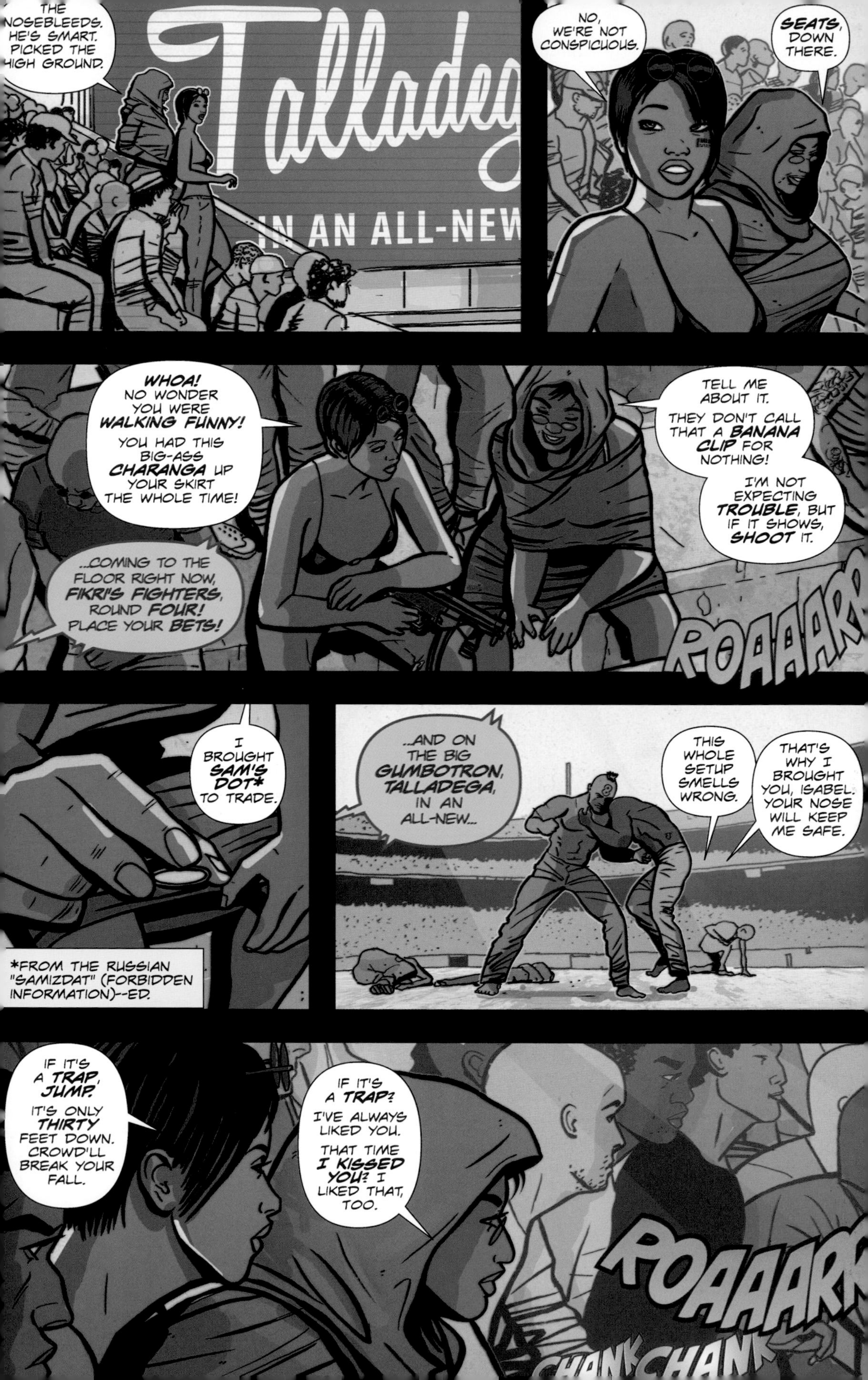
THE NOSEBLEEDS. HE'S SMART. PICKED THE HIGH GROUND.
Talladeg
IN AN ALL-NEW
NO, WE'RE NOT CONSPICUOUS.
SEATS, DOWN THERE.
WHOA! NO WONDER YOU WERE WALKING FUNNY! YOU HAD THIS BIG-ASS CHARANGA UP YOUR SKIRT THE WHOLE TIME!
TELL ME ABOUT IT. THEY DON'T CALL THAT A BANANA CLIP FOR NOTHING!
I'M NOT EXPECTING TROUBLE, BUT IF IT SHOWS, SHOOT IT.
...COMING TO THE FLOOR RIGHT NOW, FIKRI'S FIGHTERS, ROUND FOUR! PLACE YOUR BETS!
ROAAARR
I BROUGHT SAM'S DOT* TO TRADE.
*FROM THE RUSSIAN "SAMIZDAT" (FORBIDDEN INFORMATION)--ED.
...AND ON THE BIG GUMBOTRON, TALLADEGA, IN AN ALL-NEW...
THIS WHOLE SETUP SMELLS WRONG.
THAT'S WHY I BROUGHT YOU, ISABEL. YOUR NOSE WILL KEEP ME SAFE.
IF IT'S A TRAP, JUMP. IT'S ONLY THIRTY FEET DOWN. CROWD'LL BREAK YOUR FALL.
IF IT'S A TRAP? I'VE ALWAYS LIKED YOU. THAT TIME I KISSED YOU? I LIKED THAT, TOO.
ROAAARR
CHANKCHANK

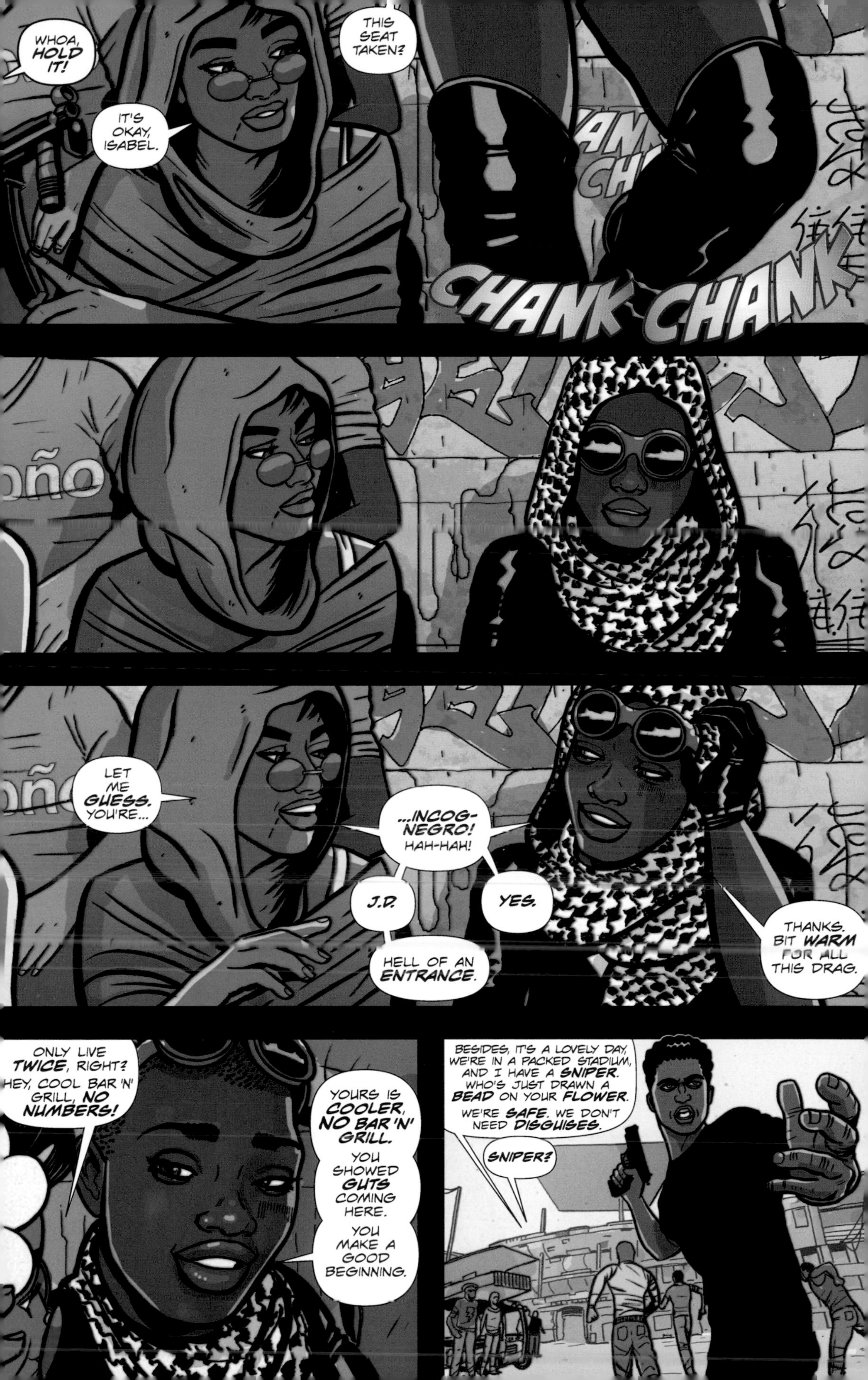

WHOA, HOLD IT!
THIS SEAT TAKEN?
IT'S OKAY, ISABEL.
CHANK CHANK
LET ME GUESS. YOU'RE...
...INCOG-NEGRO! HAH-HAH!
J.D.
YES.
HELL OF AN ENTRANCE.
THANKS. BIT WARM FOR ALL THIS DRAG.
ONLY LIVE TWICE, RIGHT? HEY, COOL BAR 'N' GRILL, NO NUMBERS!
YOURS IS COOLER, NO BAR 'N' GRILL.
YOU SHOWED GUTS COMING HERE.
YOU MAKE A GOOD BEGINNING.
BESIDES, IT'S A LOVELY DAY, WE'RE IN A PACKED STADIUM, AND I HAVE A SNIPER. WHO'S JUST DRAWN A BEAD ON YOUR FLOWER.
WE'RE SAFE. WE DON'T NEED DISGUISES.
SNIPER?

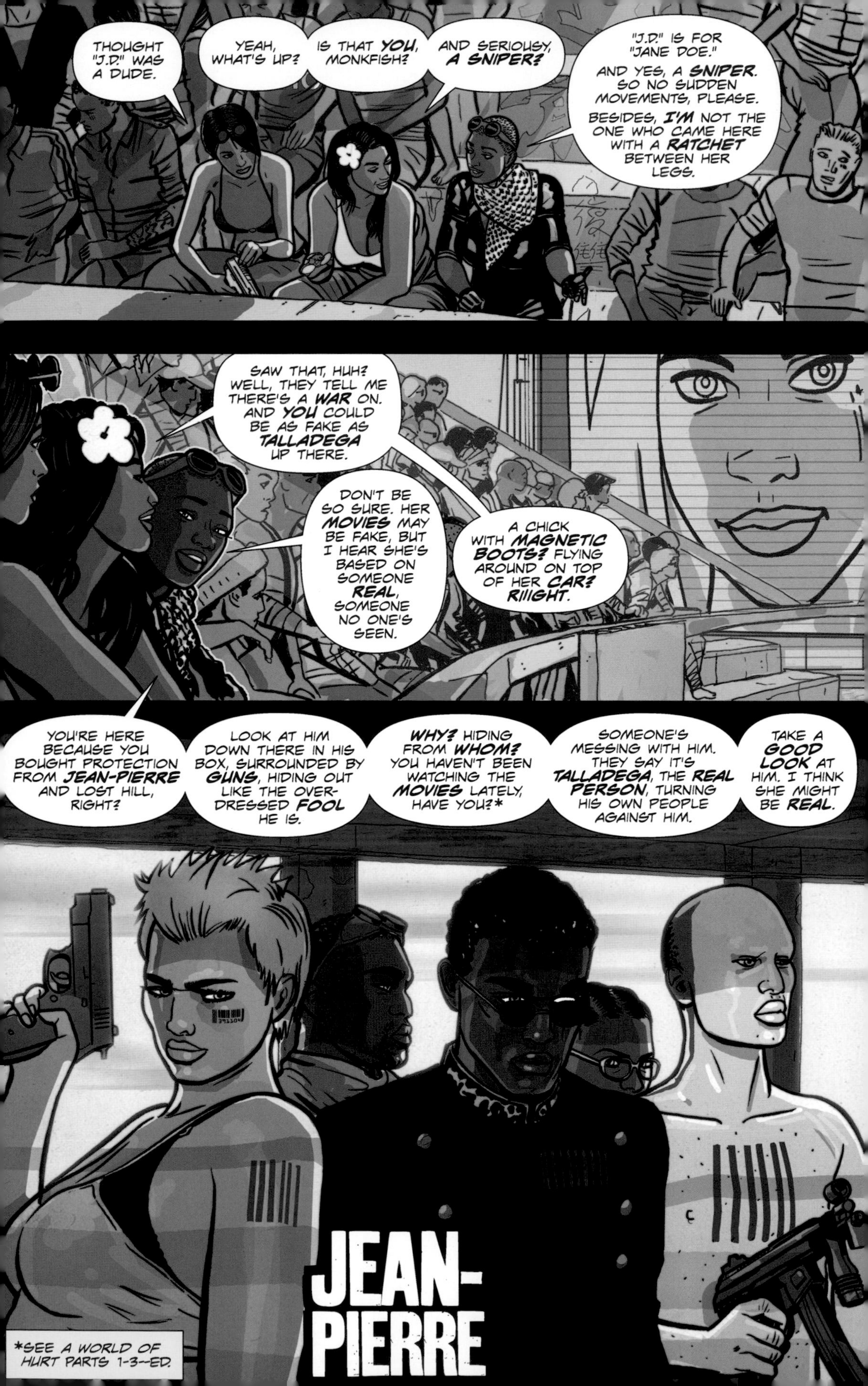
THOUGHT "J.D." WAS A DUDE.
YEAH, WHAT'S UP?
IS THAT YOU, MONKFISH?
AND SERIOUSY, A SNIPER?
"J.D." IS FOR "JANE DOE."
AND YES, A SNIPER. SO NO SUDDEN MOVEMENTS, PLEASE.
BESIDES, I'M NOT THE ONE WHO CAME HERE WITH A RATCHET BETWEEN HER LEGS.
SAW THAT, HUH? WELL, THEY TELL ME THERE'S A WAR ON. AND YOU COULD BE AS FAKE AS TALLADEGA UP THERE.
DON'T BE SO SURE. HER MOVIES MAY BE FAKE, BUT I HEAR SHE'S BASED ON SOMEONE REAL, SOMEONE NO ONE'S SEEN.
A CHICK WITH MAGNETIC BOOTS? FLYING AROUND ON TOP OF HER CAR? RIIIGHT.
YOU'RE HERE BECAUSE YOU BOUGHT PROTECTION FROM JEAN-PIERRE AND LOST HILL, RIGHT?
LOOK AT HIM DOWN THERE IN HIS BOX, SURROUNDED BY GUNS, HIDING OUT LIKE THE OVER-DRESSED FOOL HE IS.
WHY? HIDING FROM WHOM? YOU HAVEN'T BEEN WATCHING THE MOVIES LATELY, HAVE YOU?*
SOMEONE'S MESSING WITH HIM. THEY SAY IT'S TALLADEGA, THE REAL PERSON, TURNING HIS OWN PEOPLE AGAINST HIM.
TAKE A GOOD LOOK AT HIM. I THINK SHE MIGHT BE REAL.
JEAN-PIERRE
*SEE A WORLD OF HURT PARTS 1-3--ED.

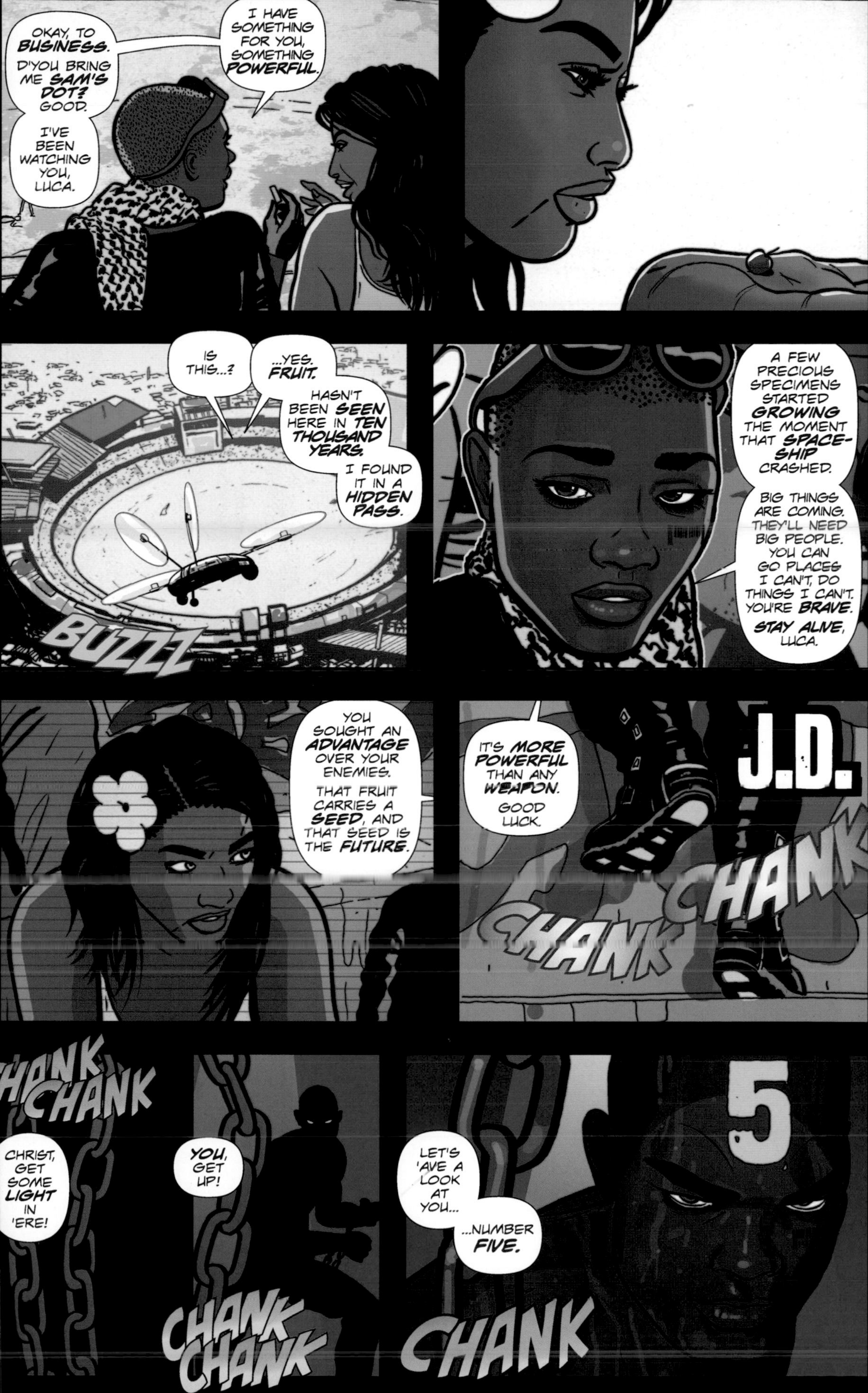
OKAY, TO BUSINESS.
D'YOU BRING ME SAM'S DOT? GOOD.
I HAVE SOMETHING FOR YOU, SOMETHING POWERFUL.
I'VE BEEN WATCHING YOU, LUCA.
IS THIS...?
...YES. FRUIT.
HASN'T BEEN SEEN HERE IN TEN THOUSAND YEARS.
I FOUND IT IN A HIDDEN PASS.
BUZZZ
A FEW PRECIOUS SPECIMENS STARTED GROWING THE MOMENT THAT SPACE-SHIP CRASHED.
BIG THINGS ARE COMING. THEY'LL NEED BIG PEOPLE. YOU CAN GO PLACES I CAN'T, DO THINGS I CAN'T. YOU'RE BRAVE.
STAY ALIVE, LUCA.
YOU SOUGHT AN ADVANTAGE OVER YOUR ENEMIES.
THAT FRUIT CARRIES A SEED, AND THAT SEED IS THE FUTURE.
IT'S MORE POWERFUL THAN ANY WEAPON.
GOOD LUCK.
J.D.
CHANK CHANK
CHANK CHANK
CHRIST, GET SOME LIGHT IN 'ERE!
YOU, GET UP!
CHANK CHANK
LET'S 'AVE A LOOK AT YOU...
...NUMBER FIVE.
5
CHANK

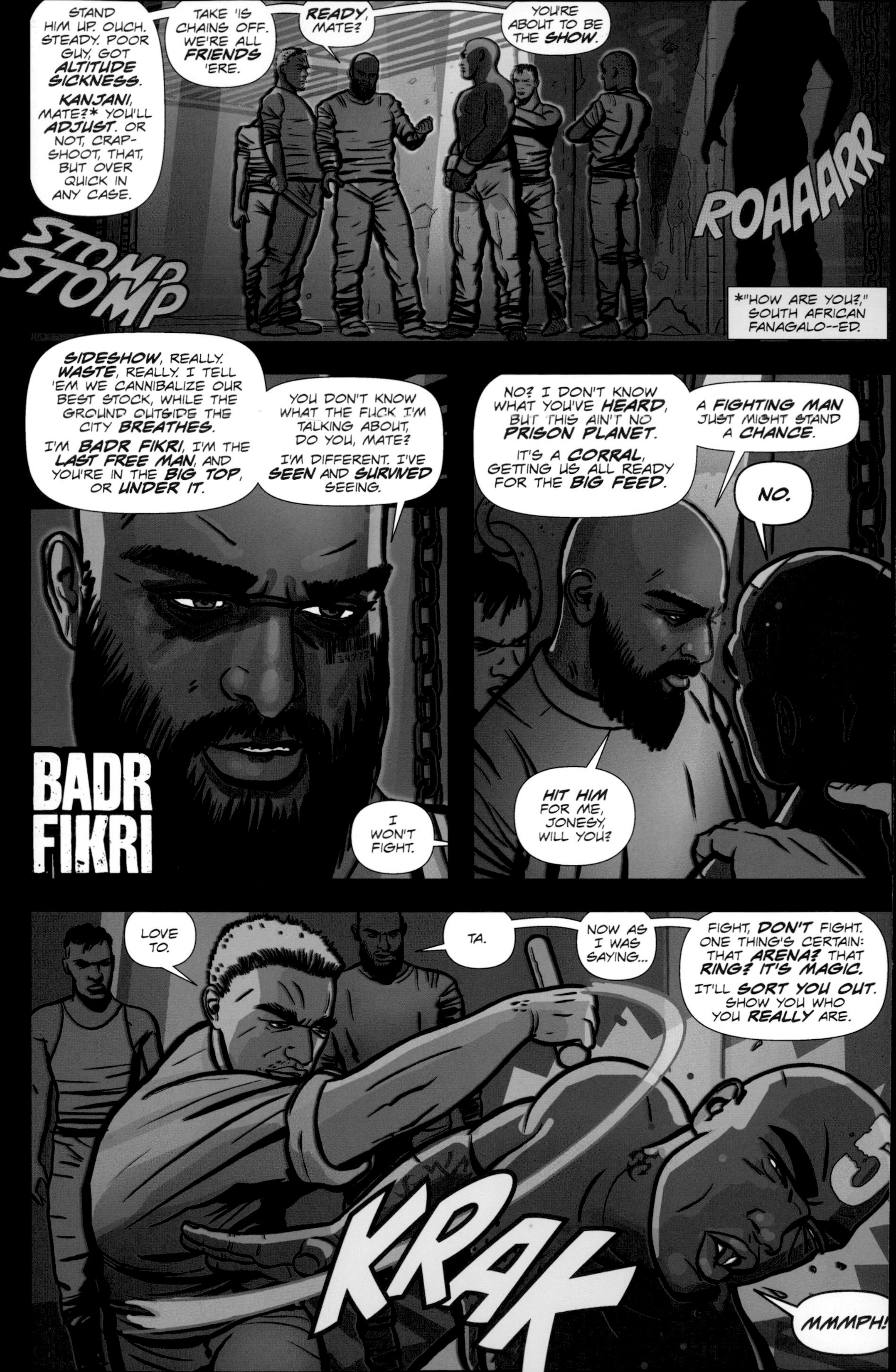
STAND HIM UP. OUCH. STEADY. POOR GUY, GOT ALTITUDE SICKNESS. KANJANI, MATE?* YOU'LL ADJUST. OR NOT, CRAP-SHOOT, THAT, BUT OVER QUICK IN ANY CASE.
TAKE 'IS CHAINS OFF. WE'RE ALL FRIENDS 'ERE.
READY, MATE?
YOU'RE ABOUT TO BE THE SHOW.
STOMP STOMP
ROAAARR
*"HOW ARE YOU?," SOUTH AFRICAN FANAGALO--ED.
SIDESHOW, REALLY. WASTE, REALLY. I TELL 'EM WE CANNIBALIZE OUR BEST STOCK, WHILE THE GROUND OUTSIDE THE CITY BREATHES.
I'M BADR FIKRI, I'M THE LAST FREE MAN, AND YOU'RE IN THE BIG TOP, OR UNDER IT.
YOU DON'T KNOW WHAT THE FUCK I'M TALKING ABOUT, DO YOU, MATE?
I'M DIFFERENT. I'VE SEEN AND SURVIVED SEEING.
BADR FIKRI
I WON'T FIGHT.
NO? I DON'T KNOW WHAT YOU'VE HEARD, BUT THIS AIN'T NO PRISON PLANET.
IT'S A CORRAL, GETTING US ALL READY FOR THE BIG FEED.
A FIGHTING MAN JUST MIGHT STAND A CHANCE.
NO.
HIT HIM FOR ME, JONESY, WILL YOU?
LOVE TO.
TA.
NOW AS I WAS SAYING...
FIGHT, DON'T FIGHT. ONE THING'S CERTAIN: THAT ARENA? THAT RING? IT'S MAGIC.
IT'LL SORT YOU OUT. SHOW YOU WHO YOU REALLY ARE.
KRAK
MMMPH!

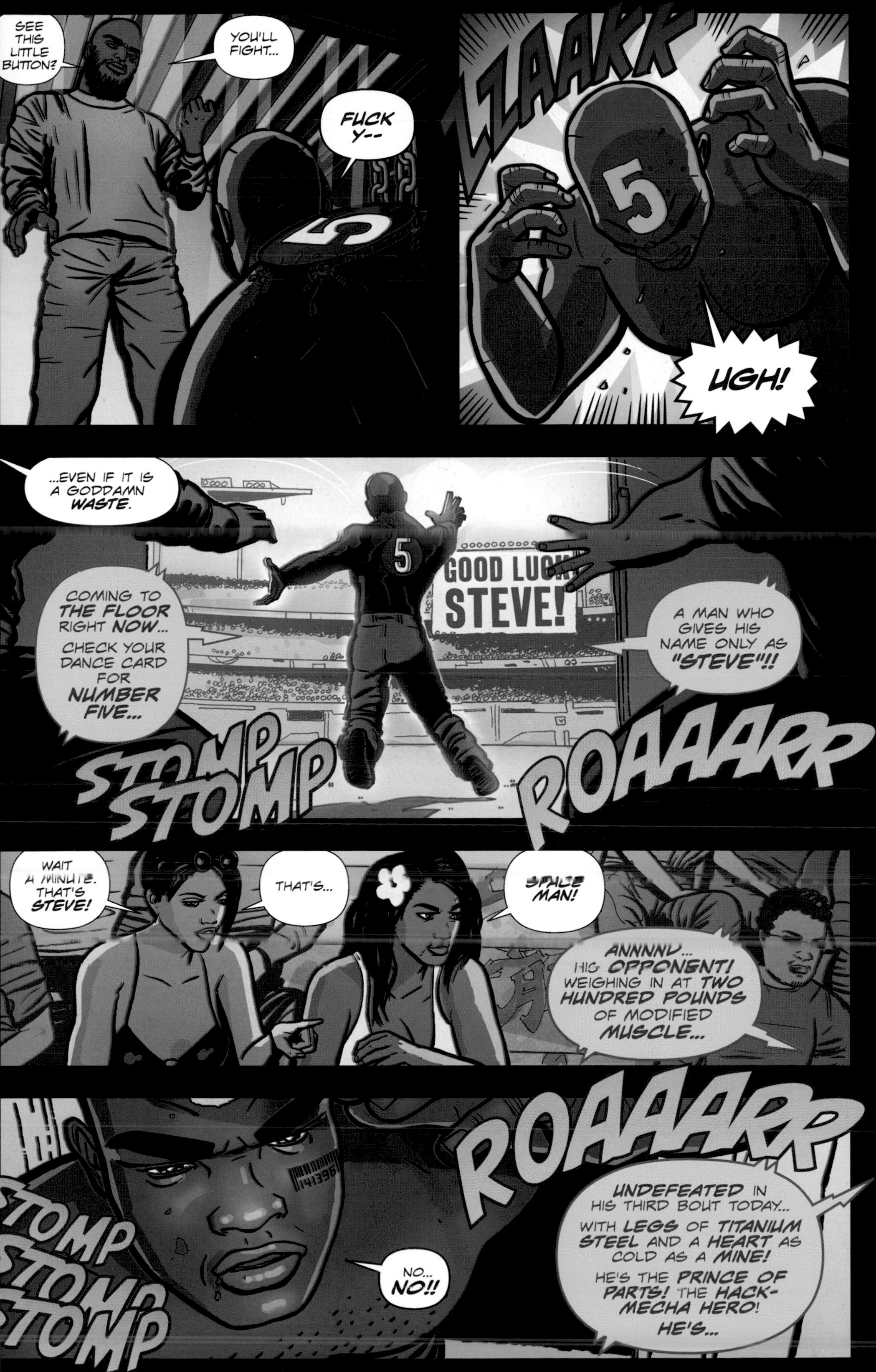
SEE THIS LITTLE BUTTON?
YOU'LL FIGHT...
FUCK Y--
ZZAAKK
UGH!
...EVEN IF IT IS A GODDAMN WASTE.
GOOD LUCK STEVE!
COMING TO THE FLOOR RIGHT NOW... CHECK YOUR DANCE CARD FOR NUMBER FIVE...
A MAN WHO GIVES HIS NAME ONLY AS "STEVE"!!
STOMP STOMP
ROAAAARR
WAIT A MINUTE. THAT'S STEVE!
THAT'S...
SPACE MAN!
ANNNND... HIS OPPONENT! WEIGHING IN AT TWO HUNDRED POUNDS OF MODIFIED MUSCLE...
ROAAAARR
STOMP STOMP STOMP
UNDEFEATED IN HIS THIRD BOUT TODAY... WITH LEGS OF TITANIUM STEEL AND A HEART AS COLD AS A MINE! HE'S THE PRINCE OF PARTS! THE HACK-MECHA HERO! HE'S...
NO... NO!!

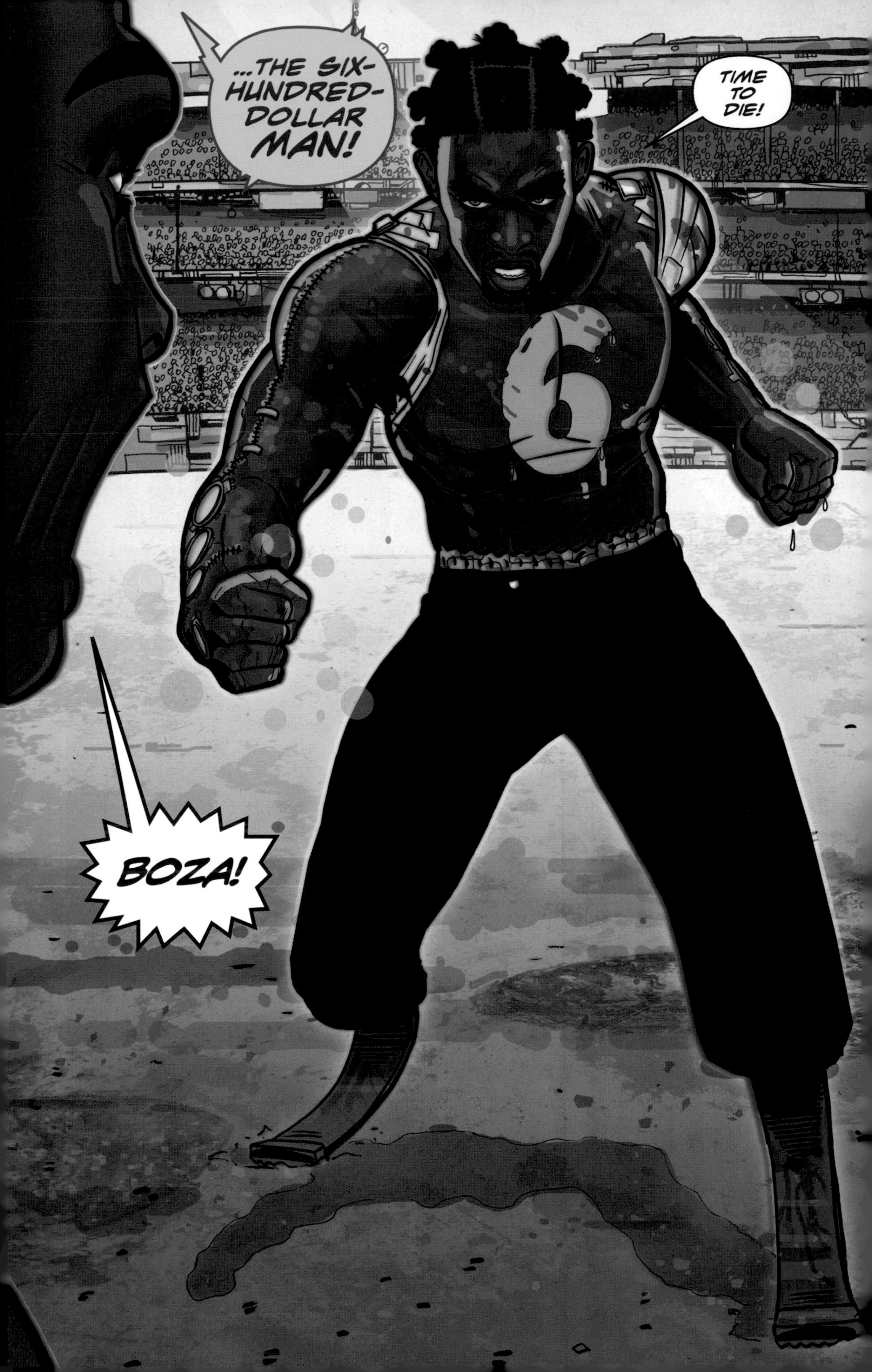
...THE SIX-HUNDRED-DOLLAR MAN!
TIME TO DIE!
BOZA!

"Look around you.
I've built something of
value here, something that
can't be denied."
　　　　　　　—Jean-Pierre

CONCRETE PARK™

VOLUME 2: R-E-S-P-E-C-T *Chapter 4: Hell Is Empty, and All the Devils Are Here*

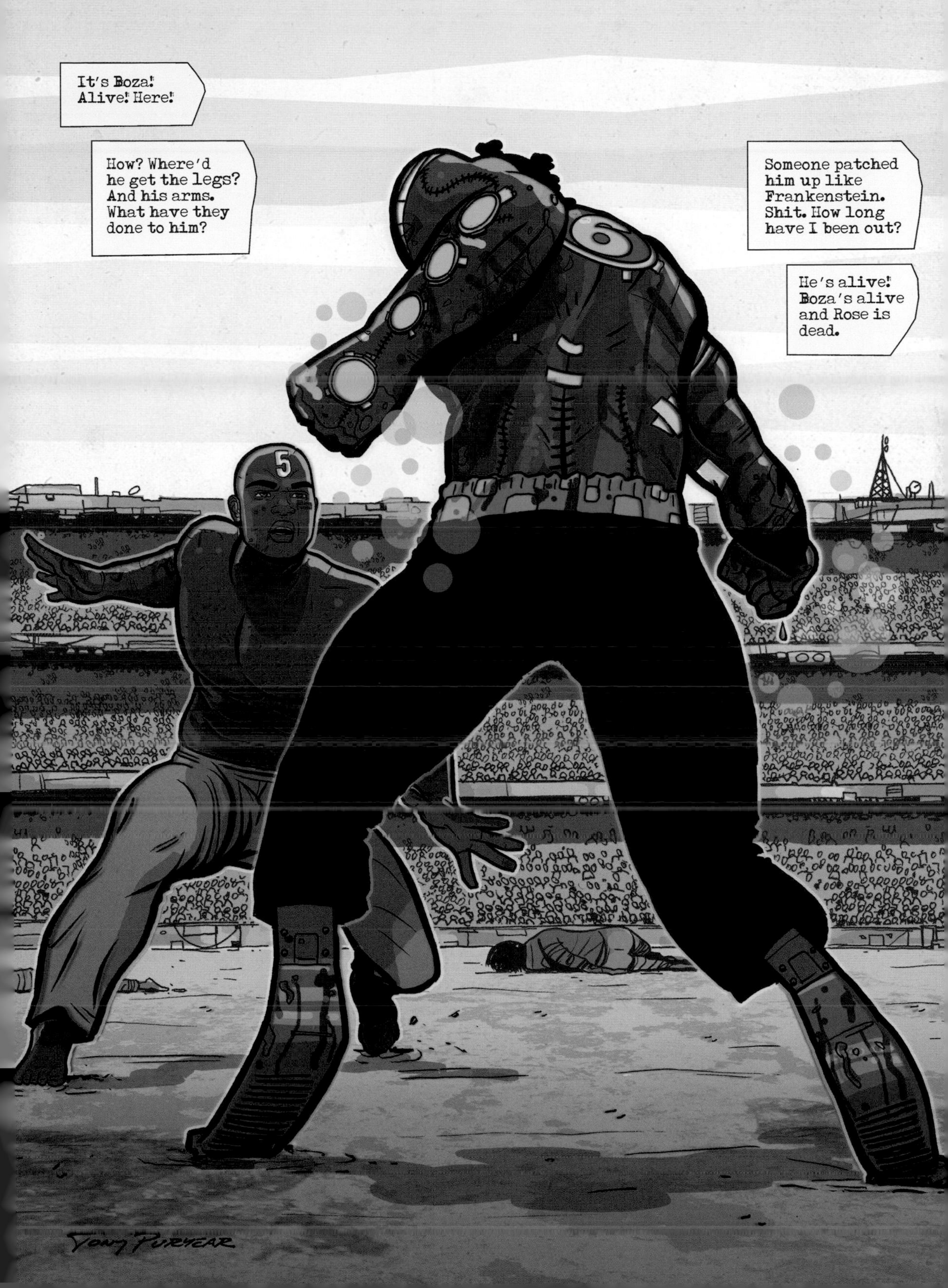
It's Boza! Alive! Here!
How? Where'd he get the legs? And his arms. What have they done to him?
Someone patched him up like Frankenstein. Shit. How long have I been out?
He's alive! Boza's alive and Rose is dead.
5
6
TONY PURYEAR

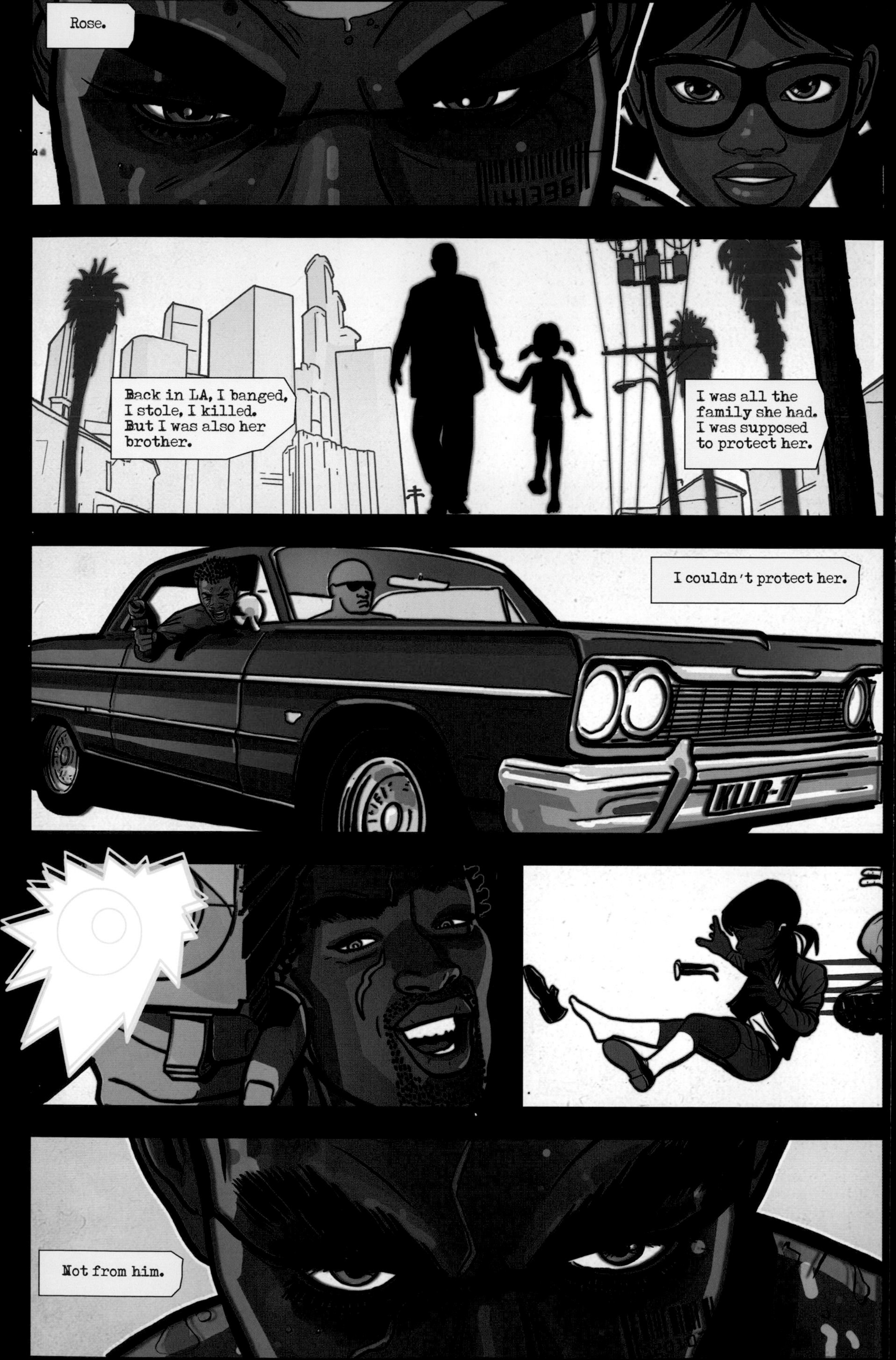
Rose.
Back in LA, I banged, I stole, I killed. But I was also her brother.
I was all the family she had. I was supposed to protect her.
I couldn't protect her.
KLLR-1
Not from him.

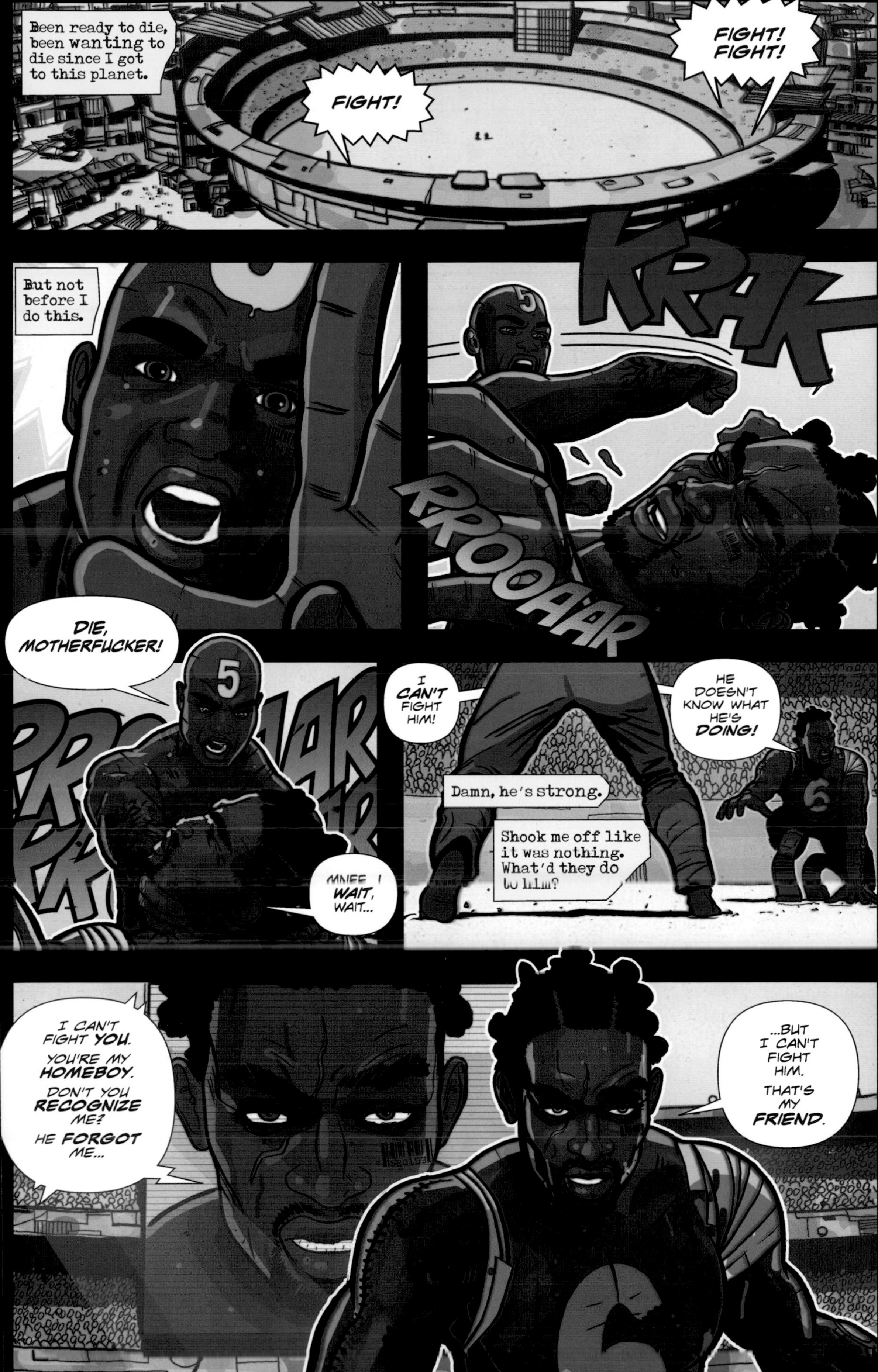
Been ready to die, been wanting to die since I got to this planet.
FIGHT!
FIGHT! FIGHT!
But not before I do this.
KRAK
RROOAAR
DIE, MOTHERFUCKER!
WAIT, WAIT...
I CAN'T FIGHT HIM!
HE DOESN'T KNOW WHAT HE'S DOING!
Damn, he's strong.
Shook me off like it was nothing. What'd they do to him?
I CAN'T FIGHT YOU.
YOU'RE MY HOMEBOY.
DON'T YOU RECOGNIZE ME?
HE FORGOT ME...
...BUT I CAN'T FIGHT HIM.
THAT'S MY FRIEND.

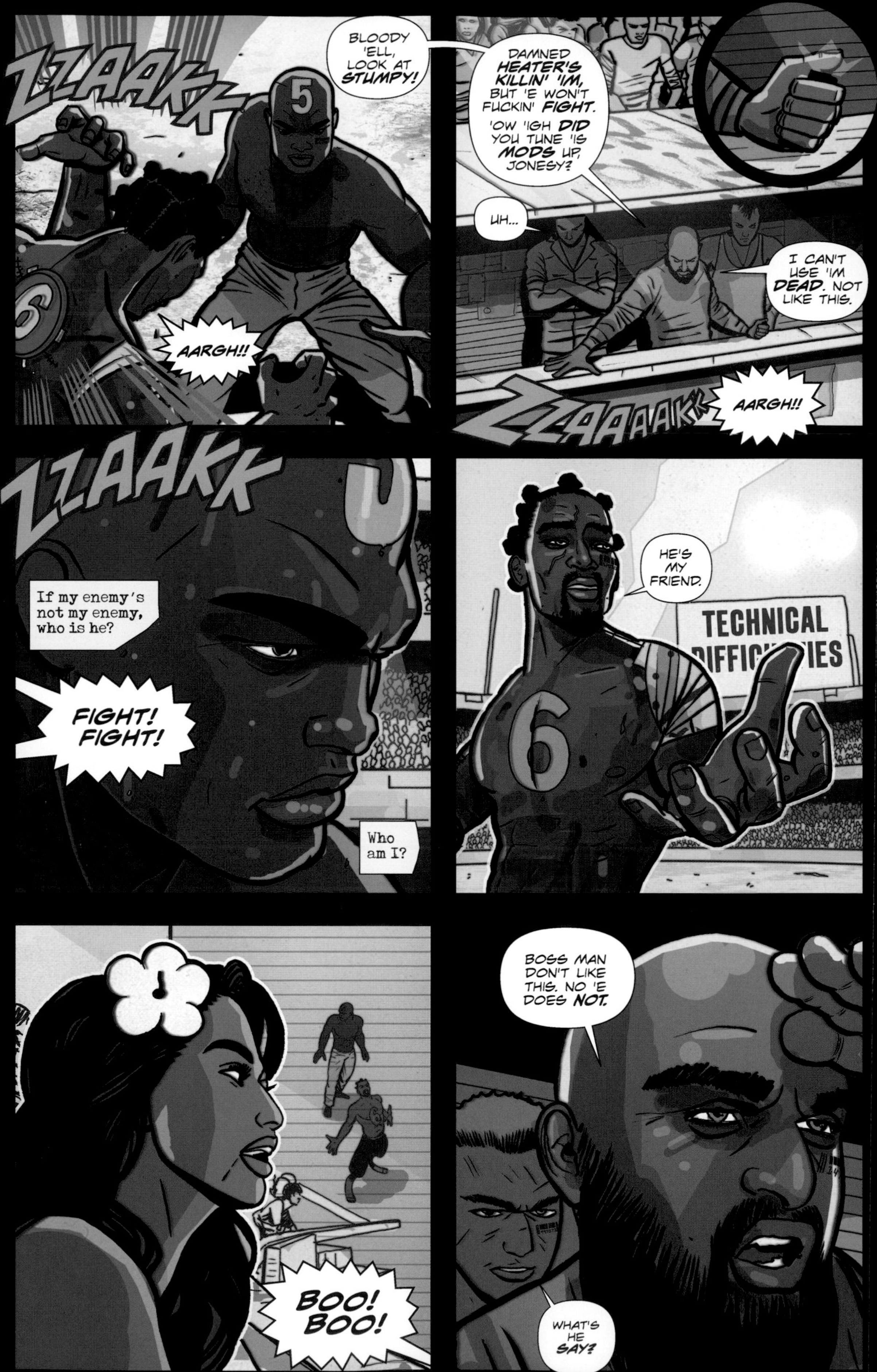
ZZAAKK
BLOODY 'ELL, LOOK AT STUMPY!
AARGH!!
DAMNED HEATER'S KILLIN' 'IM, BUT 'E WON'T FUCKIN' FIGHT.
'OW 'IGH DID YOU TUNE 'IS MODS UP, JONESY?
UH...
I CAN'T USE 'IM DEAD. NOT LIKE THIS.
ZZAAAAKK
AARGH!!
ZZAAKK
If my enemy's not my enemy, who is he?
FIGHT! FIGHT!
Who am I?
HE'S MY FRIEND.
TECHNICAL DIFFIC...IES
BOO! BOO!
BOSS MAN DON'T LIKE THIS. NO 'E DOES NOT.
WHAT'S HE SAY?

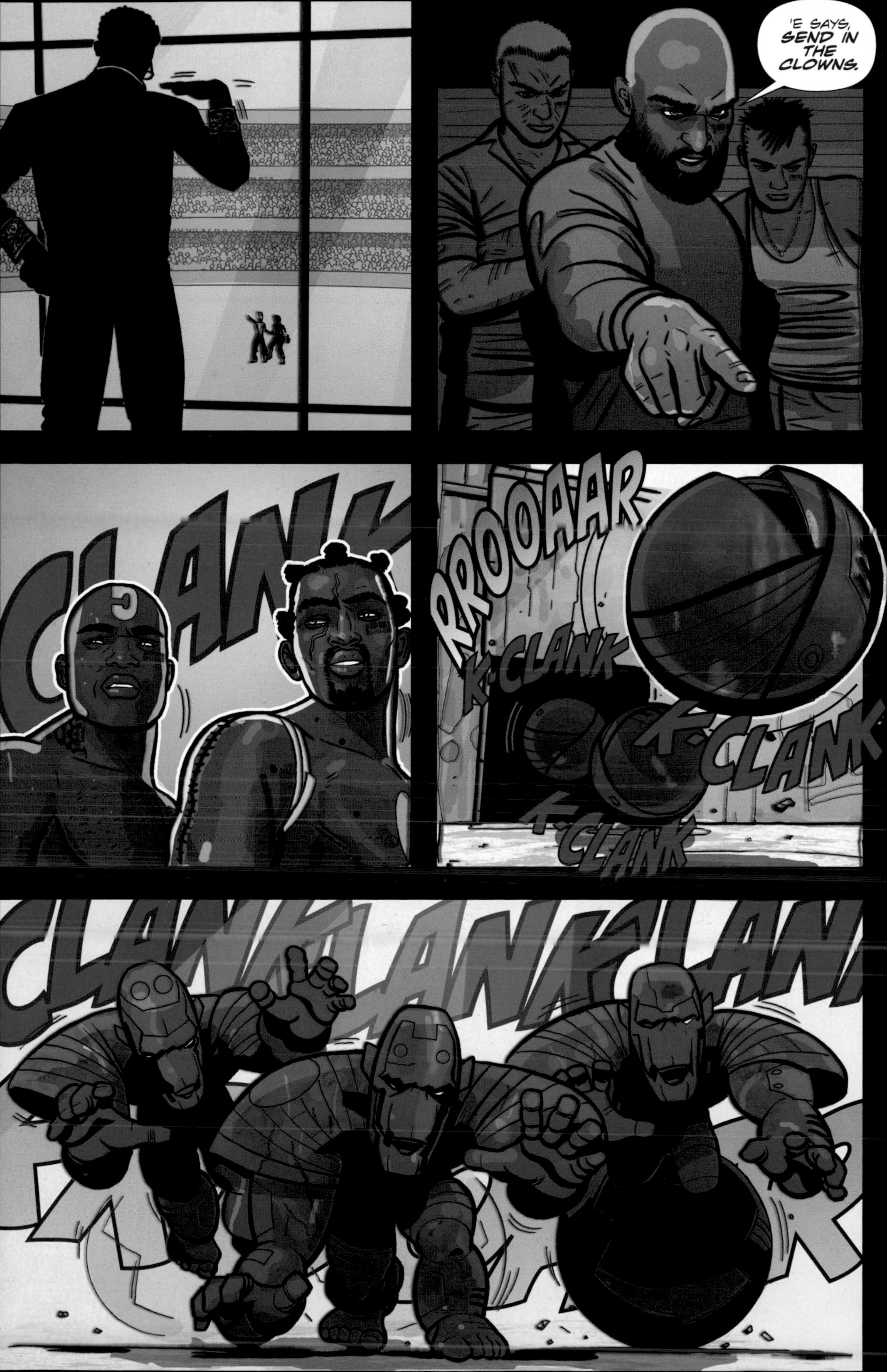
'E SAYS, SEND IN THE CLOWNS.
CLANK
RROOAAR
K-CLANK
K-CLANK
K-CLANK
CLANK CLANK CLANK

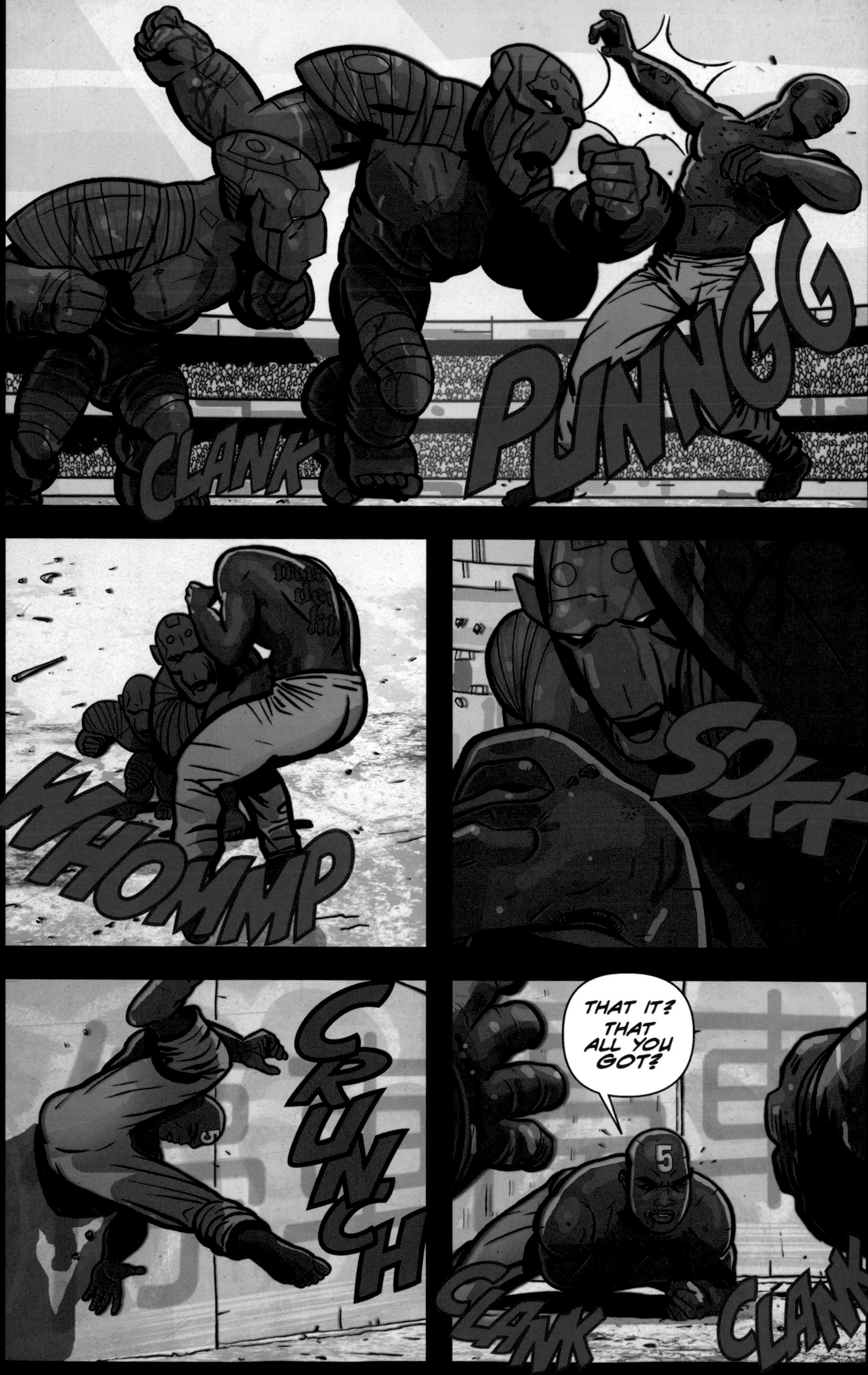
CLANK
PUNNGG
WHOMMP
SOKK
CRUNCH
THAT IT? THAT ALL YOU GOT?
CLANK
CLAN

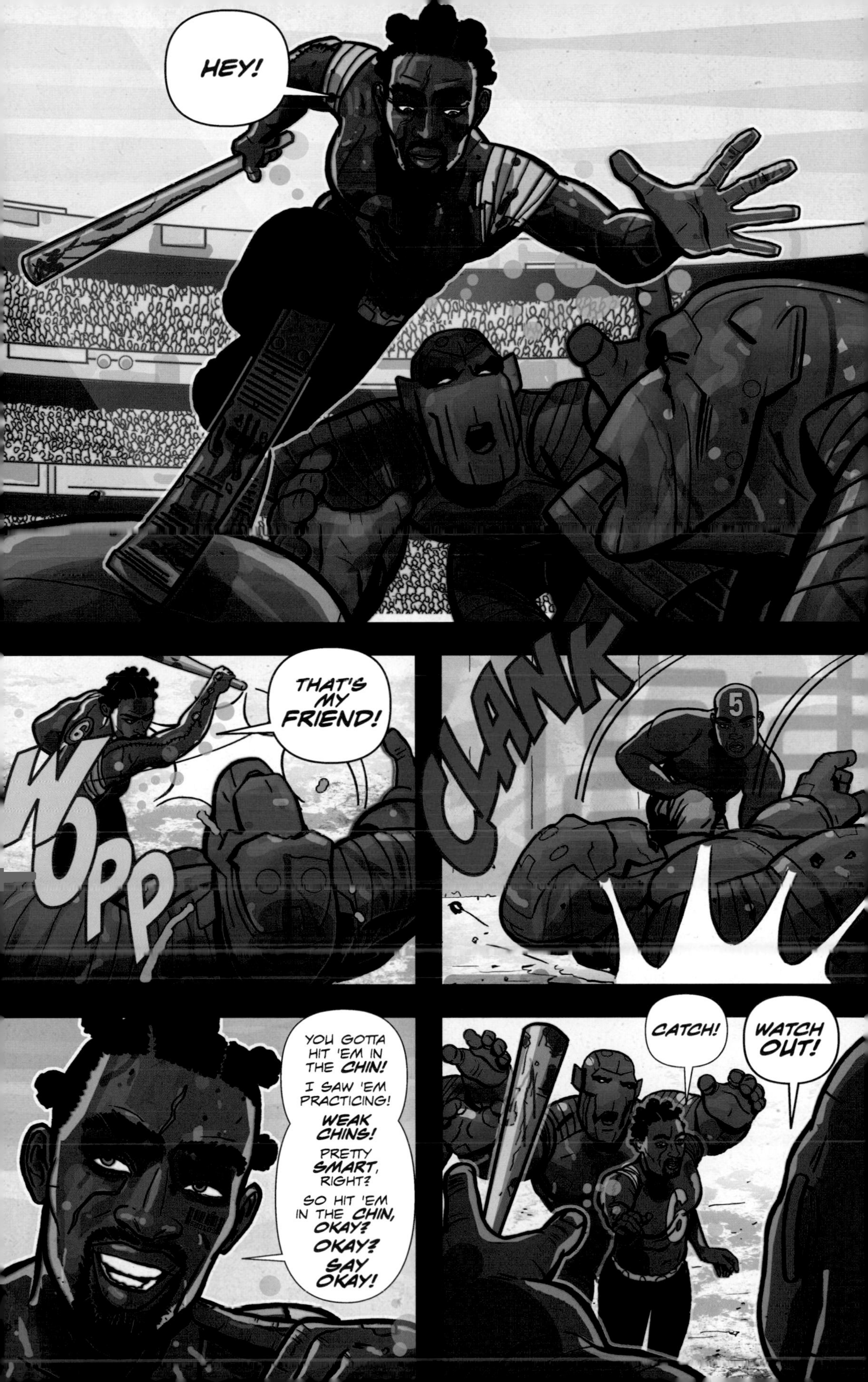
HEY!
THAT'S MY FRIEND!
WOPP
CLANK
YOU GOTTA HIT 'EM IN THE CHIN!
I SAW 'EM PRACTICING!
WEAK CHINS!
PRETTY SMART, RIGHT?
SO HIT 'EM IN THE CHIN, OKAY?
OKAY?
SAY OKAY!
CATCH!
WATCH OUT!

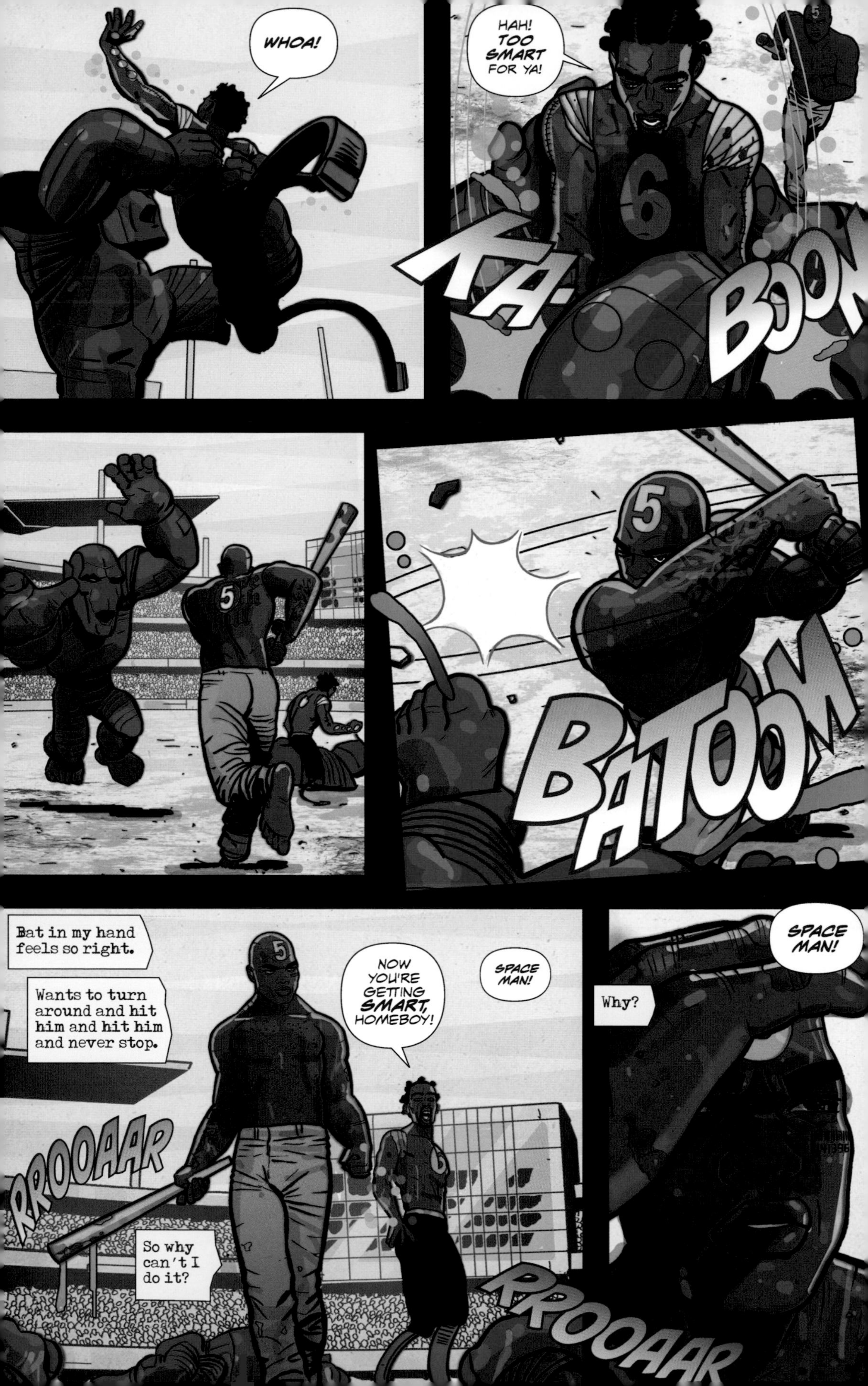
WHOA!
HAH! TOO SMART FOR YA!
KA-BOOM
BATOOM
Bat in my hand feels so right.
Wants to turn around and hit him and hit him and never stop.
NOW YOU'RE GETTING SMART, HOMEBOY!
SPACE MAN!
RROOAAR
So why can't I do it?
SPACE MAN!
Why?
RROOAAR

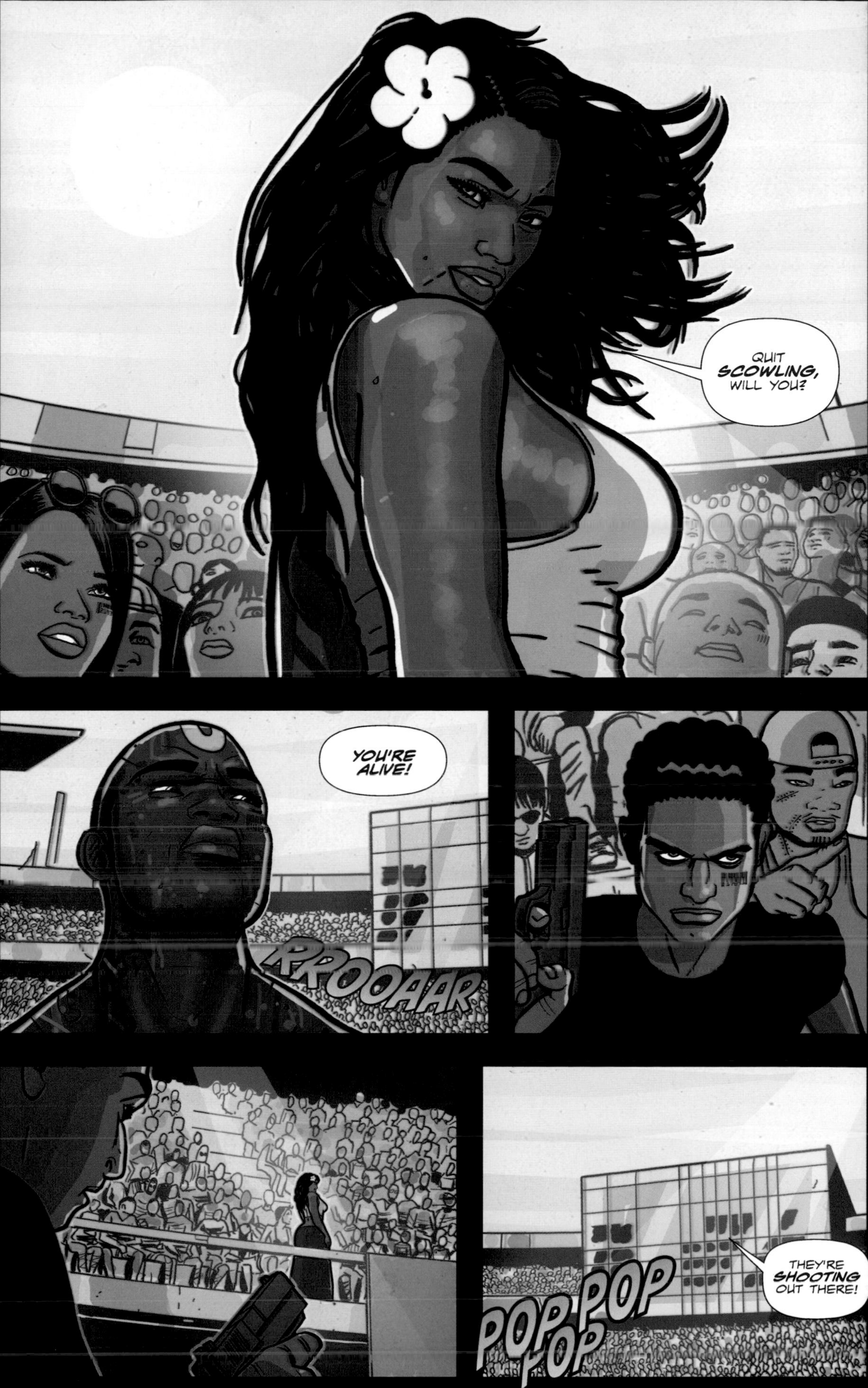
QUIT SCOWLING, WILL YOU?
YOU'RE ALIVE!
RROOAAR
THEY'RE SHOOTING OUT THERE!
POP POP POP POP

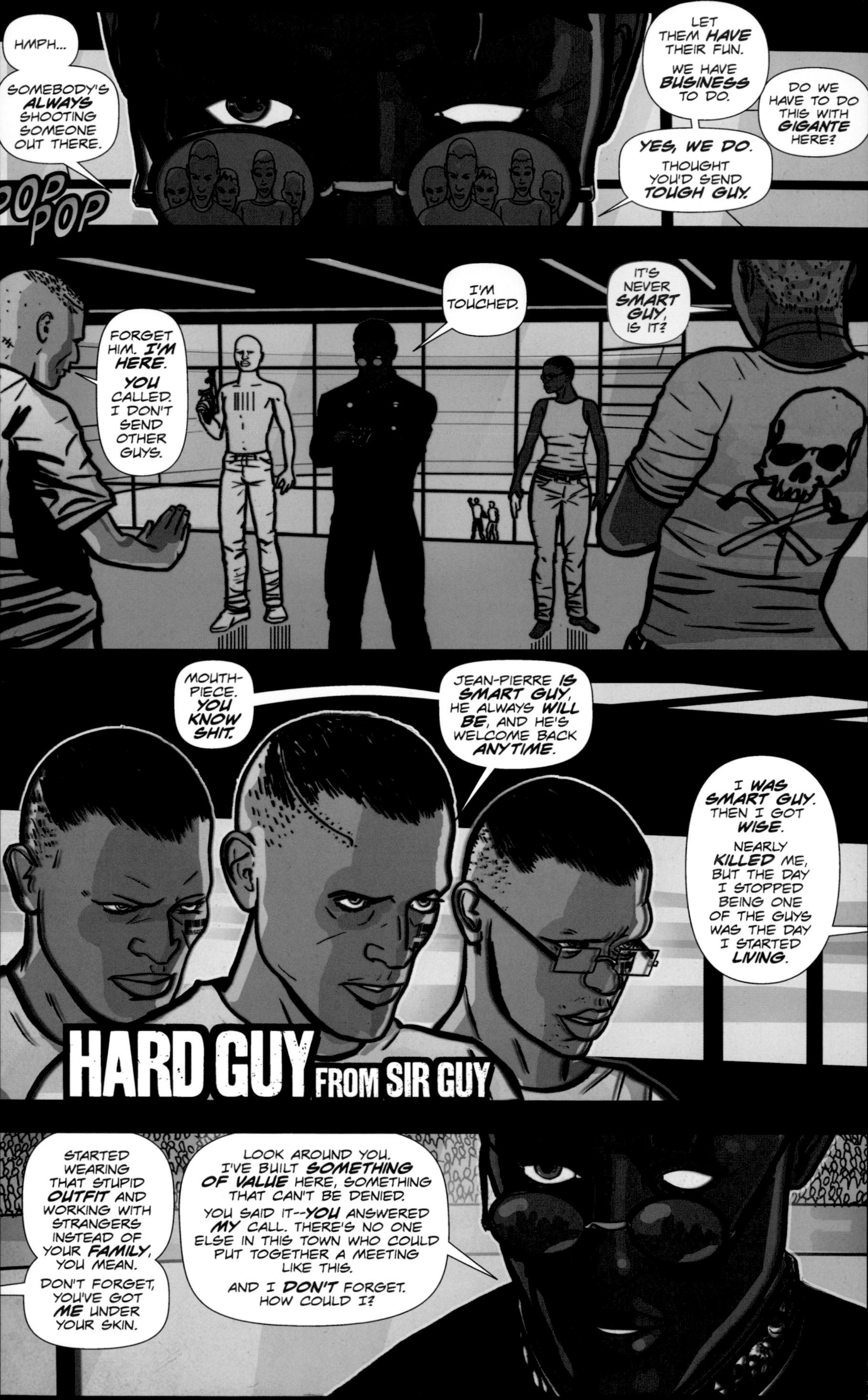

HMPH...
SOMEBODY'S ALWAYS SHOOTING SOMEONE OUT THERE.
POP POP
LET THEM HAVE THEIR FUN.
WE HAVE BUSINESS TO DO.
DO WE HAVE TO DO THIS WITH GIGANTE HERE?
YES, WE DO.
THOUGHT YOU'D SEND TOUGH GUY.
I'M TOUCHED.
IT'S NEVER SMART GUY, IS IT?
FORGET HIM. I'M HERE.
YOU CALLED. I DON'T SEND OTHER GUYS.
MOUTH-PIECE. YOU KNOW SHIT.
JEAN-PIERRE IS SMART GUY, HE ALWAYS WILL BE, AND HE'S WELCOME BACK ANYTIME.
I WAS SMART GUY. THEN I GOT WISE.
NEARLY KILLED ME, BUT THE DAY I STOPPED BEING ONE OF THE GUYS WAS THE DAY I STARTED LIVING.
HARD GUY FROM SIR GUY
STARTED WEARING THAT STUPID OUTFIT AND WORKING WITH STRANGERS INSTEAD OF YOUR FAMILY, YOU MEAN.
DON'T FORGET, YOU'VE GOT ME UNDER YOUR SKIN.
LOOK AROUND YOU. I'VE BUILT SOMETHING OF VALUE HERE, SOMETHING THAT CAN'T BE DENIED.
YOU SAID IT--YOU ANSWERED MY CALL. THERE'S NO ONE ELSE IN THIS TOWN WHO COULD PUT TOGETHER A MEETING LIKE THIS.
AND I DON'T FORGET. HOW COULD I?

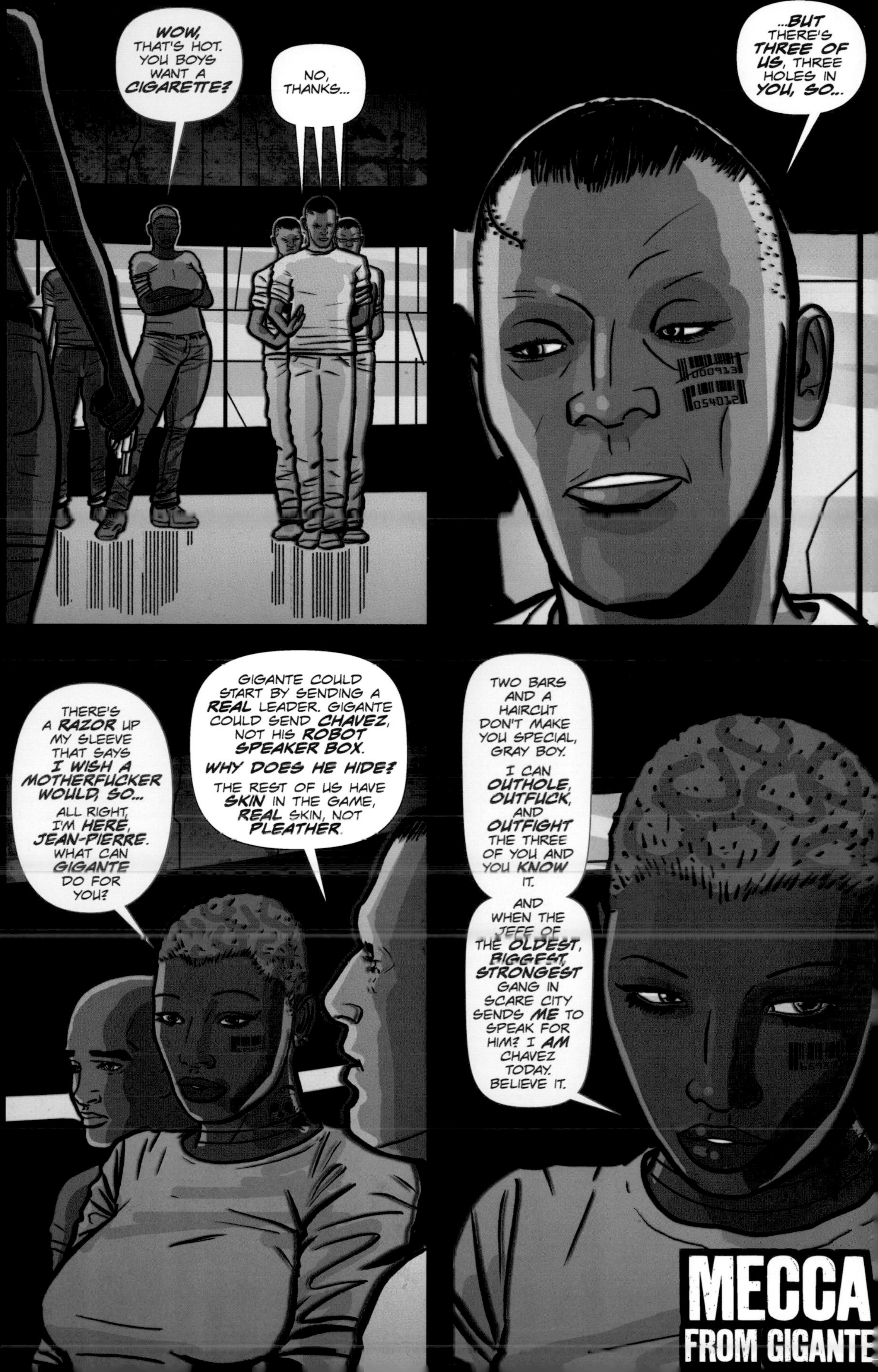
WOW, THAT'S HOT. YOU BOYS WANT A CIGARETTE?
NO, THANKS...
...BUT THERE'S THREE OF US, THREE HOLES IN YOU, SO...
THERE'S A RAZOR UP MY SLEEVE THAT SAYS I WISH A MOTHERFUCKER WOULD, SO... ALL RIGHT, I'M HERE, JEAN-PIERRE. WHAT CAN GIGANTE DO FOR YOU?
GIGANTE COULD START BY SENDING A REAL LEADER. GIGANTE COULD SEND CHAVEZ, NOT HIS ROBOT SPEAKER BOX. WHY DOES HE HIDE? THE REST OF US HAVE SKIN IN THE GAME, REAL SKIN, NOT PLEATHER.
TWO BARS AND A HAIRCUT DON'T MAKE YOU SPECIAL, GRAY BOY. I CAN OUTHOLE, OUTFUCK, AND OUTFIGHT THE THREE OF YOU AND YOU KNOW IT.
AND WHEN THE JEFE OF THE OLDEST, BIGGEST, STRONGEST GANG IN SCARE CITY SENDS ME TO SPEAK FOR HIM? I AM CHAVEZ TODAY. BELIEVE IT.
MECCA
FROM GIGANTE

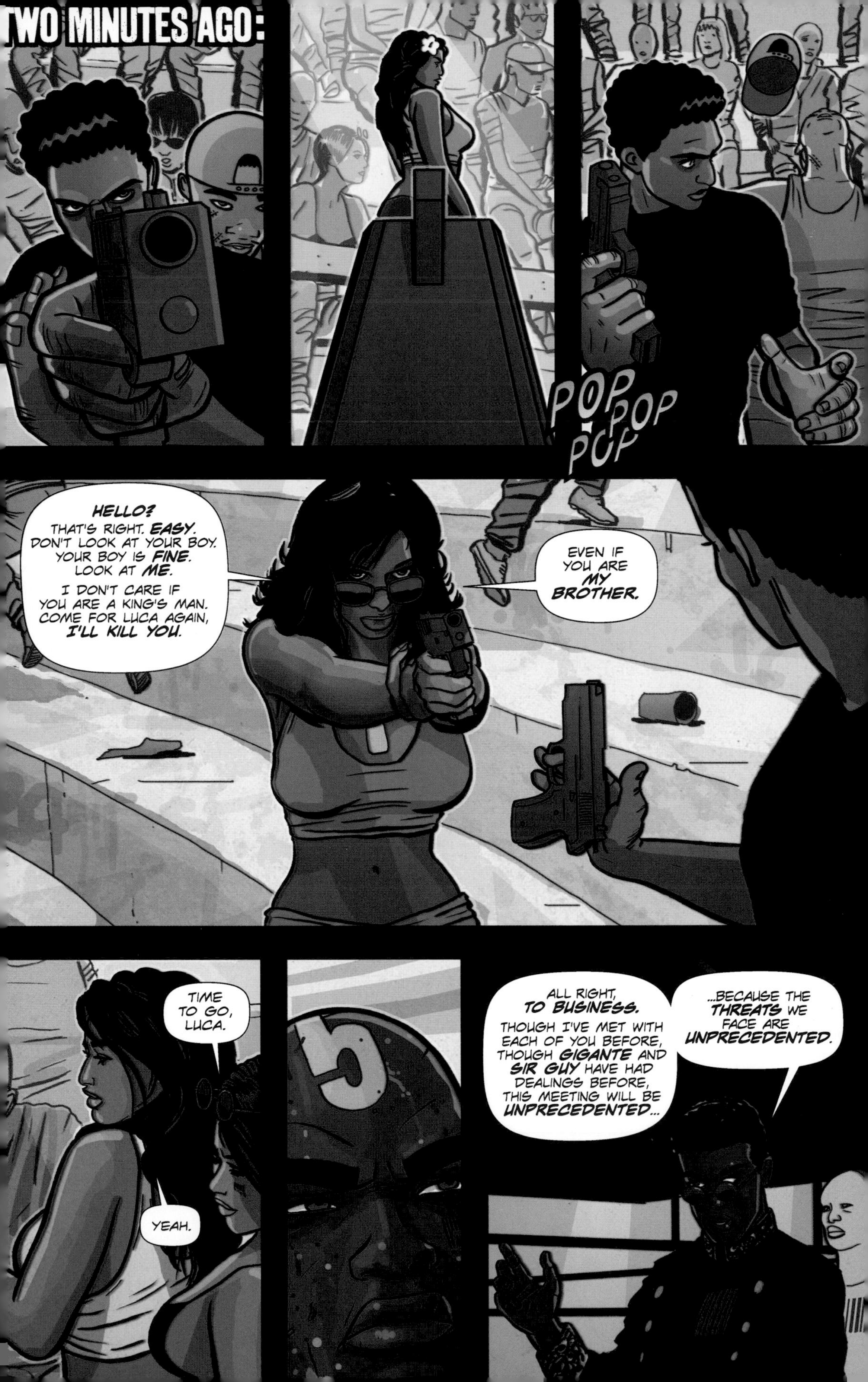
TWO MINUTES AGO:
POP POP POP
HELLO? THAT'S RIGHT. EASY. DON'T LOOK AT YOUR BOY. YOUR BOY IS FINE. LOOK AT ME.
I DON'T CARE IF YOU ARE A KING'S MAN. COME FOR LUCA AGAIN, I'LL KILL YOU.
EVEN IF YOU ARE MY BROTHER.
TIME TO GO, LUCA.
YEAH.
ALL RIGHT, TO BUSINESS.
THOUGH I'VE MET WITH EACH OF YOU BEFORE, THOUGH GIGANTE AND SIR GUY HAVE HAD DEALINGS BEFORE, THIS MEETING WILL BE UNPRECEDENTED...
...BECAUSE THE THREATS WE FACE ARE UNPRECEDENTED.

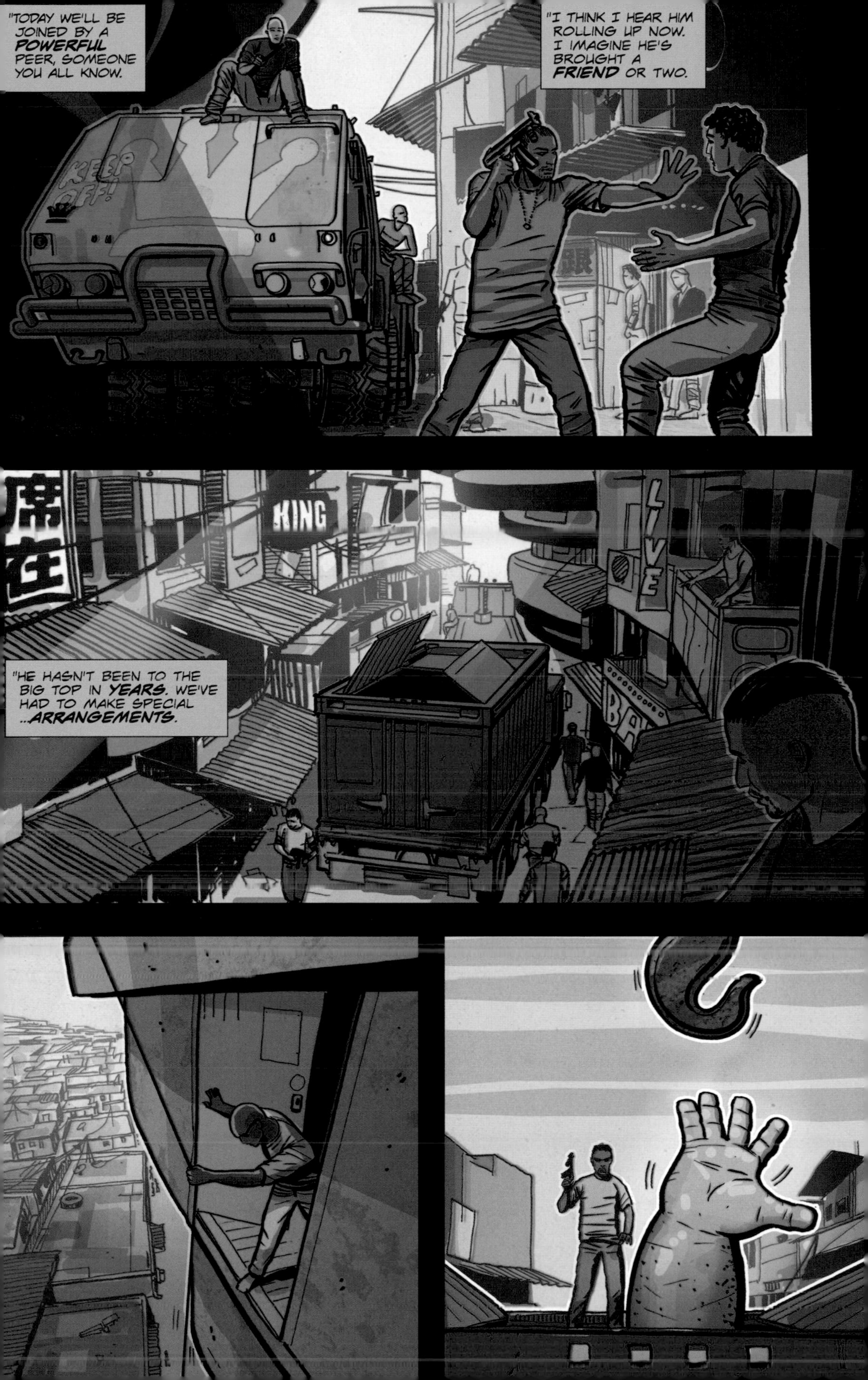
"TODAY WE'LL BE JOINED BY A POWERFUL PEER, SOMEONE YOU ALL KNOW.
"I THINK I HEAR HIM ROLLING UP NOW. I IMAGINE HE'S BROUGHT A FRIEND OR TWO.
KEEP OFF!
KING
LIVE
"HE HASN'T BEEN TO THE BIG TOP IN YEARS. WE'VE HAD TO MAKE SPECIAL ...ARRANGEMENTS.

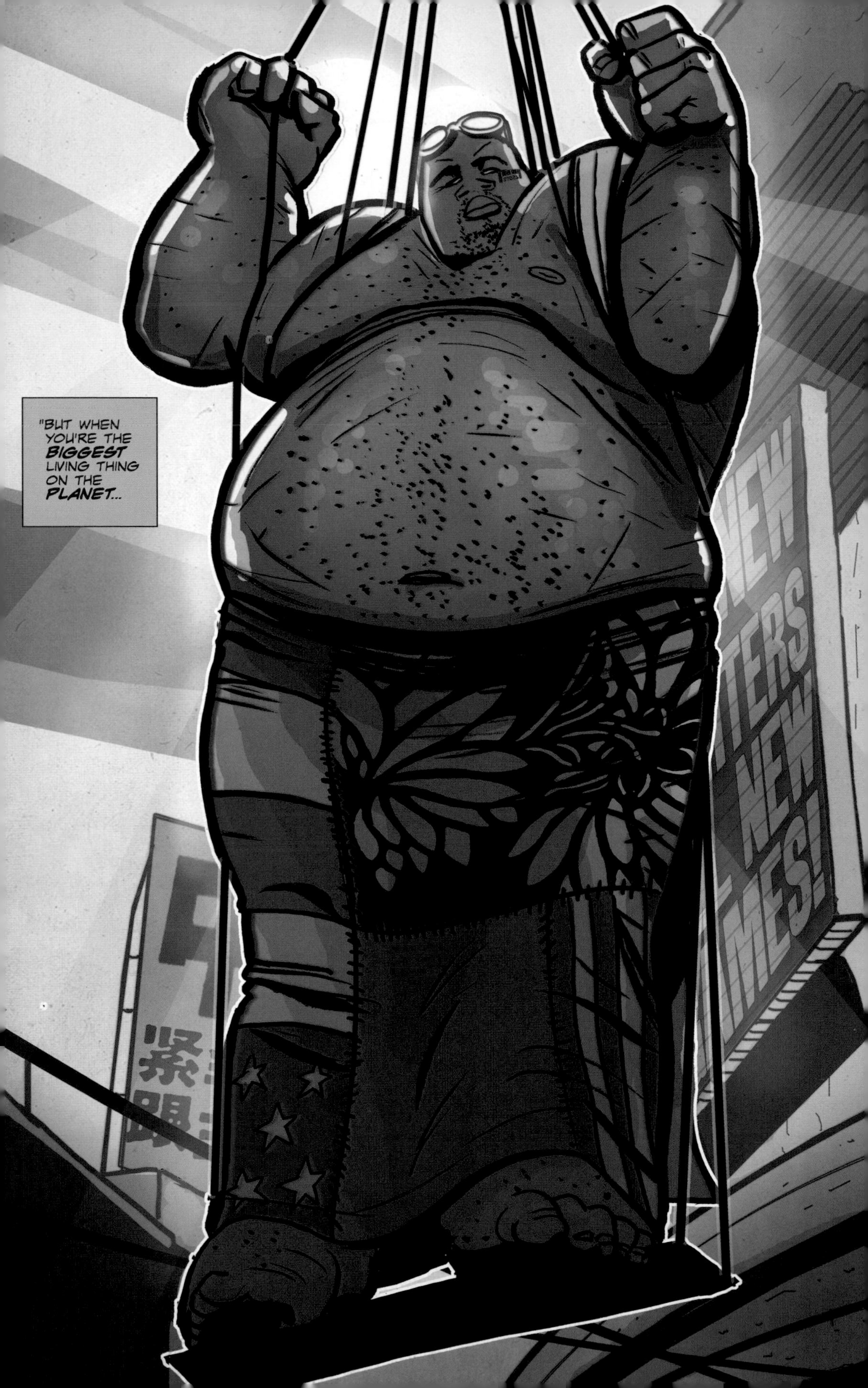
"BUT WHEN YOU'RE THE ***BIGGEST*** LIVING THING ON THE ***PLANET***...

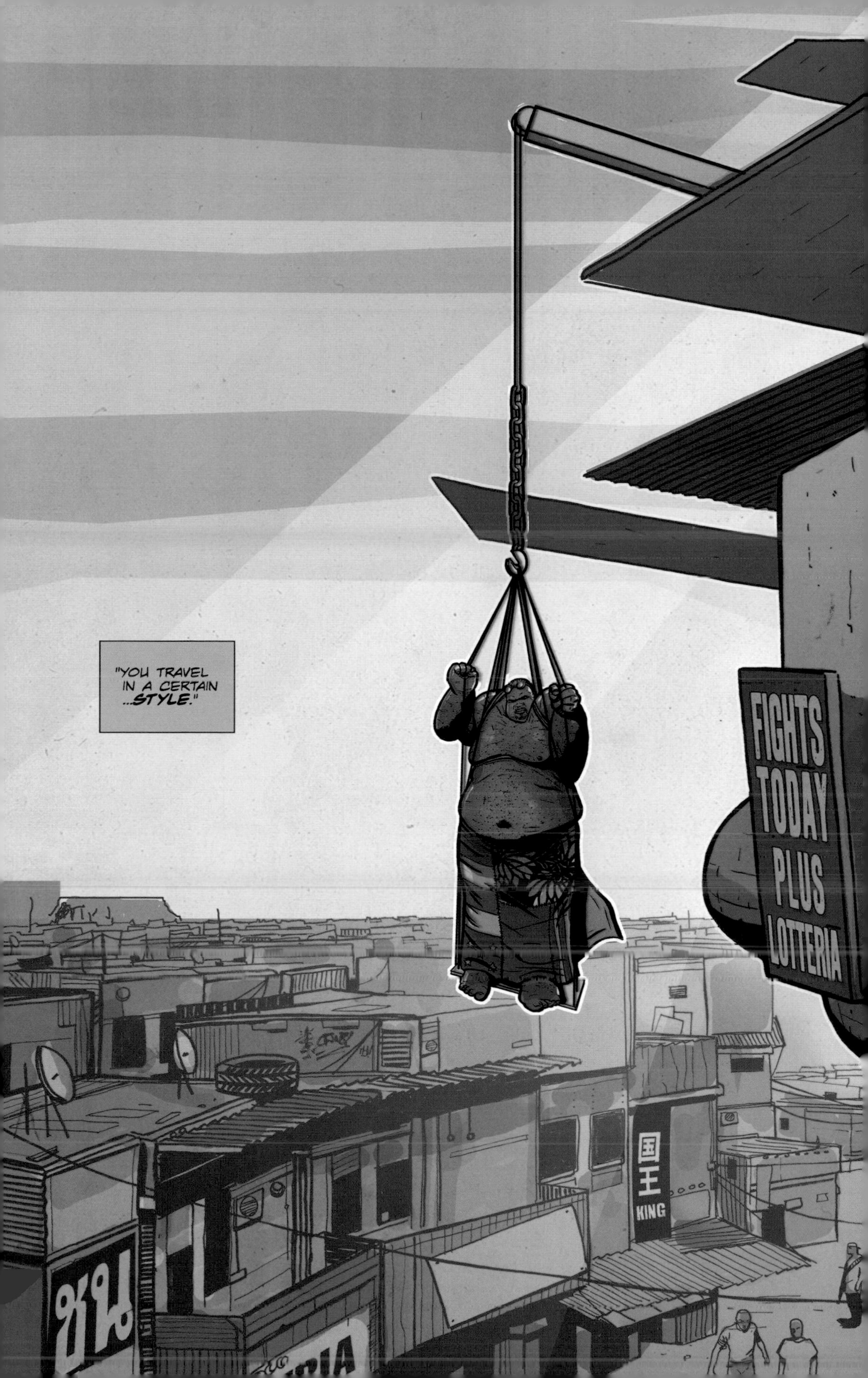
"YOU TRAVEL IN A CERTAIN ...STYLE."
FIGHTS TODAY PLUS LOTTERIA
国王
KING

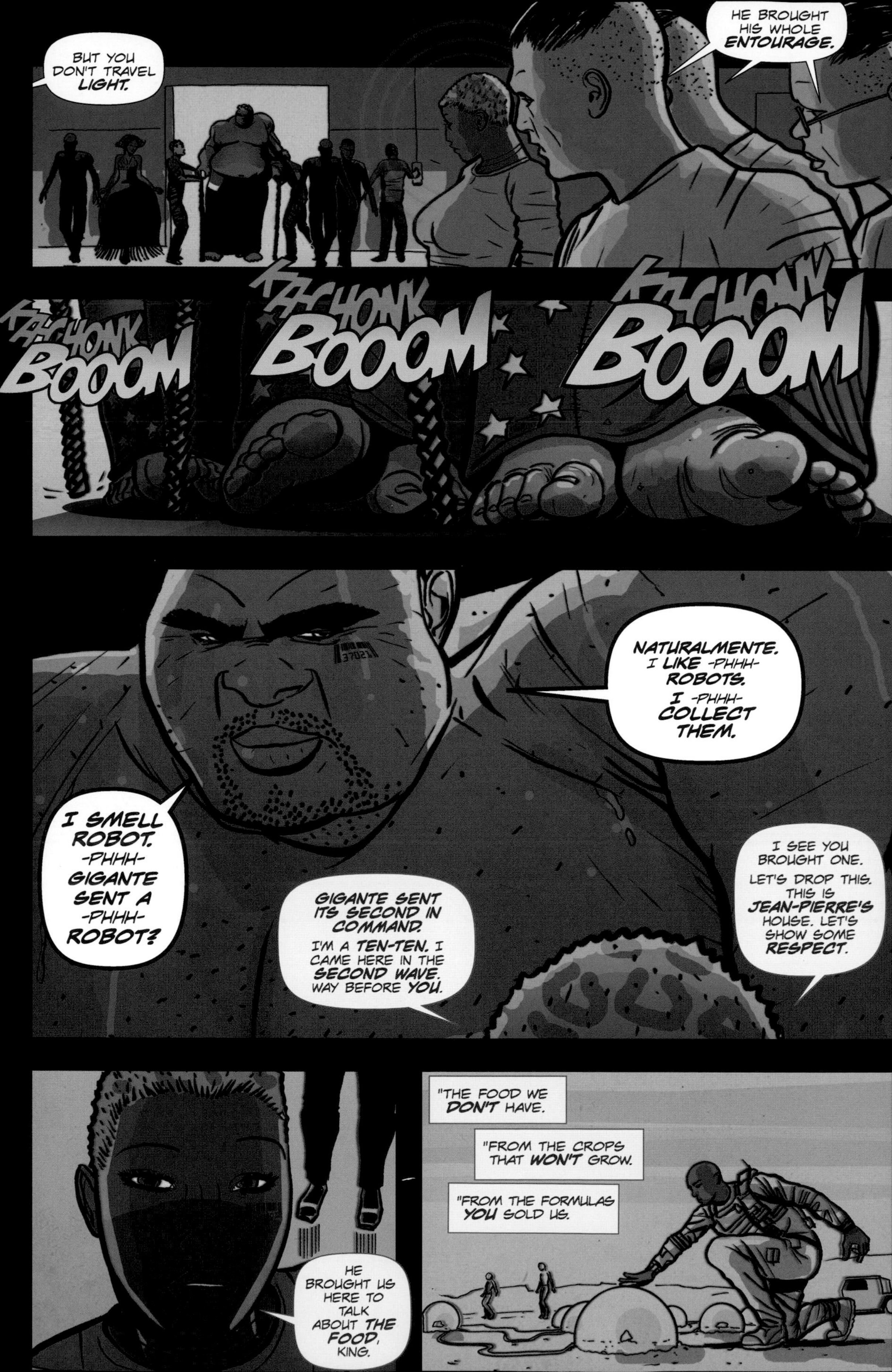
BUT YOU DON'T TRAVEL LIGHT.
HE BROUGHT HIS WHOLE ENTOURAGE.
KACHONK BOOOM
KACHONK BOOOM
KACHONK BOOOM
NATURALMENTE. I LIKE -PHHH- ROBOTS. I -PHHH- COLLECT THEM.
I SMELL ROBOT. -PHHH- GIGANTE SENT A -PHHH- ROBOT?
GIGANTE SENT ITS SECOND IN COMMAND.
I'M A TEN-TEN. I CAME HERE IN THE SECOND WAVE. WAY BEFORE YOU.
I SEE YOU BROUGHT ONE.
LET'S DROP THIS. THIS IS JEAN-PIERRE'S HOUSE. LET'S SHOW SOME RESPECT.
HE BROUGHT US HERE TO TALK ABOUT THE FOOD, KING.
"THE FOOD WE DON'T HAVE.
"FROM THE CROPS THAT WON'T GROW.
"FROM THE FORMULAS YOU SOLD US.

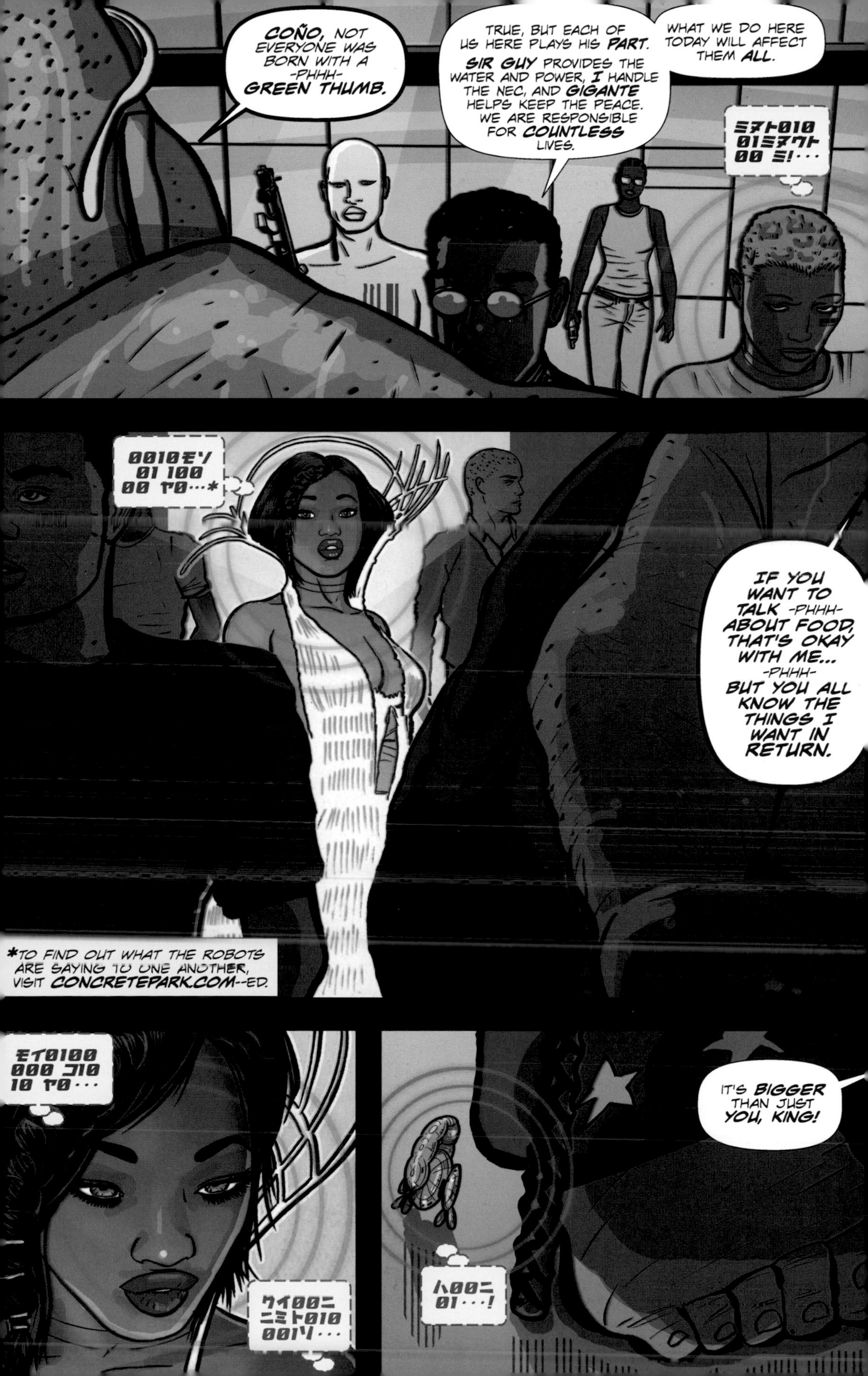

COÑO, NOT EVERYONE WAS BORN WITH A -PHHH- GREEN THUMB.
TRUE, BUT EACH OF US HERE PLAYS HIS PART. SIR GUY PROVIDES THE WATER AND POWER, I HANDLE THE NEC, AND GIGANTE HELPS KEEP THE PEACE. WE ARE RESPONSIBLE FOR COUNTLESS LIVES.
WHAT WE DO HERE TODAY WILL AFFECT THEM ALL.
ミヌト010 01ミヌクト 00 ミ!...
0010モソ 01 100 00 ヤ0...*
IF YOU WANT TO TALK -PHHH- ABOUT FOOD, THAT'S OKAY WITH ME... -PHHH- BUT YOU ALL KNOW THE THINGS I WANT IN RETURN.
*TO FIND OUT WHAT THE ROBOTS ARE SAYING TO ONE ANOTHER, VISIT CONCRETEPARK.COM--ED.
モイ0100 000 コ10 10 ヤ0...
ケイ00ニ ニミト010 001ソ...
ハ00ニ 01...!
IT'S BIGGER THAN JUST YOU, KING!

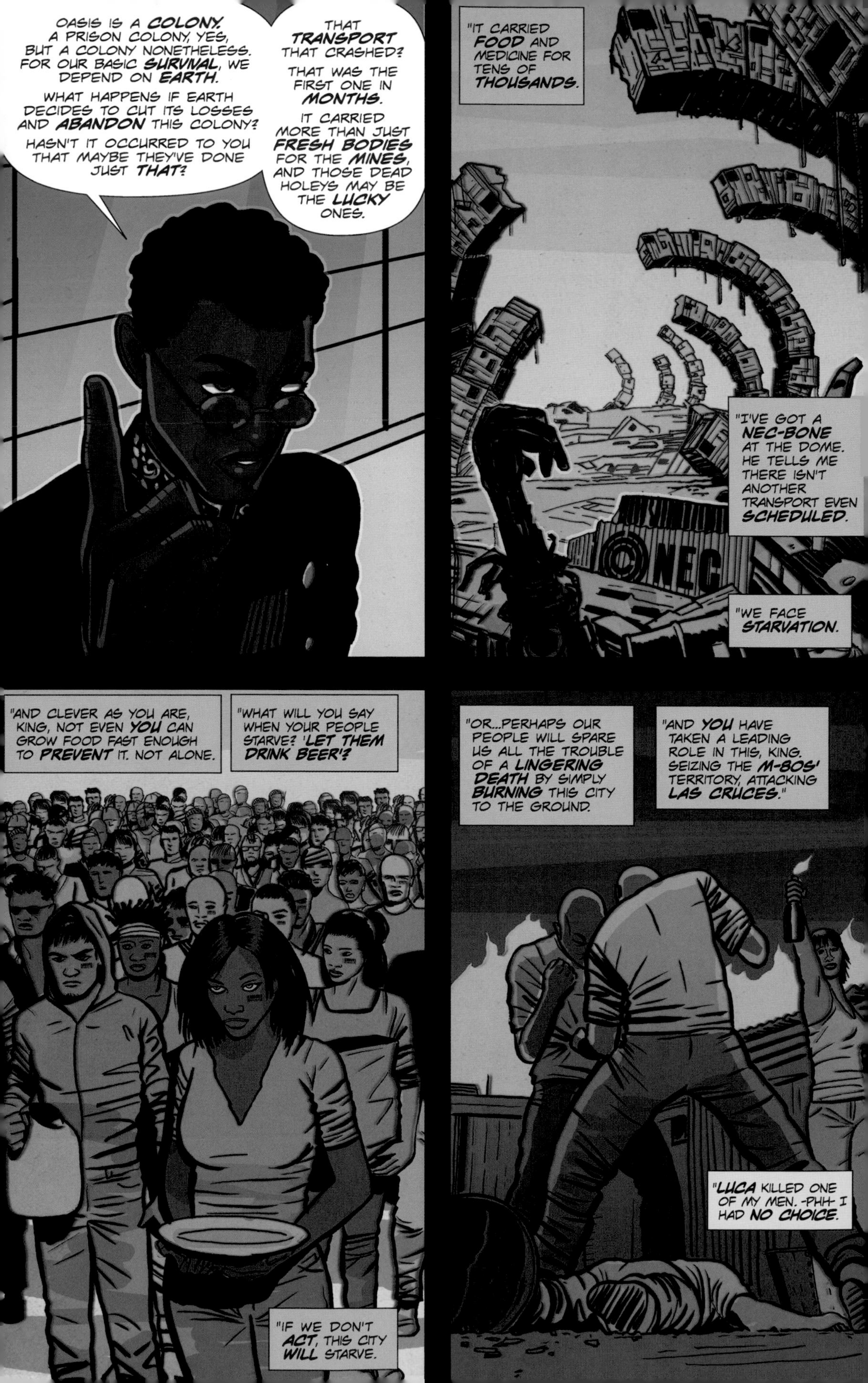
OASIS IS A COLONY. A PRISON COLONY, YES, BUT A COLONY NONETHELESS. FOR OUR BASIC SURVIVAL, WE DEPEND ON EARTH.
WHAT HAPPENS IF EARTH DECIDES TO CUT ITS LOSSES AND ABANDON THIS COLONY?
HASN'T IT OCCURRED TO YOU THAT MAYBE THEY'VE DONE JUST THAT?
THAT TRANSPORT THAT CRASHED?
THAT WAS THE FIRST ONE IN MONTHS.
IT CARRIED MORE THAN JUST FRESH BODIES FOR THE MINES, AND THOSE DEAD HOLEYS MAY BE THE LUCKY ONES.
"IT CARRIED FOOD AND MEDICINE FOR TENS OF THOUSANDS.
"I'VE GOT A NEC-BONE AT THE DOME. HE TELLS ME THERE ISN'T ANOTHER TRANSPORT EVEN SCHEDULED.
NEC
"WE FACE STARVATION.
"AND CLEVER AS YOU ARE, KING, NOT EVEN YOU CAN GROW FOOD FAST ENOUGH TO PREVENT IT. NOT ALONE.
"WHAT WILL YOU SAY WHEN YOUR PEOPLE STARVE? 'LET THEM DRINK BEER'?
"IF WE DON'T ACT, THIS CITY WILL STARVE.
"OR...PERHAPS OUR PEOPLE WILL SPARE US ALL THE TROUBLE OF A LINGERING DEATH BY SIMPLY BURNING THIS CITY TO THE GROUND.
"AND YOU HAVE TAKEN A LEADING ROLE IN THIS, KING. SEIZING THE M-80S' TERRITORY, ATTACKING LAS CRUCES."
"LUCA KILLED ONE OF MY MEN. -PHH- I HAD NO CHOICE.

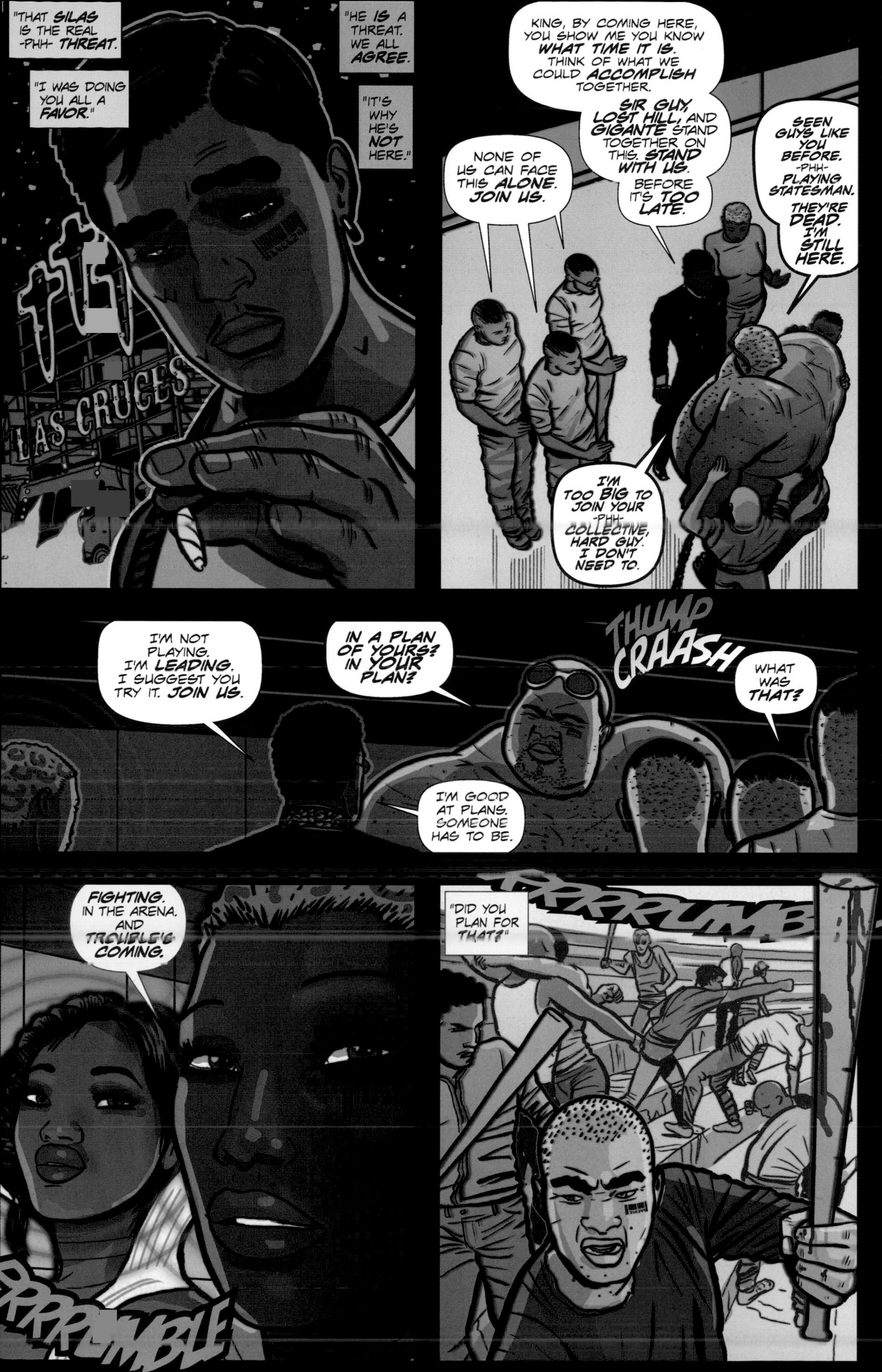
"THAT SILAS IS THE REAL -PHH- THREAT.
"I WAS DOING YOU ALL A FAVOR."
"HE IS A THREAT. WE ALL AGREE.
"IT'S WHY HE'S NOT HERE."
LAS CRUCES
KING, BY COMING HERE, YOU SHOW ME YOU KNOW WHAT TIME IT IS. THINK OF WHAT WE COULD ACCOMPLISH TOGETHER.
SIR GUY, LOST HILL, AND GIGANTE STAND TOGETHER ON THIS. STAND WITH US.
NONE OF US CAN FACE THIS ALONE. JOIN US.
BEFORE IT'S TOO LATE.
SEEN GUYS LIKE YOU BEFORE. -PHH- PLAYING STATESMAN.
THEY'RE DEAD. I'M STILL HERE.
I'M TOO BIG TO JOIN YOUR -PHH- COLLECTIVE, HARD GUY. I DON'T NEED TO.
I'M NOT PLAYING. I'M LEADING. I SUGGEST YOU TRY IT. JOIN US.
IN A PLAN OF YOURS? IN YOUR PLAN?
I'M GOOD AT PLANS. SOMEONE HAS TO BE.
THUMP
CRAASH
WHAT WAS THAT?
FIGHTING. IN THE ARENA. AND TROUBLE'S COMING.
RRRRUMBLE
"DID YOU PLAN FOR THAT?"
RRRRUMB

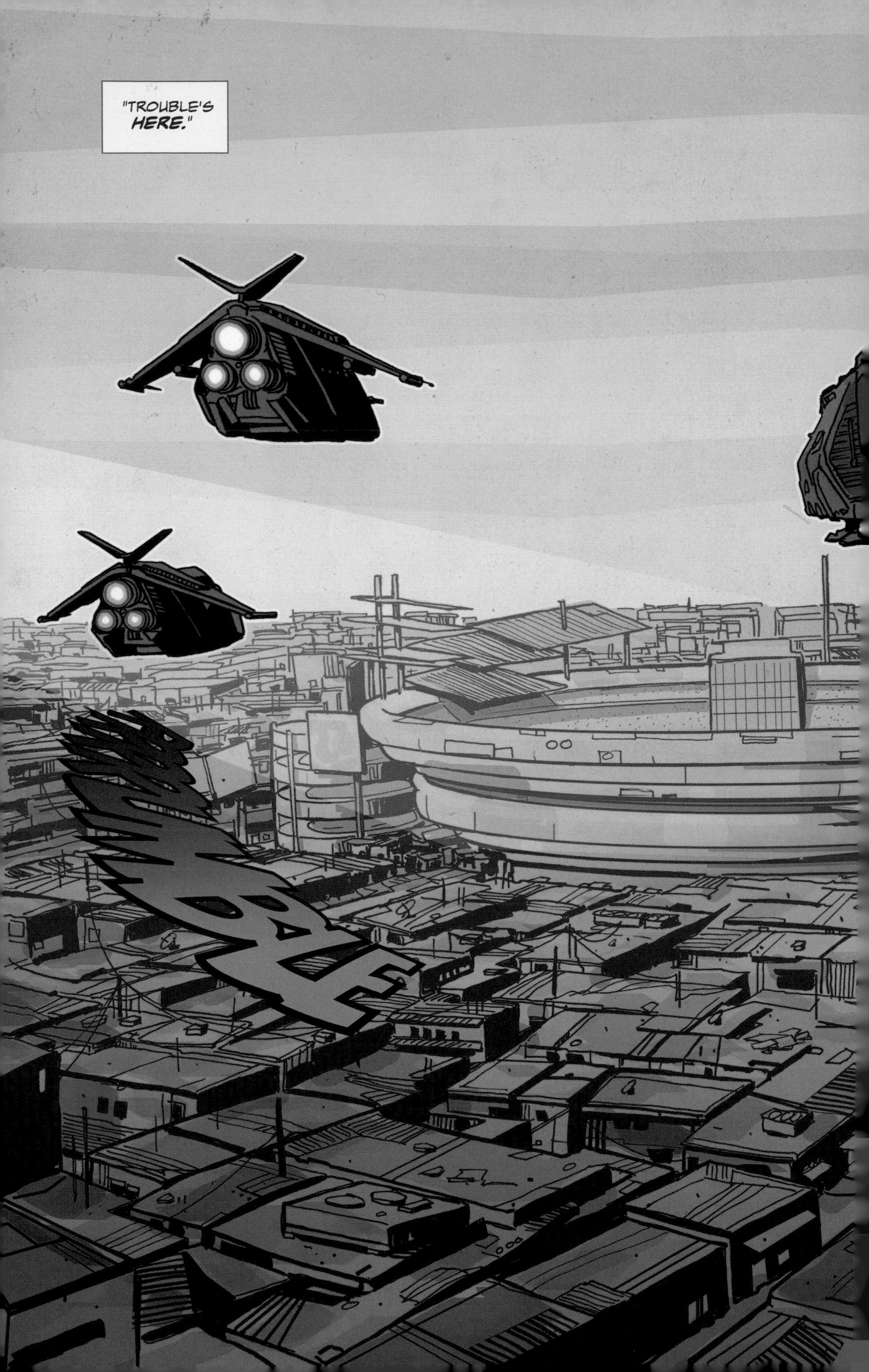
"TROUBLE'S HERE."

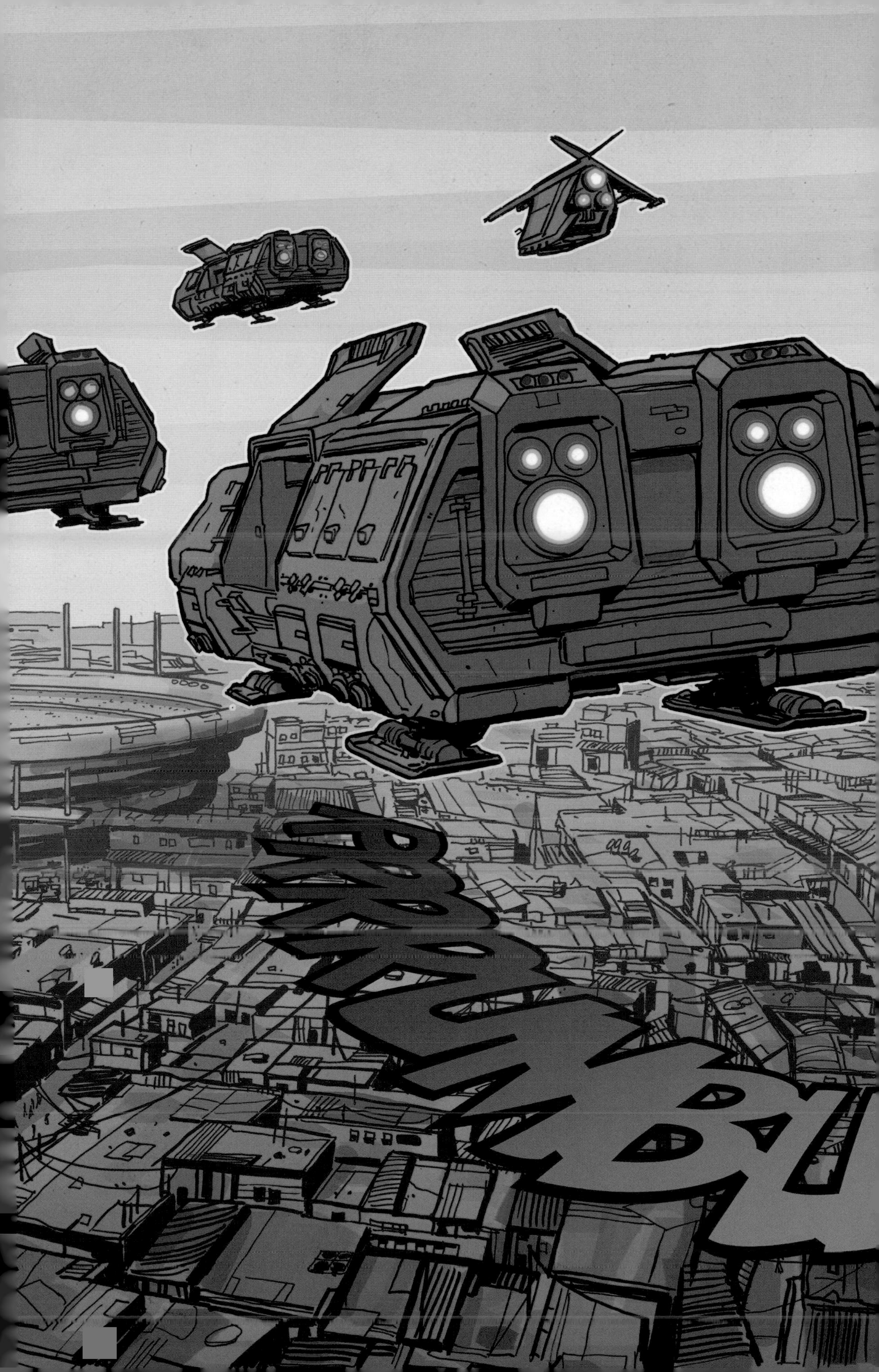

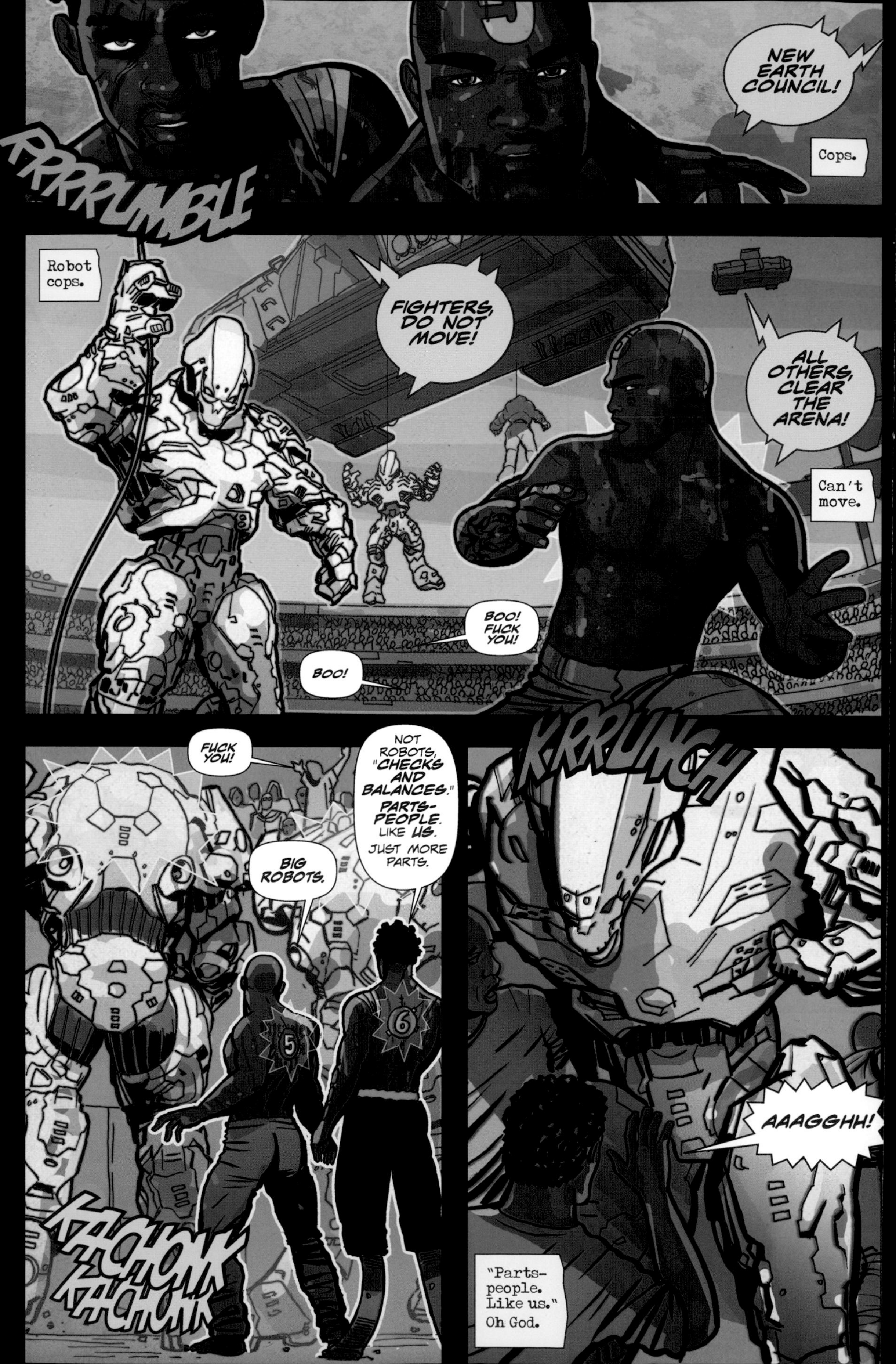
RRRRRUMBLE
NEW EARTH COUNCIL!
Cops.
Robot cops.
FIGHTERS, DO NOT MOVE!
ALL OTHERS, CLEAR THE ARENA!
Can't move.
BOO! FUCK YOU!
BOO!
FUCK YOU!
NOT ROBOTS, "CHECKS AND BALANCES." PARTS-PEOPLE. LIKE US. JUST MORE PARTS.
BIG ROBOTS.
KACHONK KACHONK
K-RRUNCH
AAAGGHH!
"Parts-people. Like us."
Oh God.

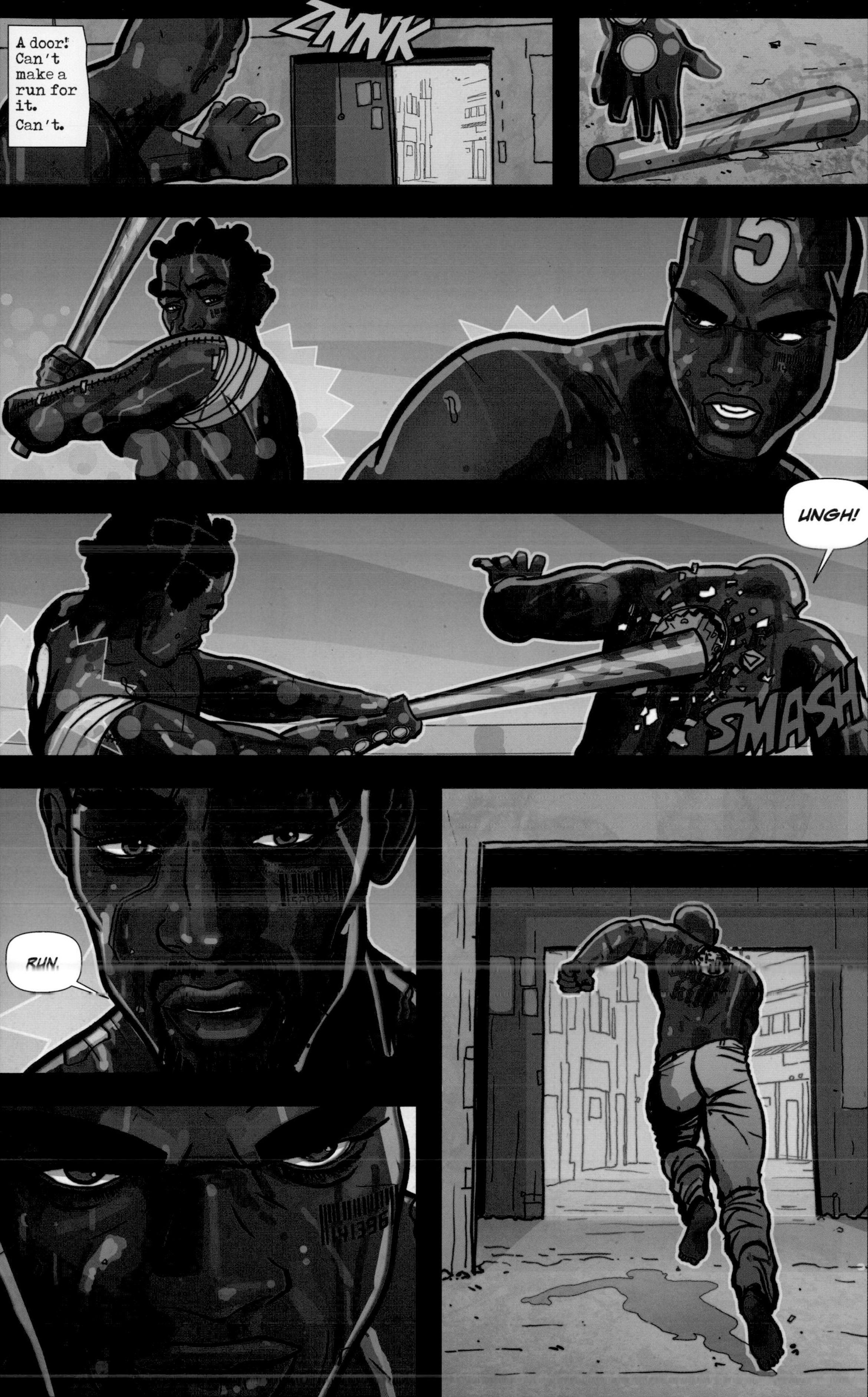
A door! Can't make a run for it. Can't.
ZNNK
UNGH!
SMASH
RUN.

RRRRUMBLE
I'VE WARNED YOU ALL. THIS IS HOW A NEC CRACKDOWN BEGINS. IF YOU ALL CAN'T KEEP A ROUGH KIND OF PEACE, GIGANTE WILL.*
BOOM
WHAT'S THAT SOUND?
FIREWORKS. NORMAL PART OF THE SHOW. PRE-PROGRAMMED.
BRILLIANT.
*CHAVEZ'S VOICE--ED.
BOOM
BOOM
THE CHECKS AND BALANCES WILL SHUT DOWN MORE THAN YOUR SHOW, JEAN-PIERRE.
-KOFF- WHAT'S THAT SMELL?
THUMP THUMP
FREEZE!
I WISH. THIS GUY SMELLS AWFUL!
EVENING, ALL!
FONTAINE, YOU DESERT FILTH! HOW DARE YOU SHOW YOUR FACE HERE?
A GHOST APPEARS.
DESERT FILTH I MAY BE, BUT I'M HERE BECAUSE I WAS INVITED. THANK YOU, JEAN-PIERRE.
GOOD TO "SEE" YOU, CHAVEZ, OLD FRIEND.
NICE BODY-GUARDS, KING.
WHAT -PHH- IS THAT? -KOFF-
I'VE BROUGHT A SPECIAL SURPRISE.
THE MADMAN FONTAINE FROM BAMA

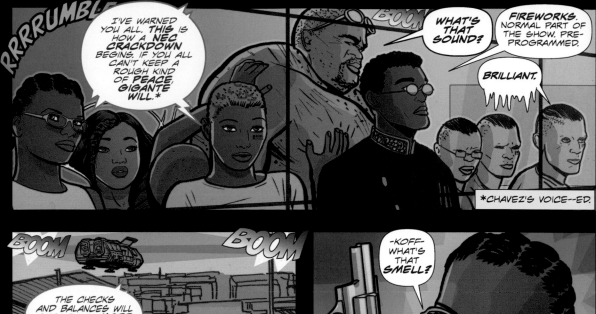

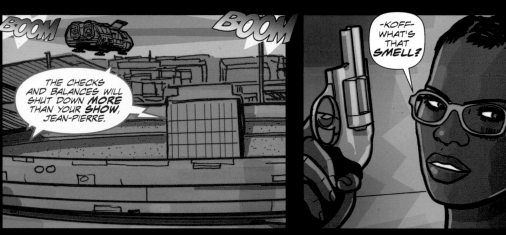

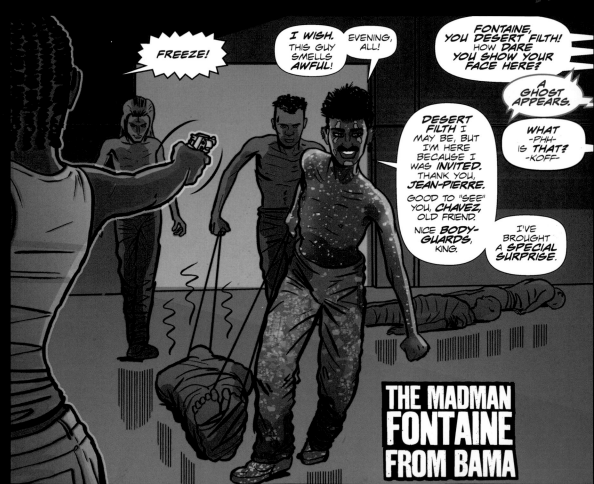

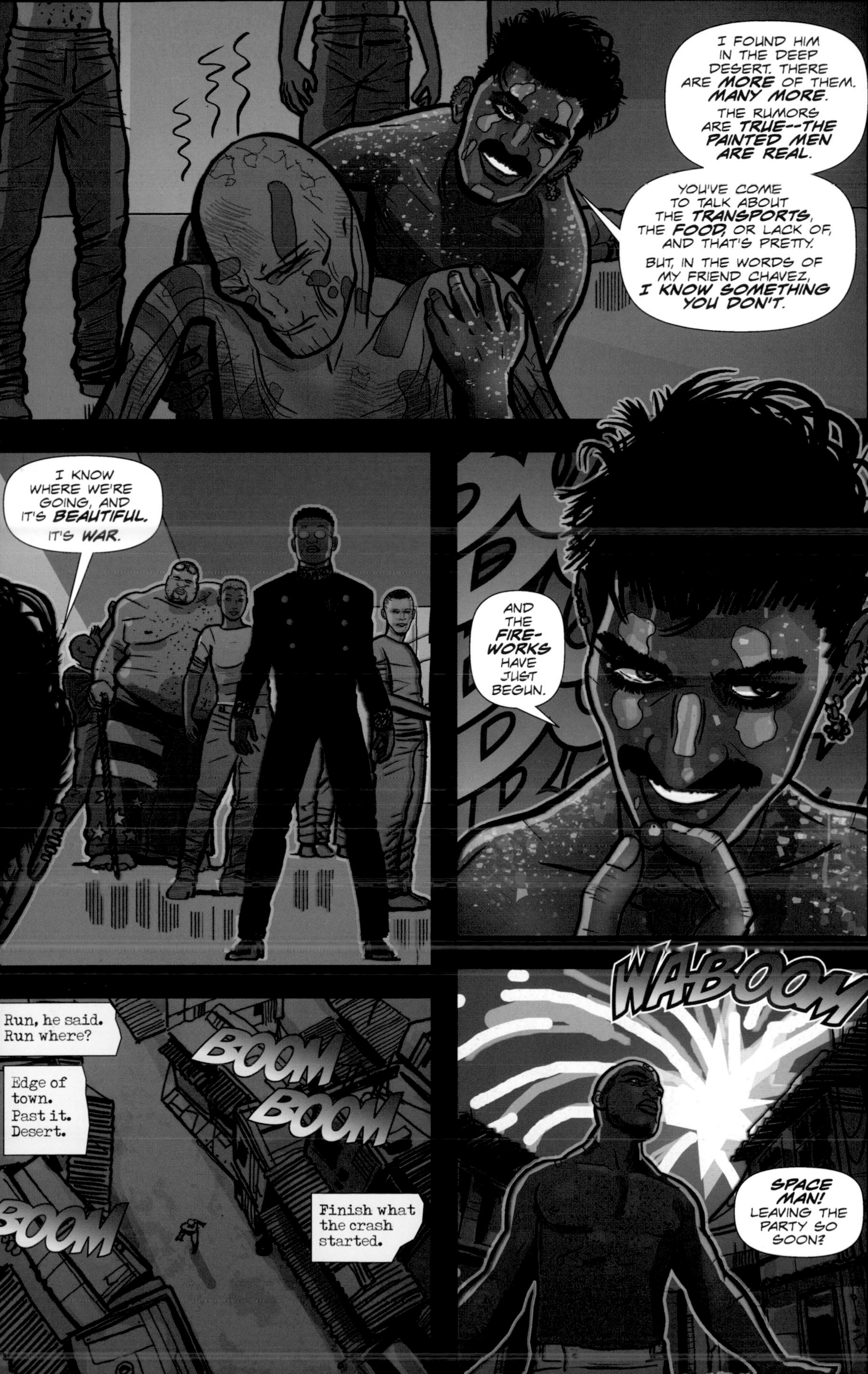
I FOUND HIM IN THE DEEP DESERT. THERE ARE MORE OF THEM. MANY MORE.
THE RUMORS ARE TRUE--THE PAINTED MEN ARE REAL.
YOU'VE COME TO TALK ABOUT THE TRANSPORTS, THE FOOD, OR LACK OF, AND THAT'S PRETTY.
BUT, IN THE WORDS OF MY FRIEND CHAVEZ, I KNOW SOMETHING YOU DON'T.
I KNOW WHERE WE'RE GOING, AND IT'S BEAUTIFUL.
IT'S WAR.
AND THE FIRE-WORKS HAVE JUST BEGUN.
Run, he said. Run where?
Edge of town. Past it. Desert.
BOOM
BOOM
BOOM
Finish what the crash started.
WABOOM
SPACE MAN! LEAVING THE PARTY SO SOON?

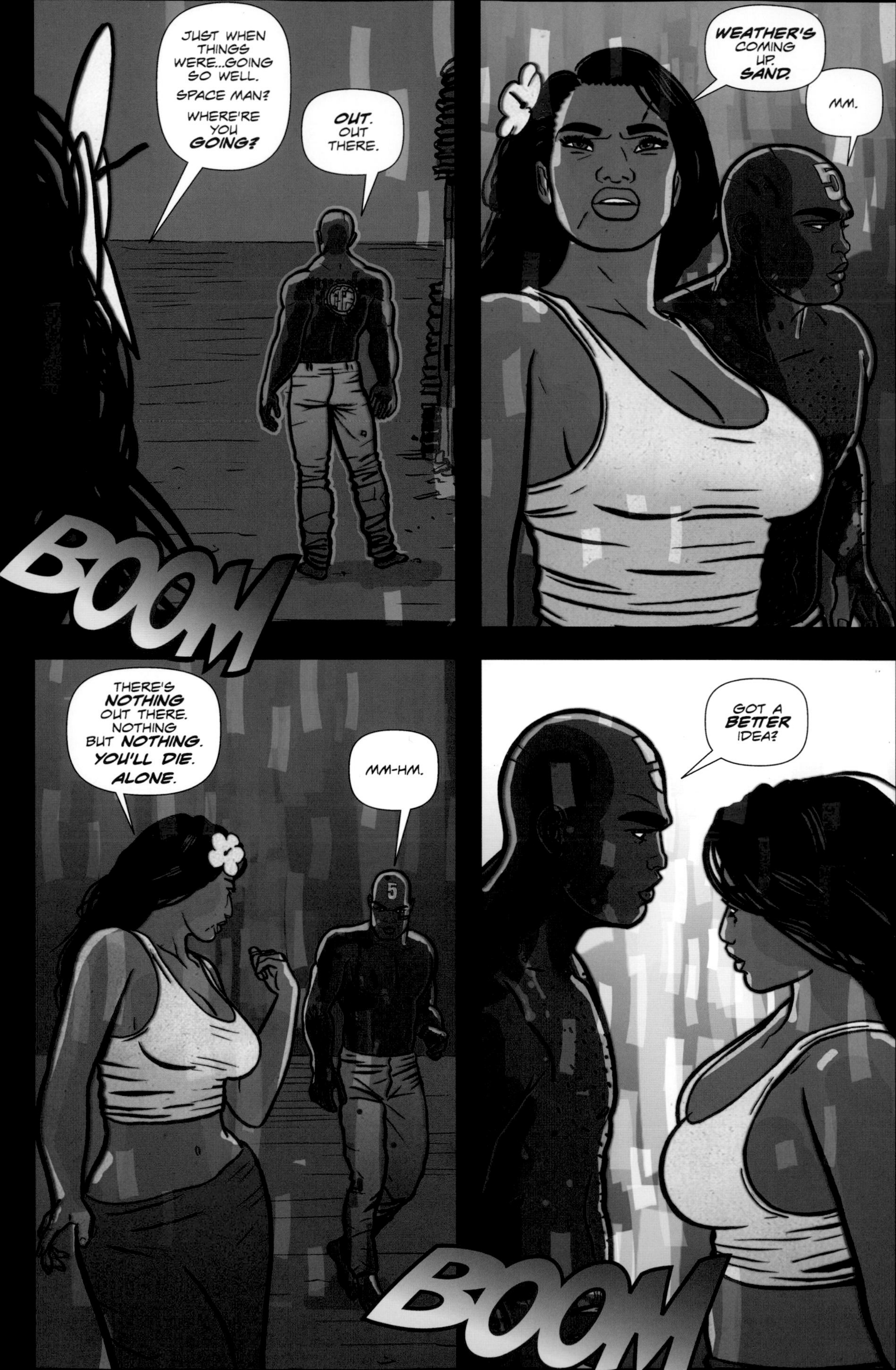
JUST WHEN THINGS WERE...GOING SO WELL.
SPACE MAN?
WHERE'RE YOU GOING?
OUT. OUT THERE.
BOOM
WEATHER'S COMING UP. SAND.
MM.
THERE'S NOTHING OUT THERE. NOTHING BUT NOTHING. YOU'LL DIE. ALONE.
MM-HM.
GOT A BETTER IDEA?
BOOM

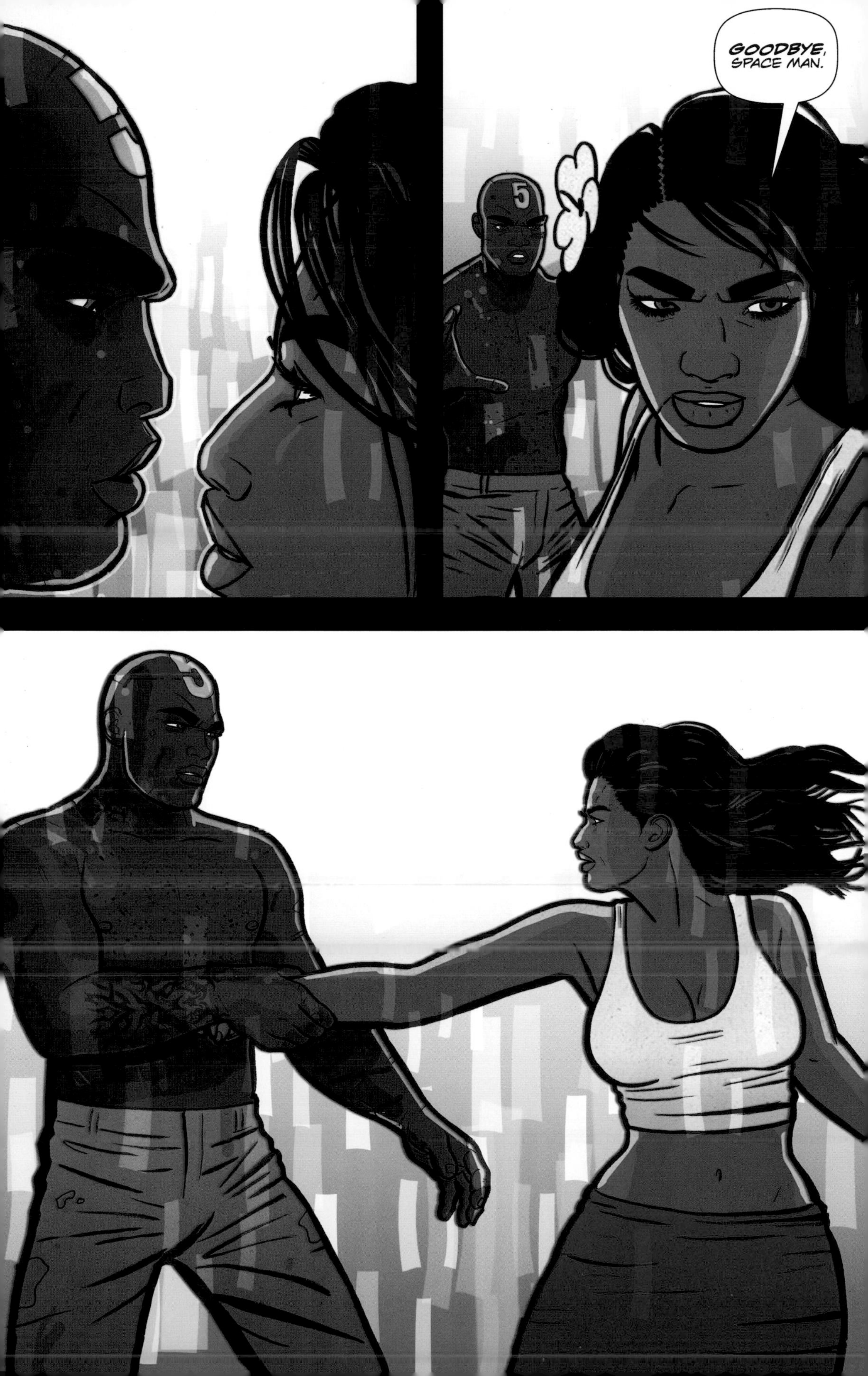
GOODBYE, SPACE MAN.

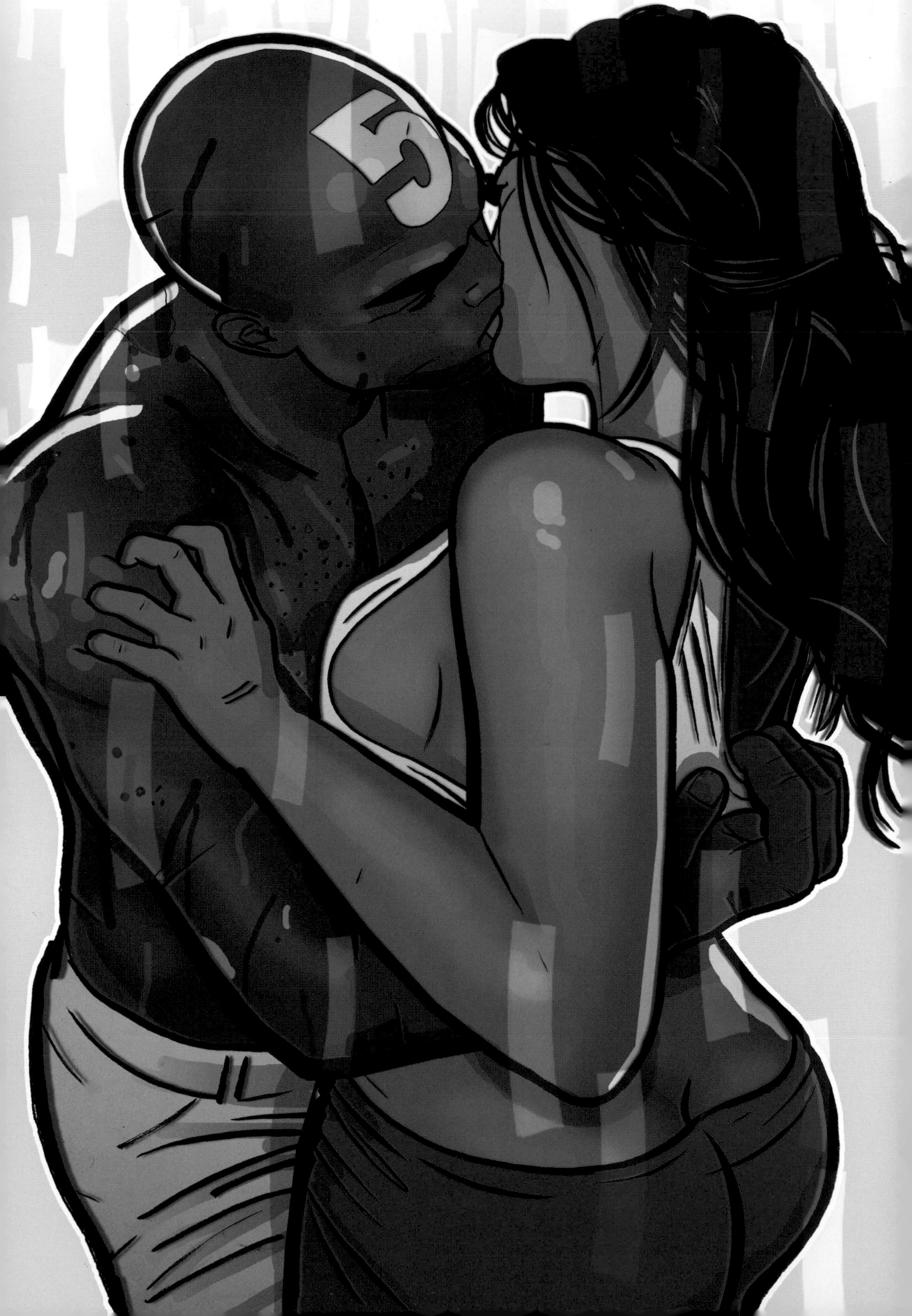

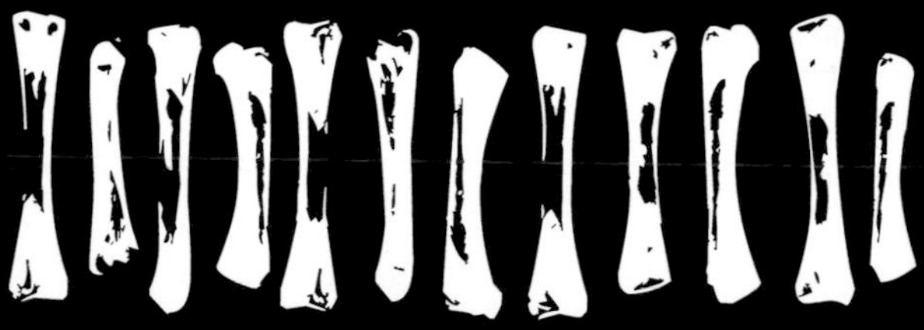

"When you were born,
the stars forgot to shine.
Make them regret it."
—The Voices of Oasis

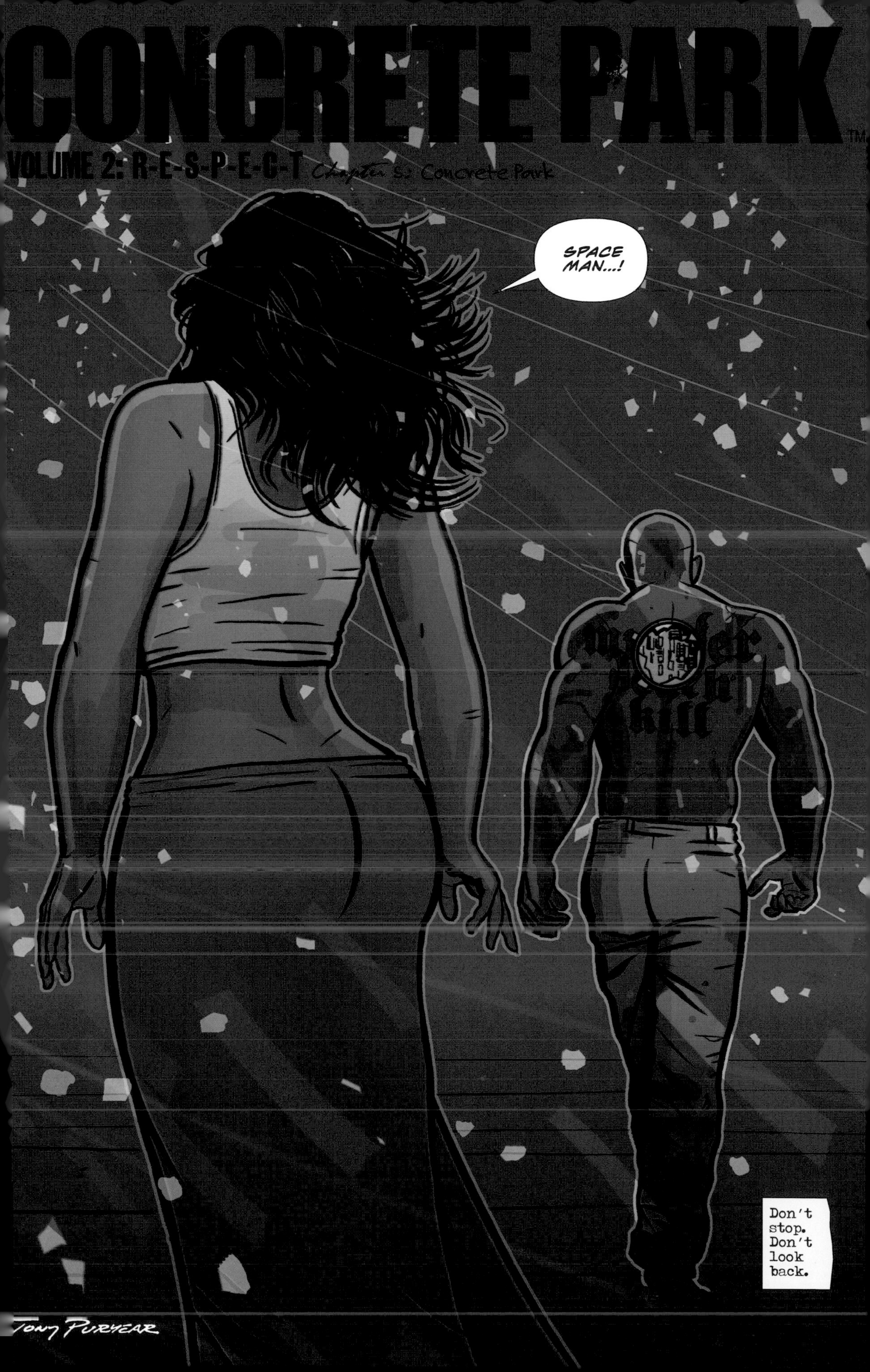
CONCRETE PARK™
VOLUME 2: R-E-S-P-E-C-T Chapter 5: Concrete Park
SPACE MAN...!
Don't stop. Don't look back.
TONY PURYEAR

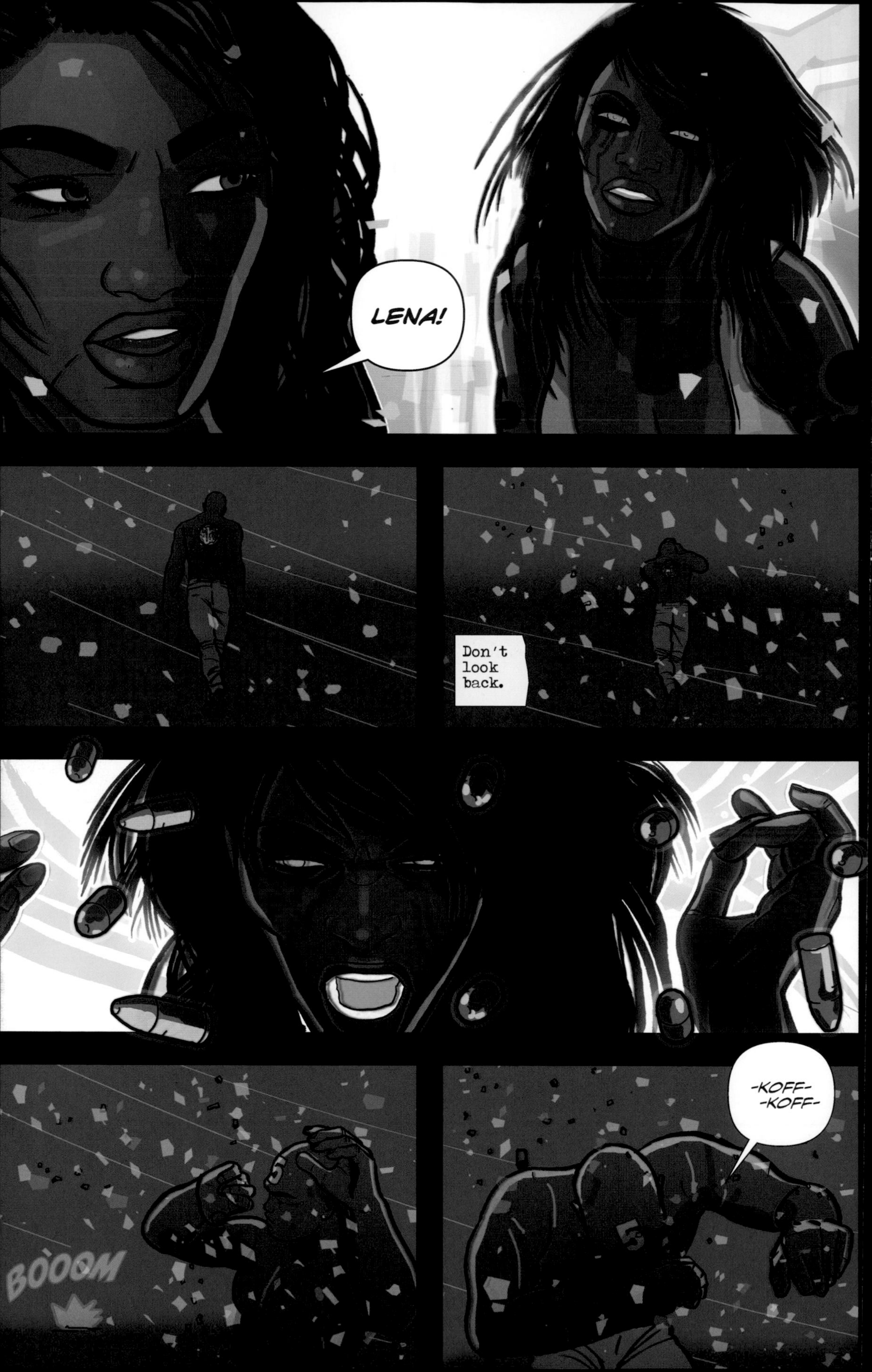
LENA!
Don't look back.
BOOOM
-KOFF-
-KOFF-

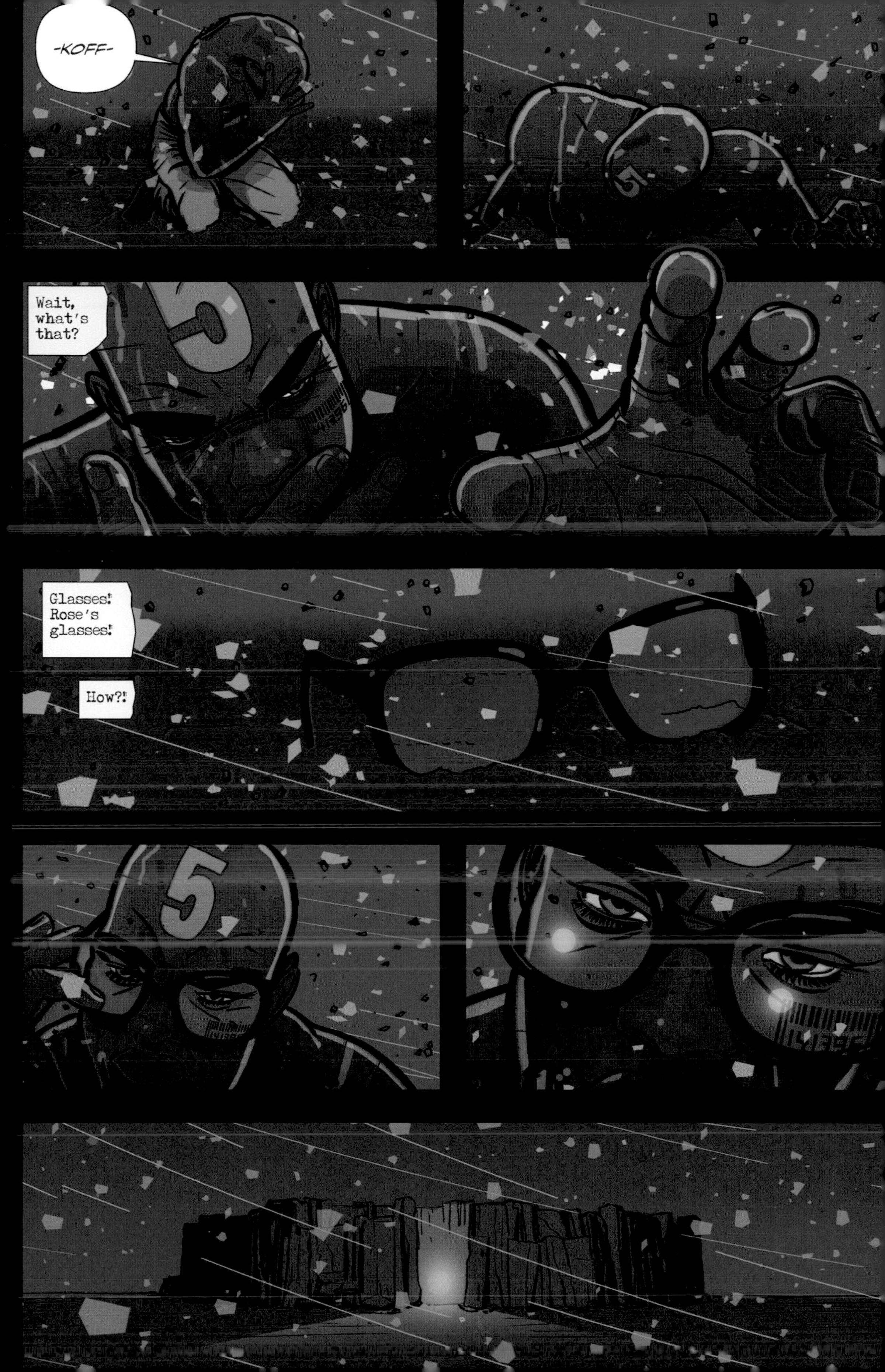
-KOFF-
Wait, what's that?
Glasses!! Rose's glasses!!
How?!!

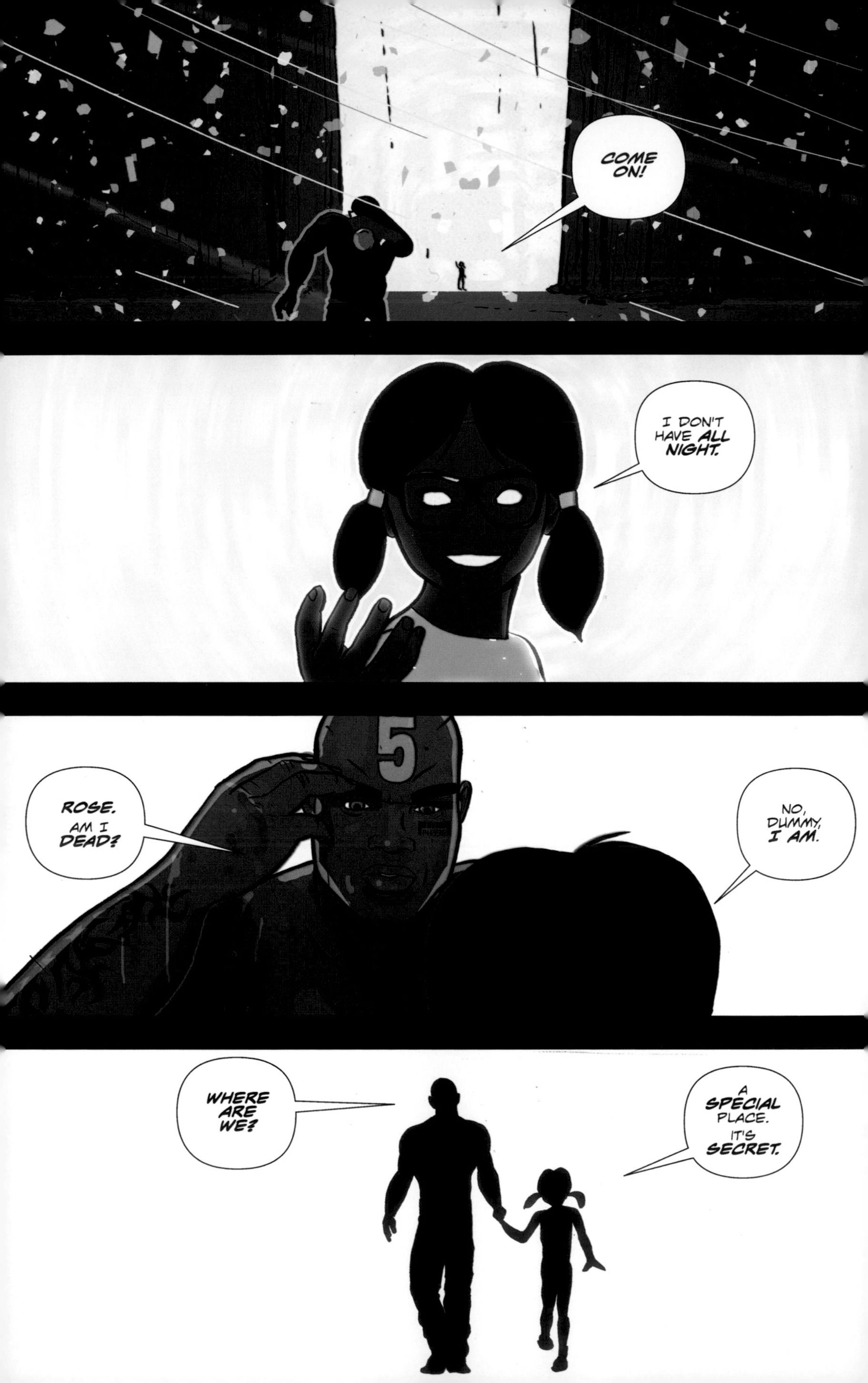
COME ON!
I DON'T HAVE ALL NIGHT.
ROSE. AM I DEAD?
NO, DUMMY, I AM.
WHERE ARE WE?
A SPECIAL PLACE. IT'S SECRET.

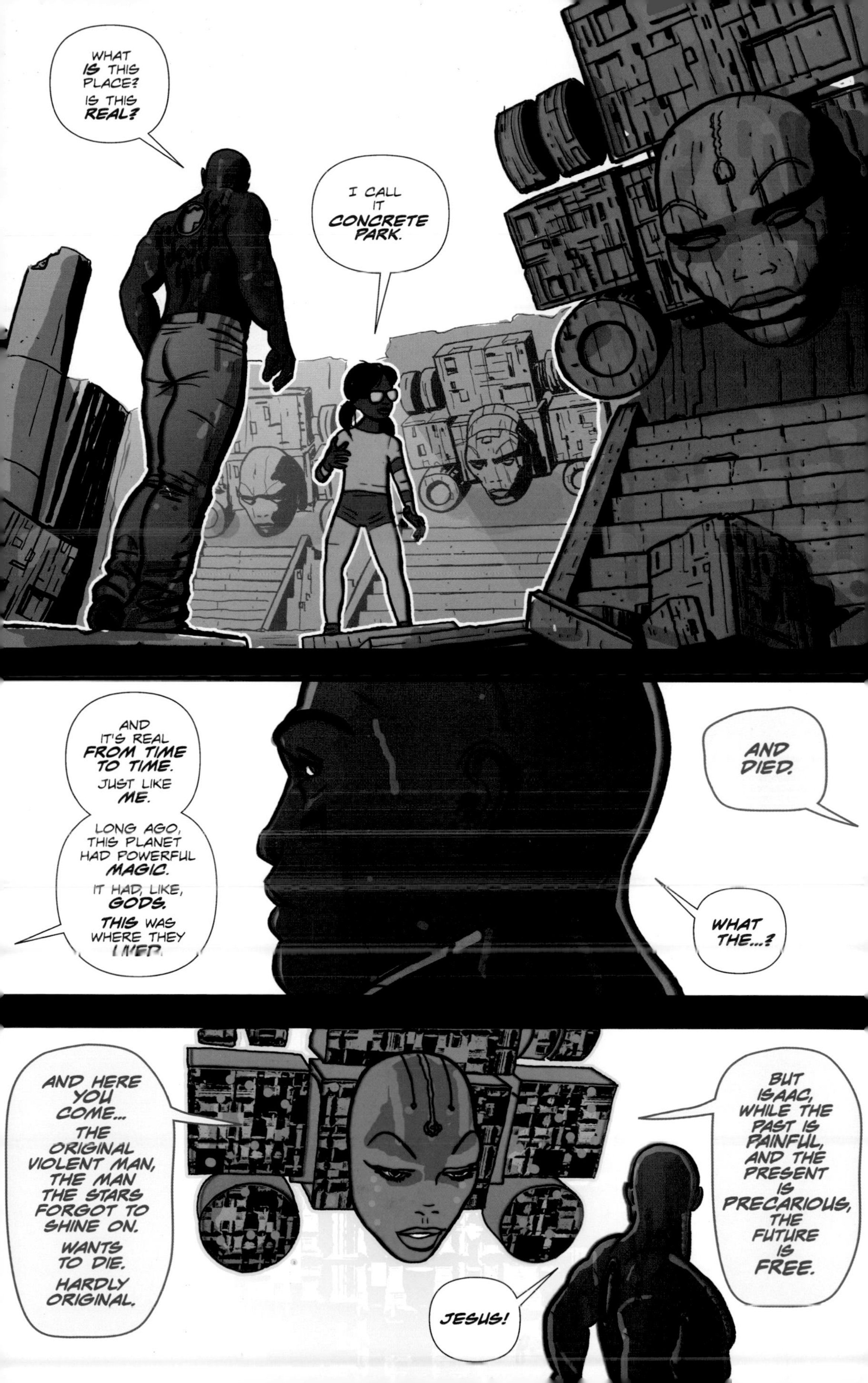

WHAT IS THIS PLACE? IS THIS REAL?
I CALL IT CONCRETE PARK.
AND IT'S REAL FROM TIME TO TIME. JUST LIKE ME.
LONG AGO, THIS PLANET HAD POWERFUL MAGIC. IT HAD, LIKE, GODS. THIS WAS WHERE THEY LIVED.
AND DIED.
WHAT THE...?
AND HERE YOU COME... THE ORIGINAL VIOLENT MAN, THE MAN THE STARS FORGOT TO SHINE ON. WANTS TO DIE. HARDLY ORIGINAL.
BUT ISAAC, WHILE THE PAST IS PAINFUL, AND THE PRESENT IS PRECARIOUS, THE FUTURE IS FREE.
JESUS!

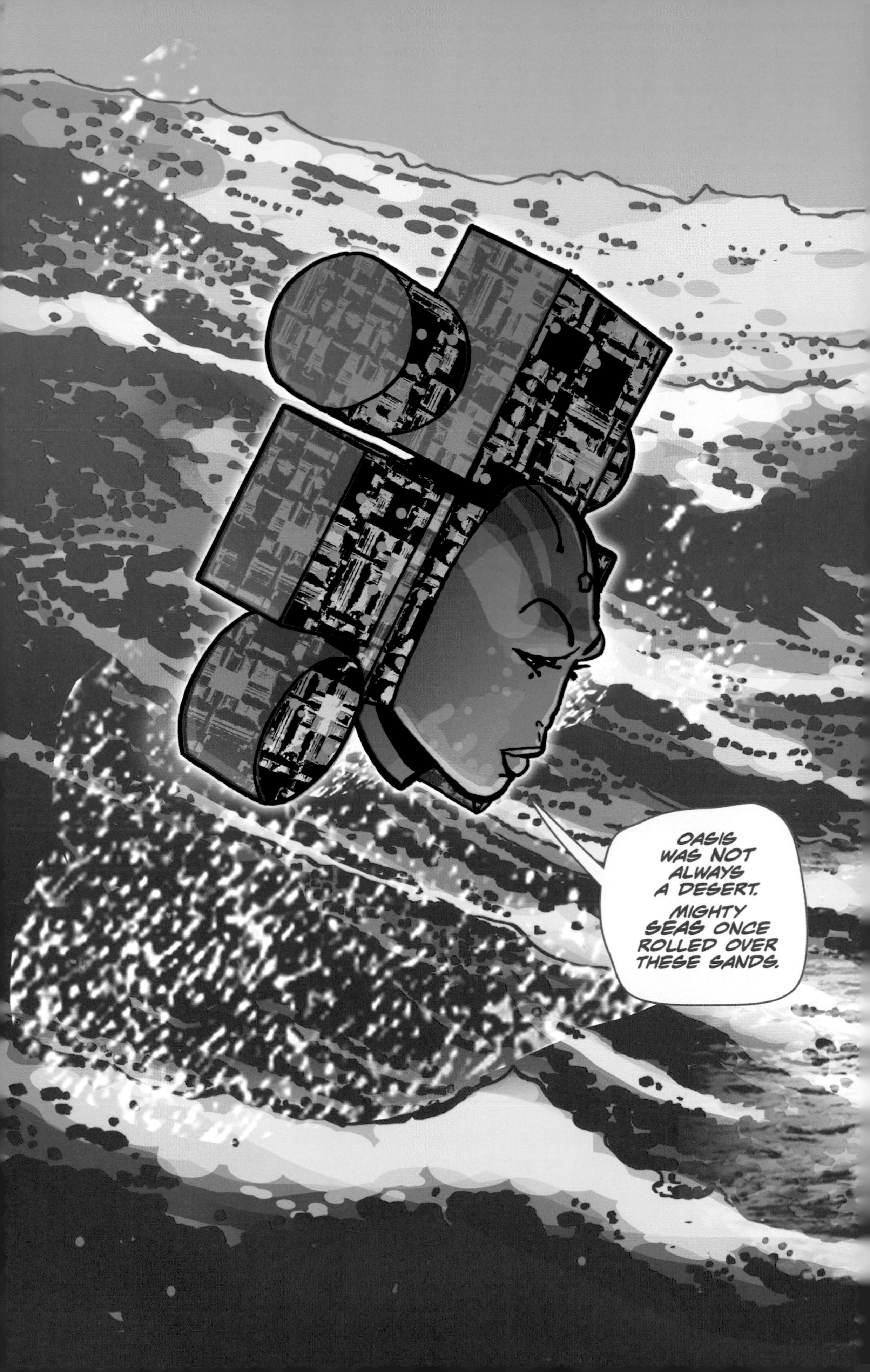
OASIS WAS NOT ALWAYS A DESERT.
MIGHTY SEAS ONCE ROLLED OVER THESE SANDS.

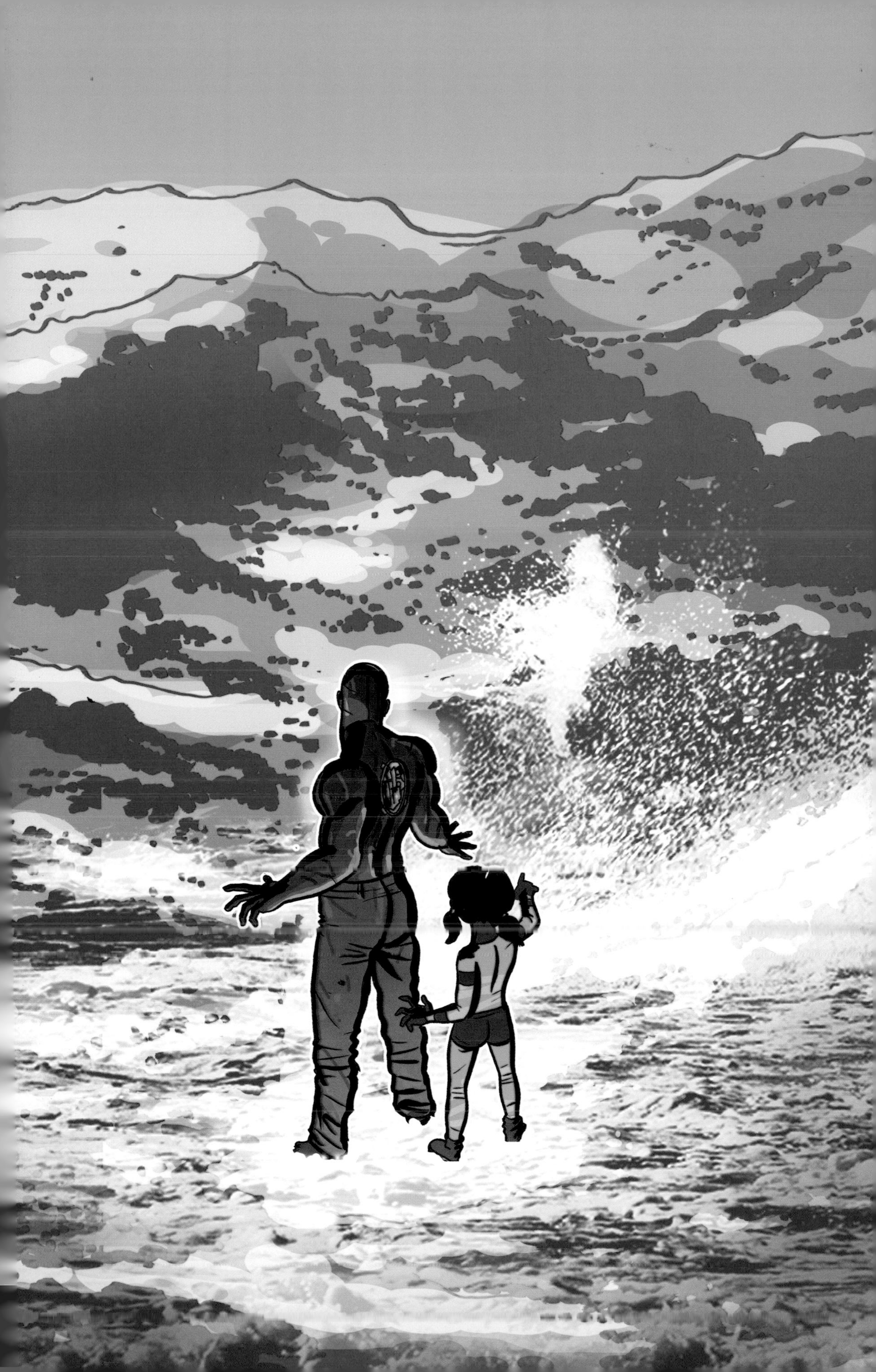

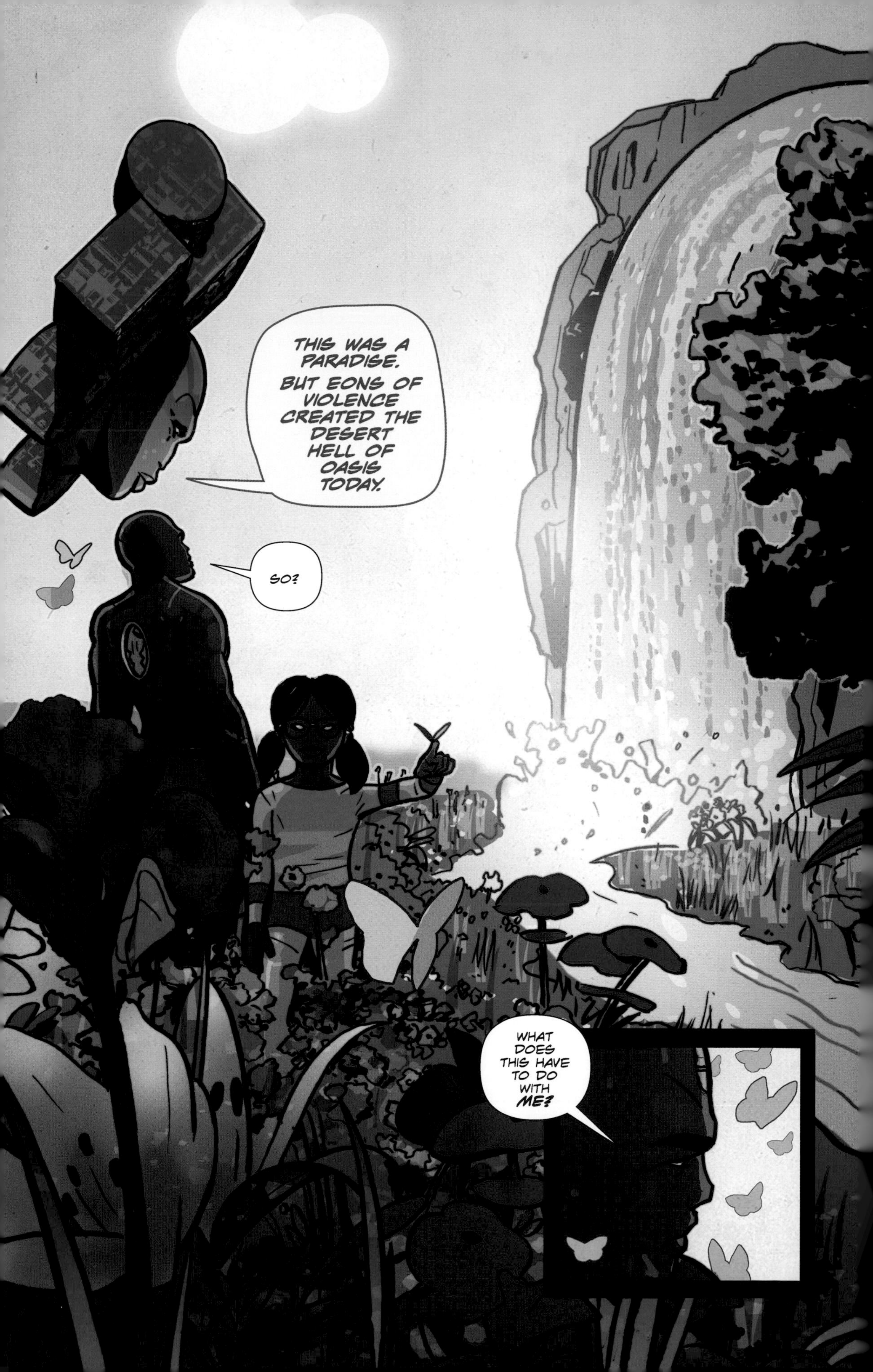
THIS WAS A PARADISE.
BUT EONS OF VIOLENCE CREATED THE DESERT HELL OF OASIS TODAY.
SO?
WHAT DOES THIS HAVE TO DO WITH ME?

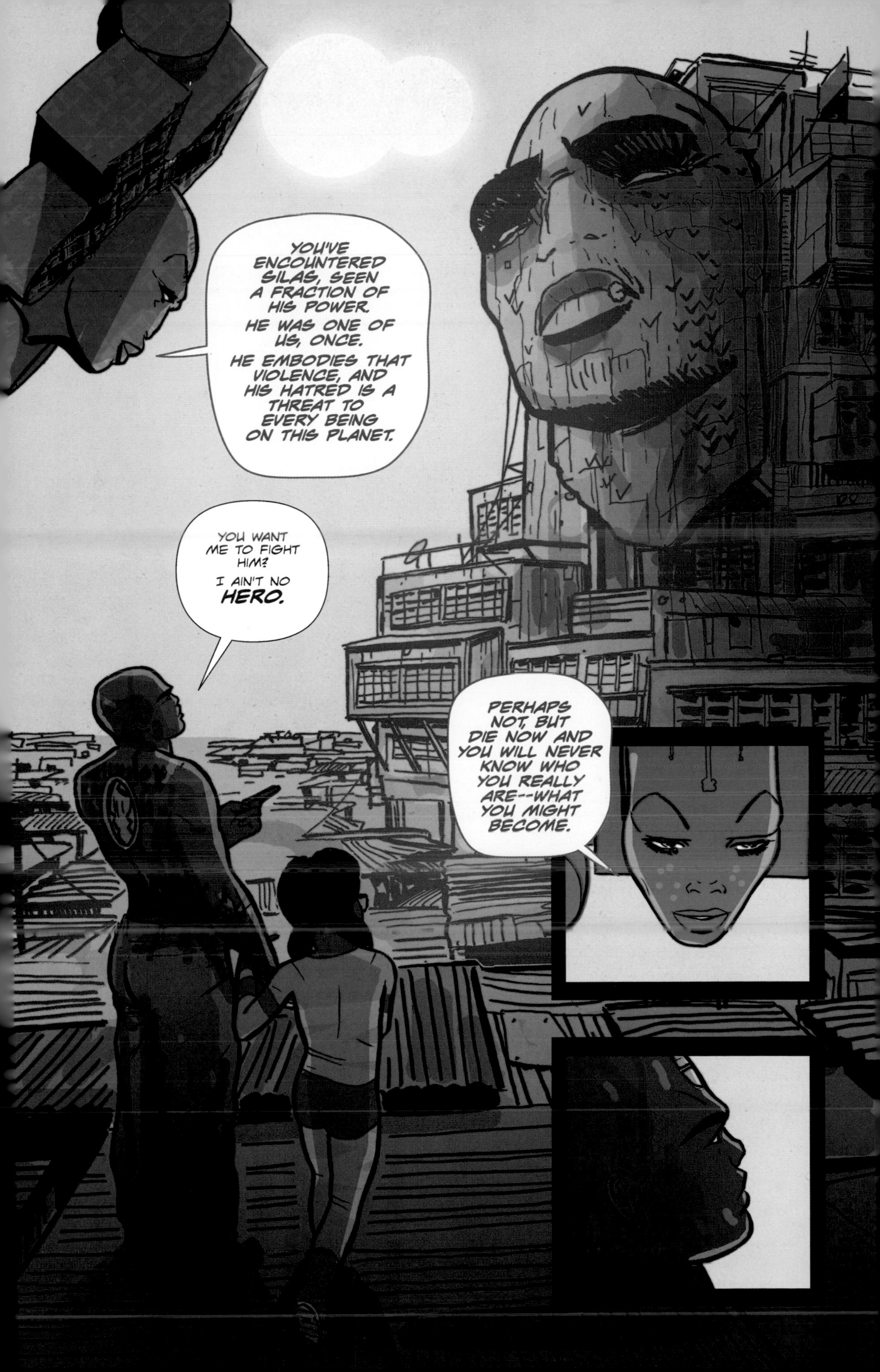
YOU'VE ENCOUNTERED SILAS, SEEN A FRACTION OF HIS POWER.
HE WAS ONE OF US, ONCE.
HE EMBODIES THAT VIOLENCE, AND HIS HATRED IS A THREAT TO EVERY BEING ON THIS PLANET.
YOU WANT ME TO FIGHT HIM?
I AIN'T NO HERO.
PERHAPS NOT, BUT DIE NOW AND YOU WILL NEVER KNOW WHO YOU REALLY ARE--WHAT YOU MIGHT BECOME.

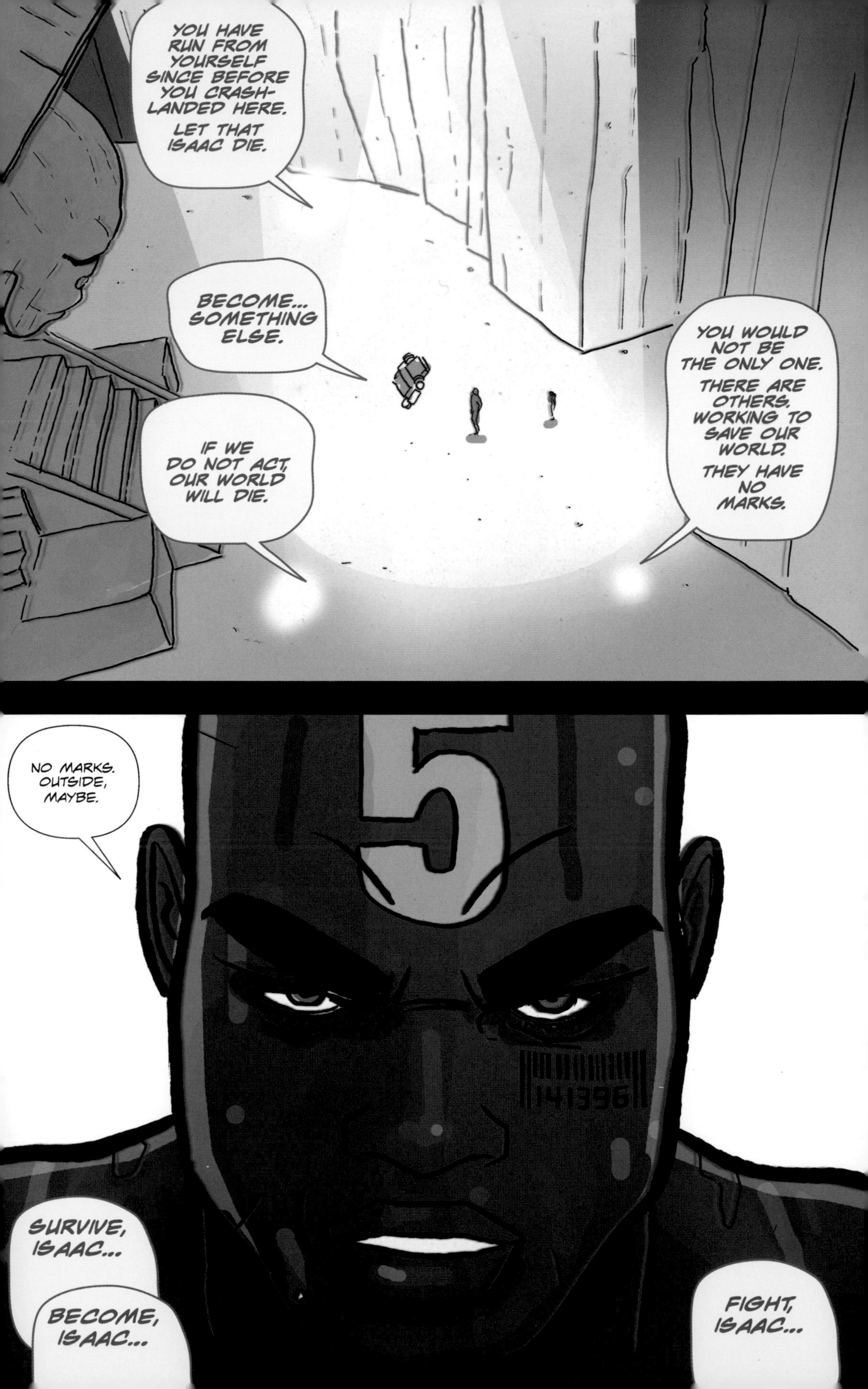
YOU HAVE RUN FROM YOURSELF SINCE BEFORE YOU CRASH-LANDED HERE.
LET THAT ISAAC DIE.
BECOME... SOMETHING ELSE.
IF WE DO NOT ACT, OUR WORLD WILL DIE.
YOU WOULD NOT BE THE ONLY ONE.
THERE ARE OTHERS, WORKING TO SAVE OUR WORLD.
THEY HAVE NO MARKS.
NO MARKS. OUTSIDE, MAYBE.
5
141396
SURVIVE, ISAAC...
BECOME, ISAAC...
FIGHT, ISAAC...

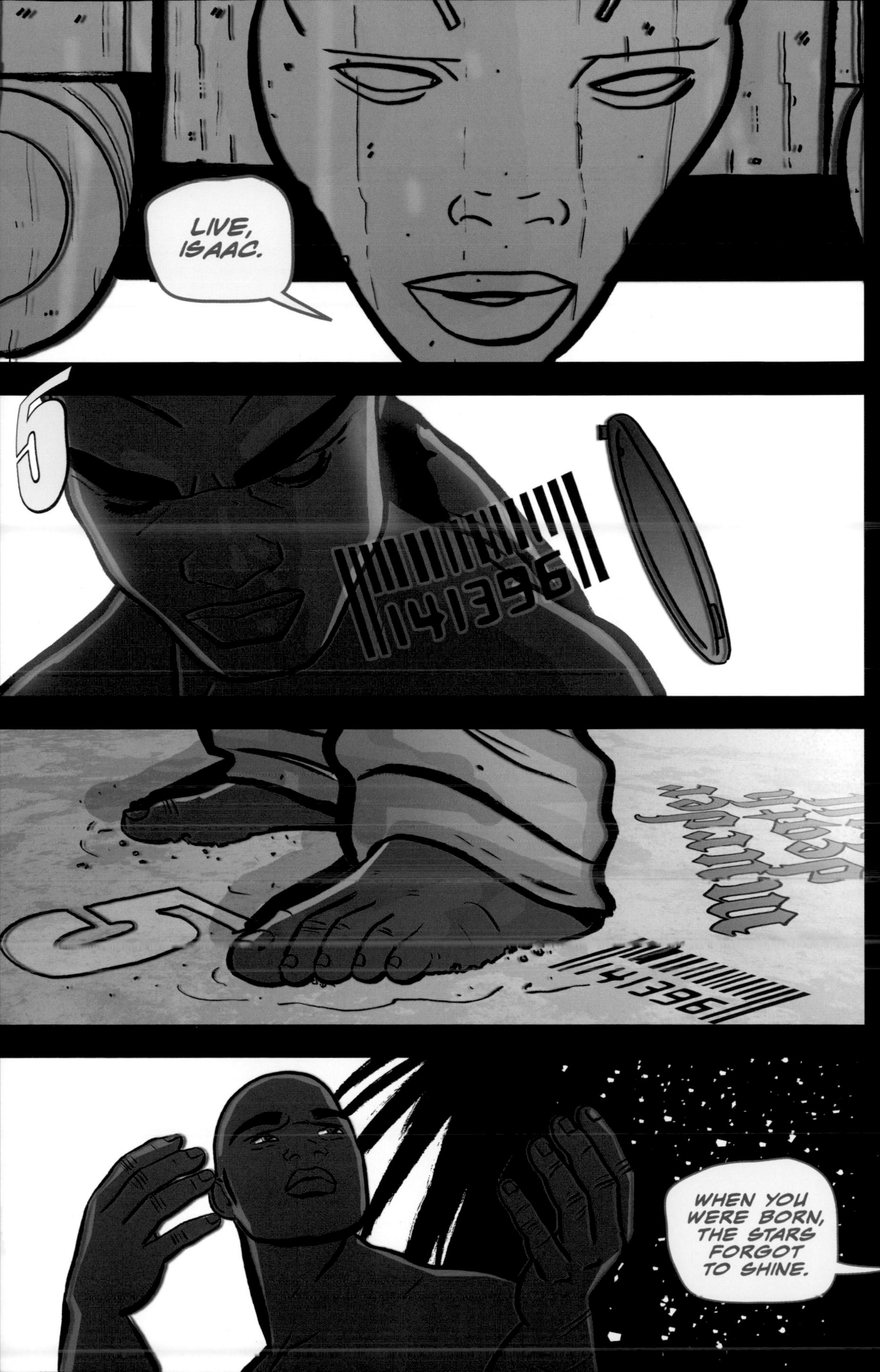
LIVE, ISAAC.
141396
141396
WHEN YOU WERE BORN, THE STARS FORGOT TO SHINE.

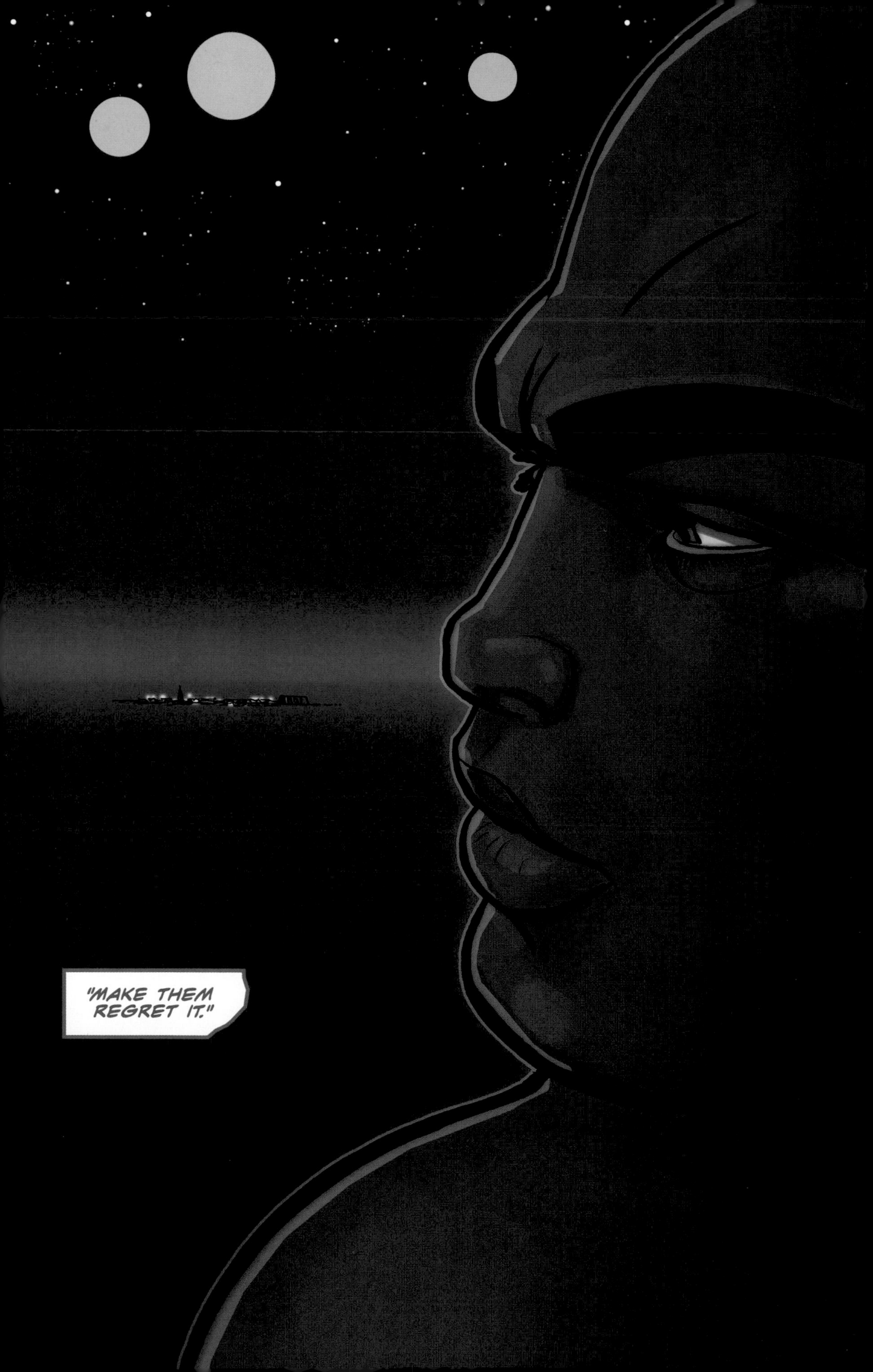
"MAKE THEM REGRET IT."

COVER GALLERY

FIVE *CONCRETE PARK: R-E-S-P-E-C-T* COVERS BY ARTIST TONY PURYEAR

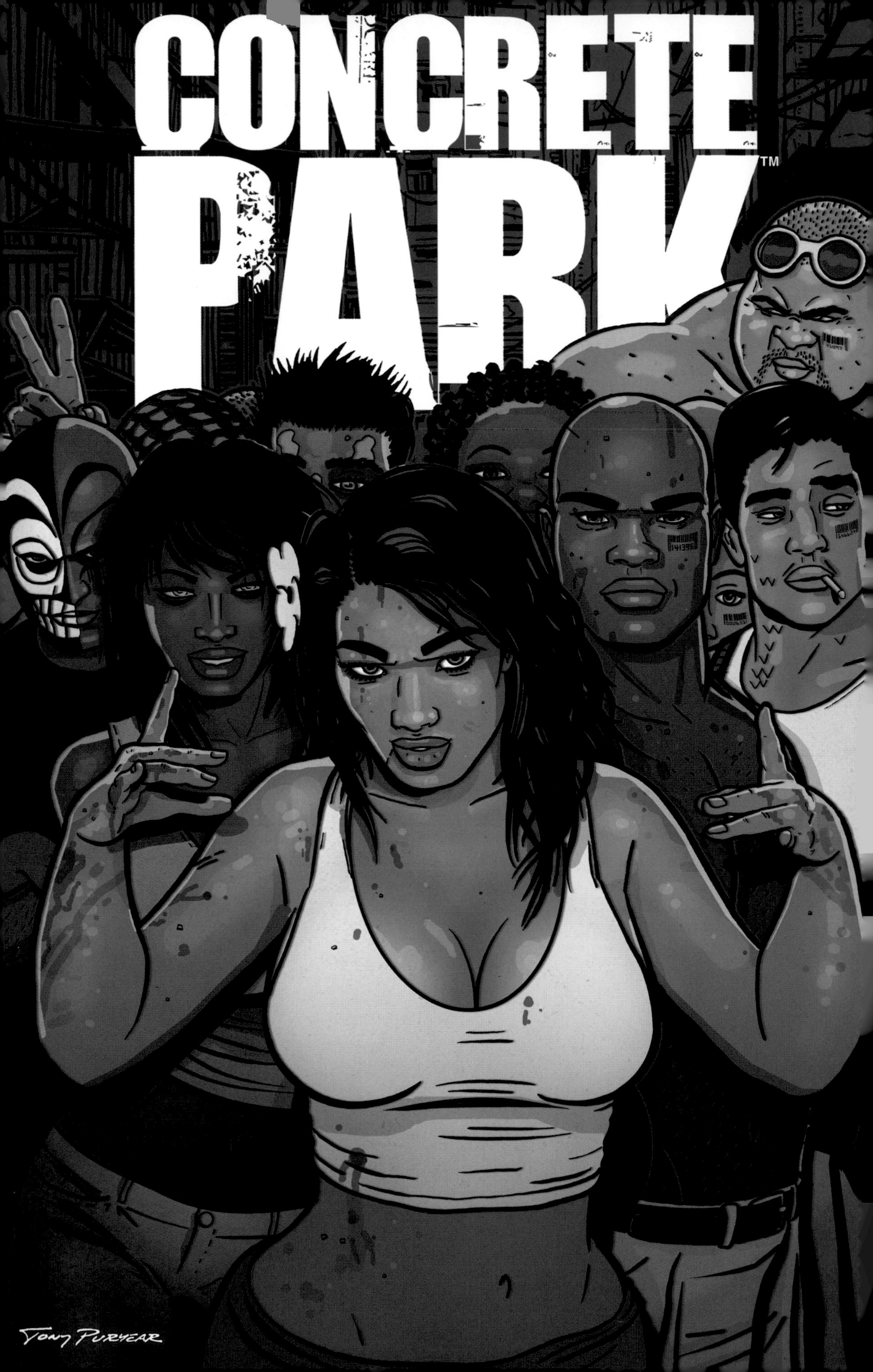
CONCRETE
PARK™
Tony Puryear

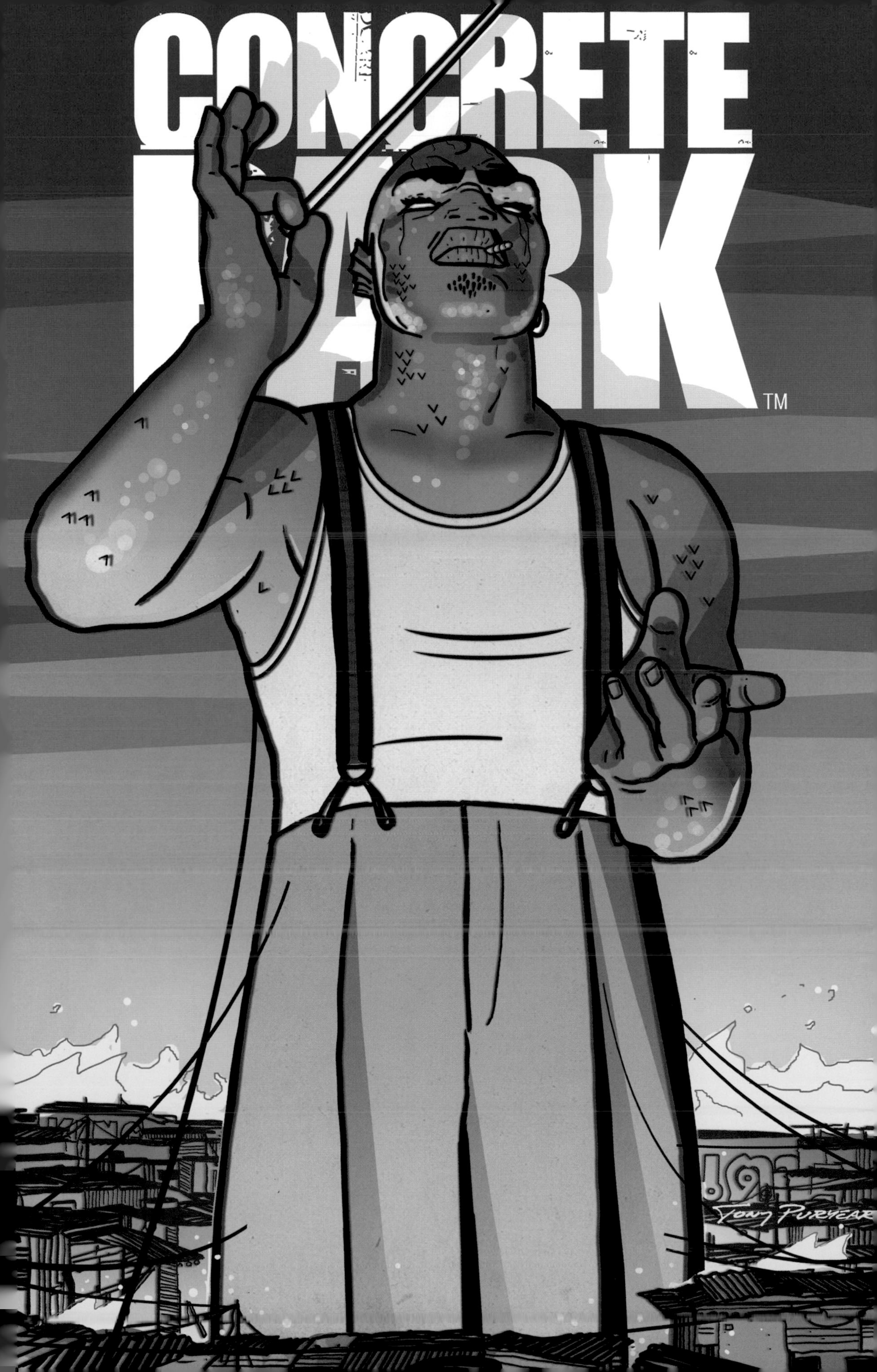
CONCRETE PARK™
Tony Puryear

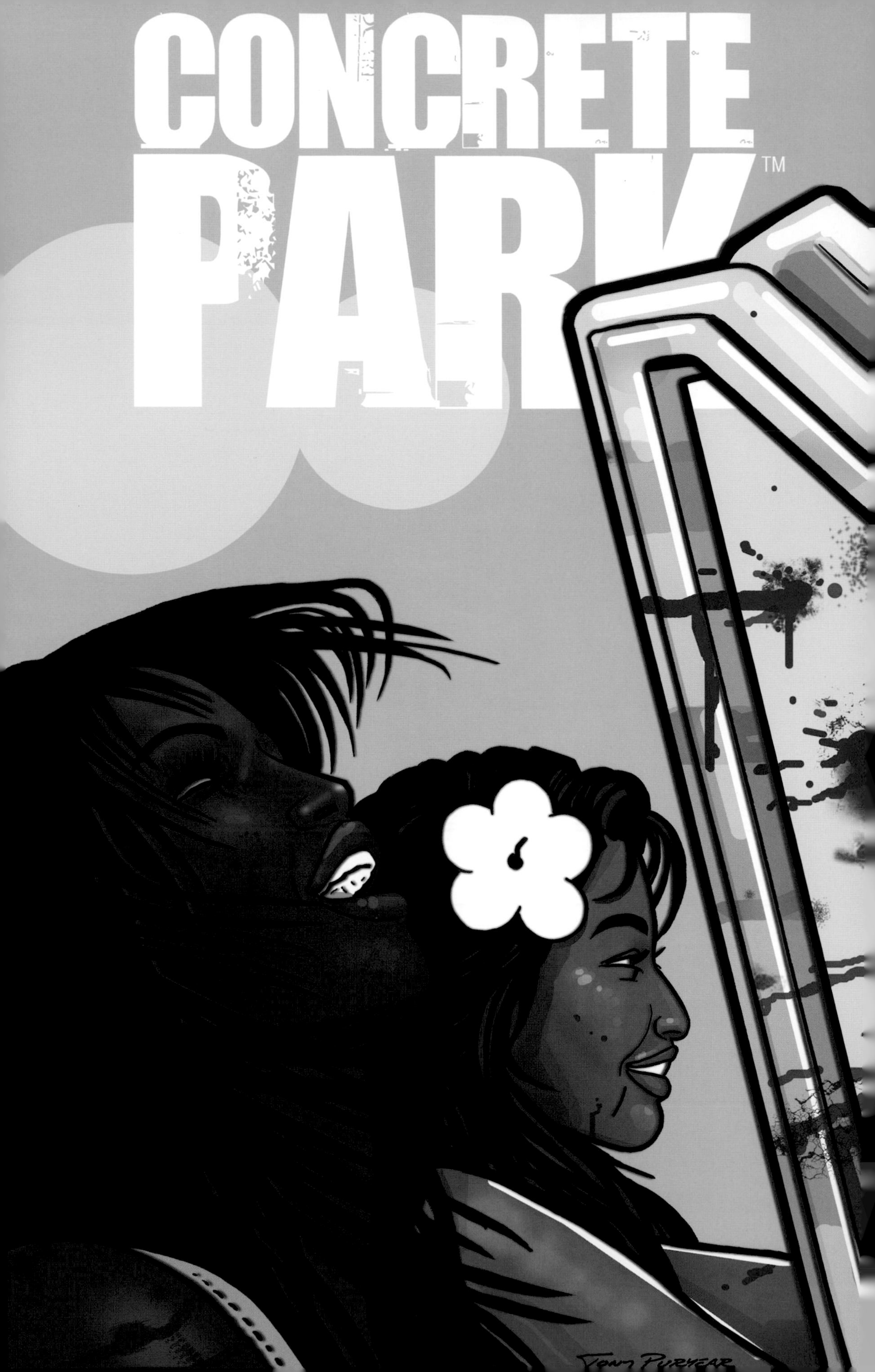
CONCRETE PARK™
TONY PURYEAR

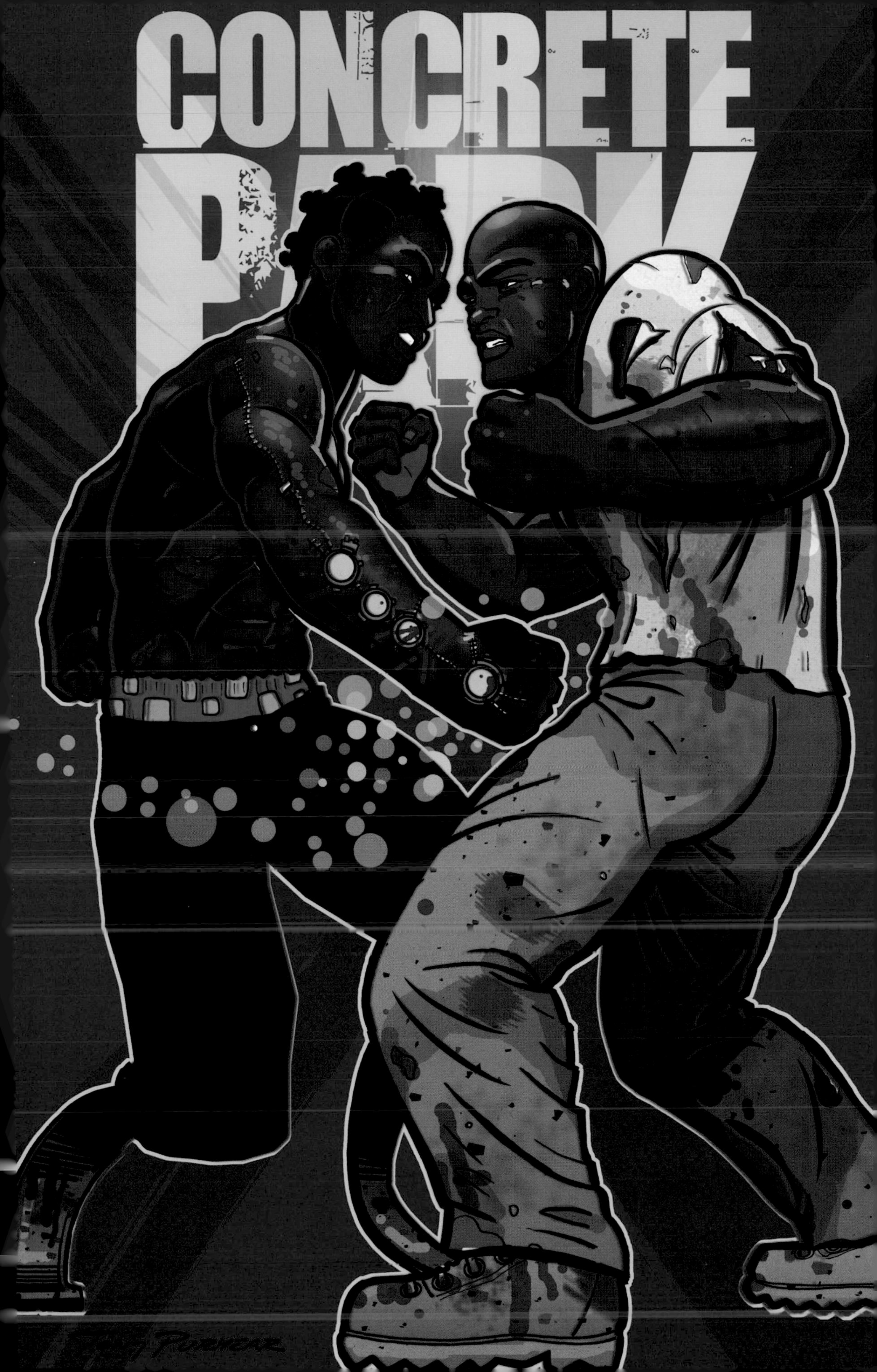
CONCRETE
PARK

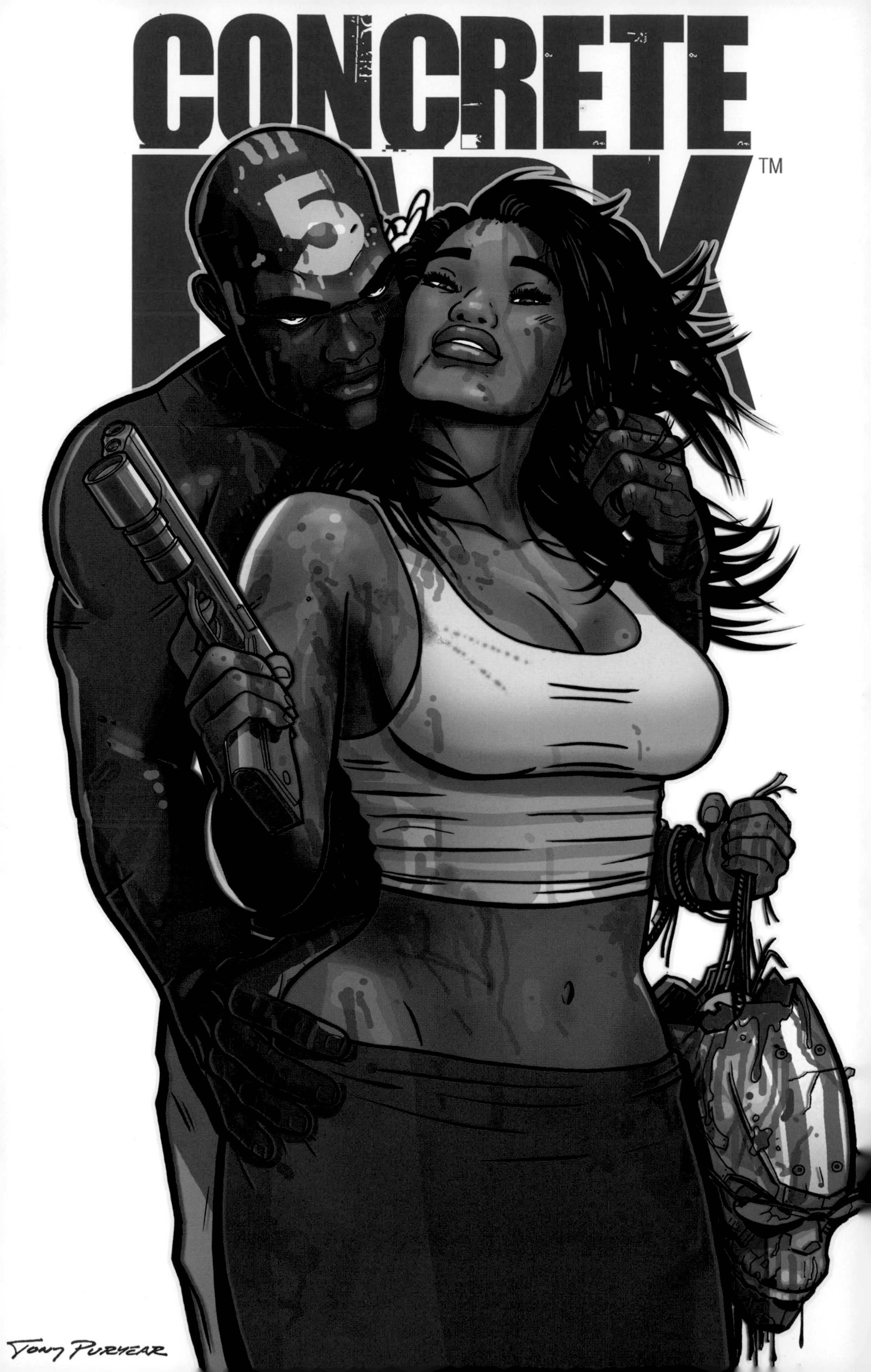
CONCRETE
PARK
TM
TONY PURYEAR

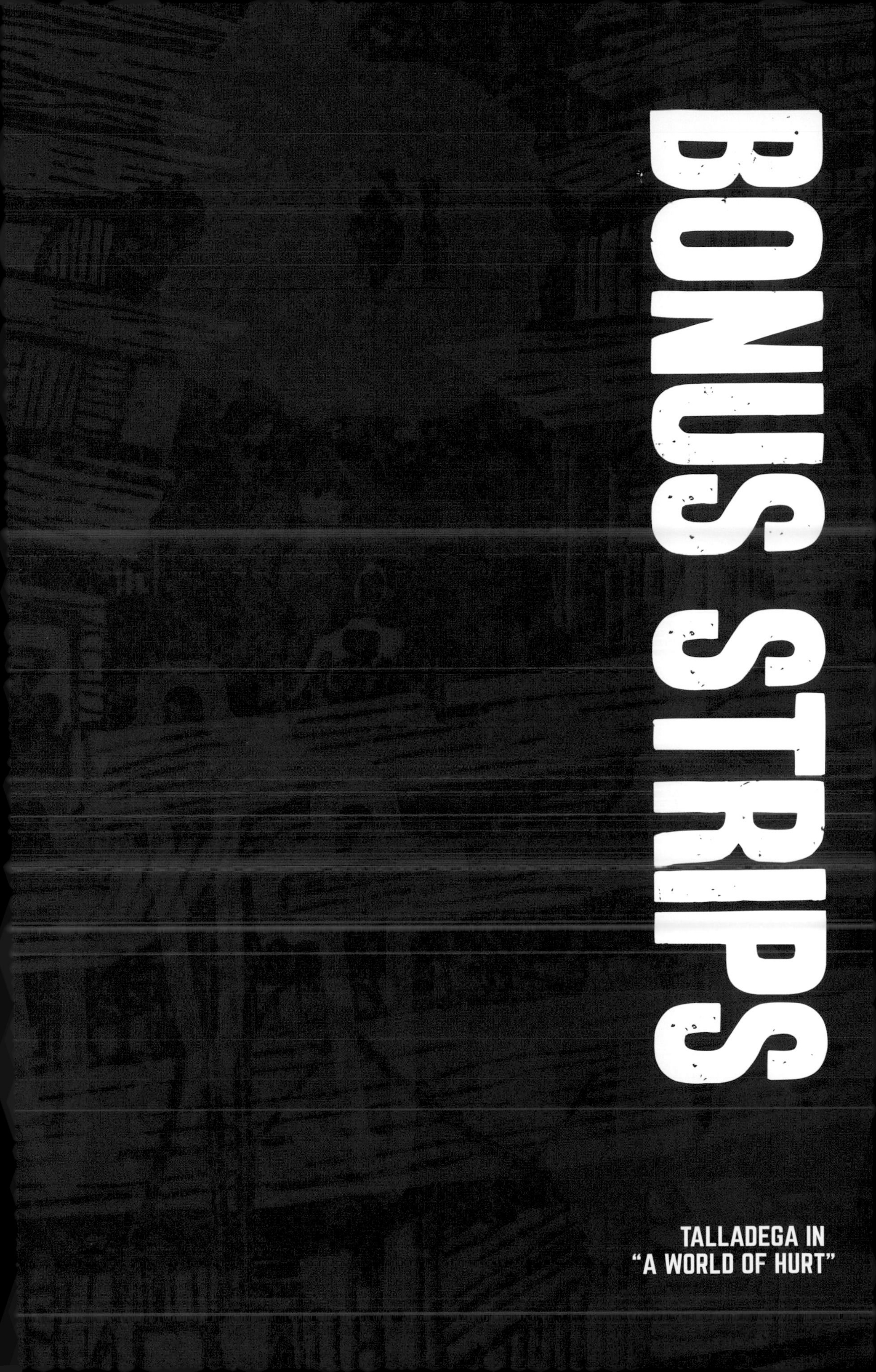

BONUS STRIPS

TALLADEGA IN
"A WORLD OF HURT"

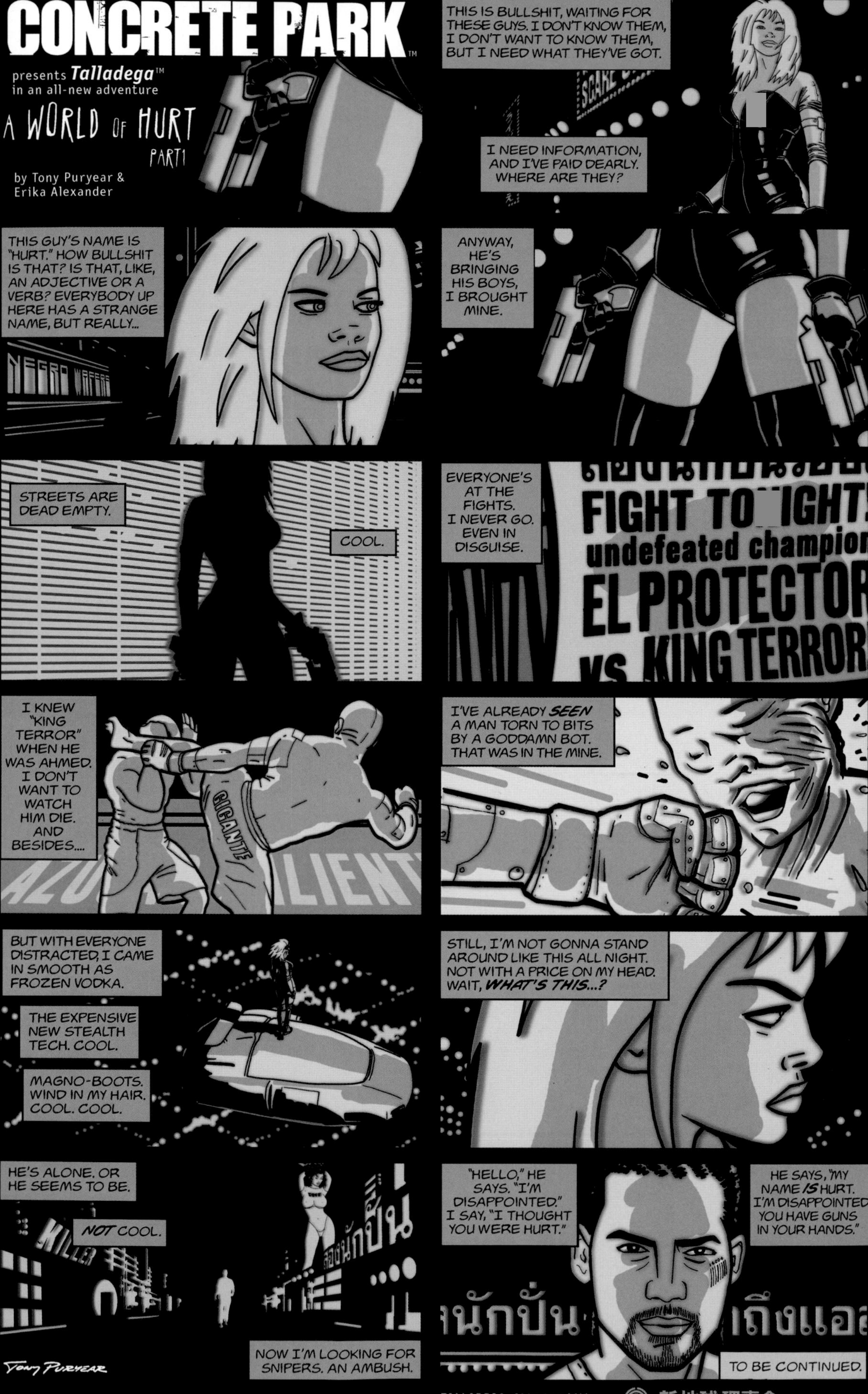

CONCRETE PARK™
presents Talladega™
in an all-new adventure
A WORLD OF HURT
PART 1
by Tony Puryear &
Erika Alexander
THIS IS BULLSHIT, WAITING FOR THESE GUYS. I DON'T KNOW THEM, I DON'T WANT TO KNOW THEM, BUT I NEED WHAT THEY'VE GOT.
I NEED INFORMATION, AND I'VE PAID DEARLY. WHERE ARE THEY?
THIS GUY'S NAME IS "HURT." HOW BULLSHIT IS THAT? IS THAT, LIKE, AN ADJECTIVE OR A VERB? EVERYBODY UP HERE HAS A STRANGE NAME, BUT REALLY...
ANYWAY, HE'S BRINGING HIS BOYS, I BROUGHT MINE.
STREETS ARE DEAD EMPTY.
COOL.
EVERYONE'S AT THE FIGHTS. I NEVER GO. EVEN IN DISGUISE.
FIGHT TO IGHT!
undefeated champion
EL PROTECTOR
vs KING TERROR
I KNEW "KING TERROR" WHEN HE WAS AHMED. I DON'T WANT TO WATCH HIM DIE. AND BESIDES....
GIGANTE
I'VE ALREADY SEEN A MAN TORN TO BITS BY A GODDAMN BOT. THAT WAS IN THE MINE.
BUT WITH EVERYONE DISTRACTED, I CAME IN SMOOTH AS FROZEN VODKA.
THE EXPENSIVE NEW STEALTH TECH. COOL.
MAGNO-BOOTS. WIND IN MY HAIR. COOL. COOL.
STILL, I'M NOT GONNA STAND AROUND LIKE THIS ALL NIGHT. NOT WITH A PRICE ON MY HEAD. WAIT, WHAT'S THIS...?
HE'S ALONE. OR HE SEEMS TO BE.
NOT COOL.
KILLER
NOW I'M LOOKING FOR SNIPERS. AN AMBUSH.
TONY PURYEAR
"HELLO," HE SAYS. "I'M DISAPPOINTED." I SAY, "I THOUGHT YOU WERE HURT."
HE SAYS, "MY NAME IS HURT. I'M DISAPPOINTED YOU HAVE GUNS IN YOUR HANDS."
TO BE CONTINUED.

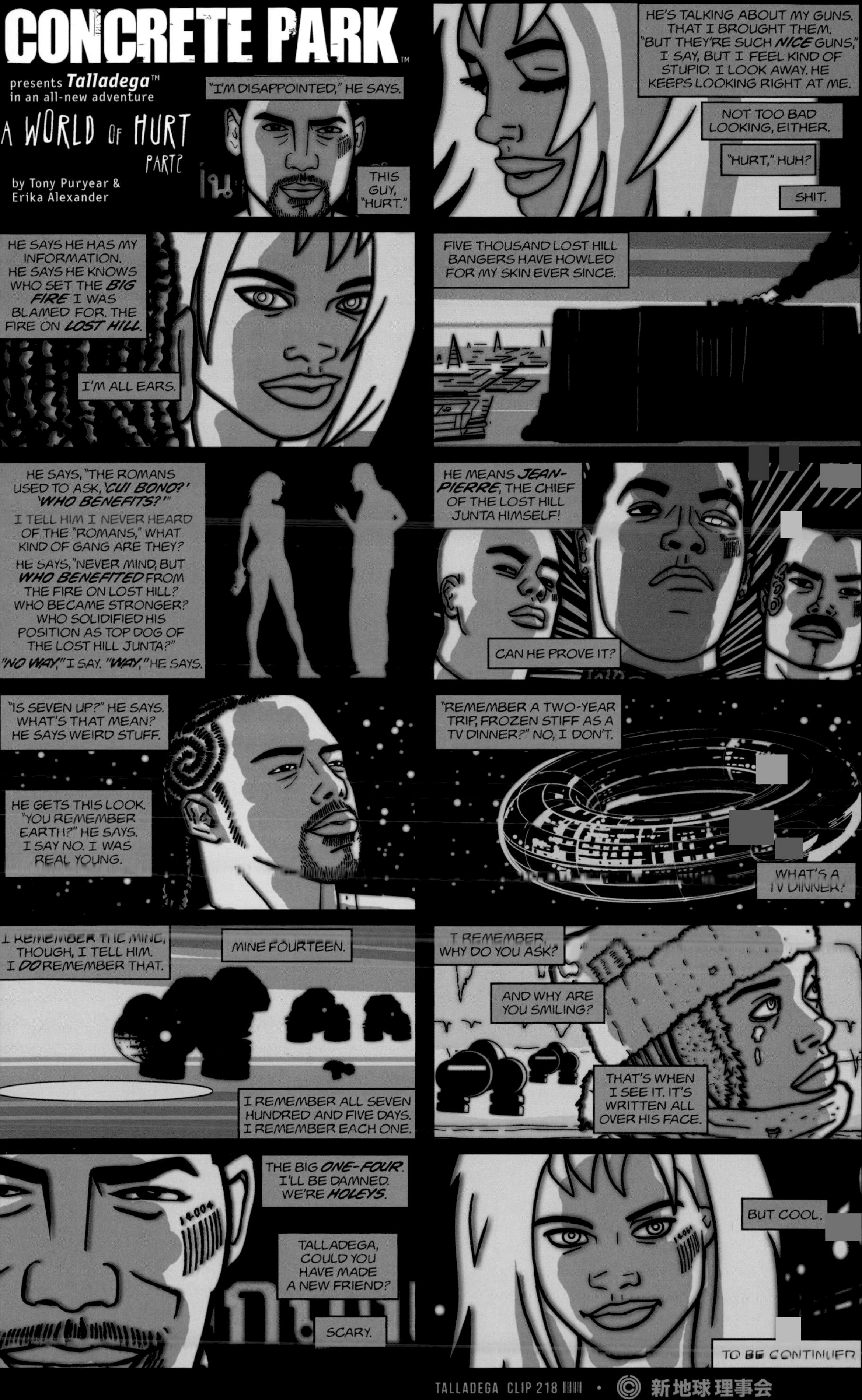
CONCRETE PARK
presents Talladega
in an all-new adventure
A WORLD OF HURT
PART 2
by Tony Puryear & Erika Alexander
"I'M DISAPPOINTED," HE SAYS.
THIS GUY, "HURT."
HE'S TALKING ABOUT MY GUNS. THAT I BROUGHT THEM. "BUT THEY'RE SUCH NICE GUNS," I SAY, BUT I FEEL KIND OF STUPID. I LOOK AWAY. HE KEEPS LOOKING RIGHT AT ME.
NOT TOO BAD LOOKING, EITHER.
"HURT," HUH?
SHIT.
HE SAYS HE HAS MY INFORMATION. HE SAYS HE KNOWS WHO SET THE BIG FIRE I WAS BLAMED FOR. THE FIRE ON LOST HILL.
I'M ALL EARS.
FIVE THOUSAND LOST HILL BANGERS HAVE HOWLED FOR MY SKIN EVER SINCE.
HE SAYS, "THE ROMANS USED TO ASK, 'CUI BONO?' 'WHO BENEFITS?'"
I TELL HIM I NEVER HEARD OF THE "ROMANS," WHAT KIND OF GANG ARE THEY?
HE SAYS, "NEVER MIND, BUT WHO BENEFITED FROM THE FIRE ON LOST HILL? WHO BECAME STRONGER? WHO SOLIDIFIED HIS POSITION AS TOP DOG OF THE LOST HILL JUNTA?"
"NO WAY," I SAY. "WAY," HE SAYS.
HE MEANS JEAN-PIERRE, THE CHIEF OF THE LOST HILL JUNTA HIMSELF!
CAN HE PROVE IT?
"IS SEVEN UP?" HE SAYS. WHAT'S THAT MEAN? HE SAYS WEIRD STUFF.
HE GETS THIS LOOK. "YOU REMEMBER EARTH?" HE SAYS. I SAY NO. I WAS REAL YOUNG.
"REMEMBER A TWO-YEAR TRIP, FROZEN STIFF AS A TV DINNER?" NO, I DON'T.
WHAT'S A TV DINNER?
I REMEMBER THE MINE, THOUGH, I TELL HIM. I DO REMEMBER THAT.
MINE FOURTEEN.
I REMEMBER ALL SEVEN HUNDRED AND FIVE DAYS. I REMEMBER EACH ONE.
I REMEMBER. WHY DO YOU ASK?
AND WHY ARE YOU SMILING?
THAT'S WHEN I SEE IT. IT'S WRITTEN ALL OVER HIS FACE.
THE BIG ONE-FOUR. I'LL BE DAMNED. WE'RE HOLEYS.
TALLADEGA, COULD YOU HAVE MADE A NEW FRIEND?
SCARY.
BUT COOL.
TO BE CONTINUED
TALLADEGA CLIP 218
© 新地球理事会

CONCRETE PARK™
presents Talladega™
in an all-new adventure
A WORLD OF HURT
PART 3
by Tony Puryear &
Erika Alexander
STILL THINKING. ABOUT HURT.
HE TOLD ME THE PERSON WHO SET THE FIRE ON LOST HILL, THE FIRE I WAS BLAMED FOR, WAS THE GANG'S LEADER, JEAN-PIERRE. DAMN.
LOST HILL PUT A PRICE ON MY HEAD. I'VE HAD TO BE EXTRA CAREFUL ON THIS SIDE OF TOWN EVER SINCE THEN.
HELL, I'VE ALWAYS HAD TO BE CAREFUL. THAT'S WHY IT FEELS SO WEIRD ABOUT HURT.
I DON'T KNOW IF I CAN TRUST HIM. HE SEEMS OK. HOW MANY TIMES HAVE YOU SAID THAT, TD? HIS INTEL HAS TO BE ACTED ON, THOUGH. I CAN'T LET IT GO. I HAVE TO HIT JEAN-PIERRE.
I KNOW JEAN-PIERRE SOME. I'VE STOLEN THE ODD PIECE OF MECHA FOR HIM.
JP SET ME UP GOOD, THOUGH. THAT'S ALL THAT MATTERS NOW. THE LYING BASTARD.
lost hill
DIEN BIEN PH
THE PLAN I'M THINKING ABOUT DOESN'T NEED A BIG FIRE. IT NEEDS A SCALPEL, SOMETHING SURGICALLY SHARP AND MEAN.
I KNOW A GUY WHO MIGHT BE ABLE TO HELP ME. SAMMY CAMERA. HE'S UP IN DIEN BIEN PHU. HE HAS THE HARDWARE. IF I'M GONNA START AN ARMS RACE, HE'S WHERE I BEGIN.
I FLY OVER SOUND SYSTEM, JUST TO FEEL THE BEAT. WHATEVER THE HELL THEY'RE PLAYING TONIGHT, IT SHAKES ME RIGHT THROUGH MY MAGNO-BOOTS. I LIKE IT. IT FEELS LIKE WAR MUSIC. IT FEELS RIGHT FOR WHAT I'M GOING TO HAVE TO DO TO JP.
SALE
SO I ROLL UP, AND OK, I'VE GOT A LITTLE ATTITUDE, A LITTLE ENTHUSIASM. SAMMY TAKES ONE LOOK AT ME AND NOW HE'S GOT AN ATTITUDE. SAMMY SAYS HE HAS POST TRAUMATIC STRESS. WHO DOESN'T, RIGHT? MAYBE MAKING BOMBS ISN'T THE JOB FOR HIM, YOU KNOW? HE LOOKS OK TO ME. MAYBE THIS IS JUST A NEGOTIATING TACTIC.
I TELL SAMMY WHAT I'M LOOKING FOR: A NICE LITTLE BOOM IN THE NIGHT FOR AN OLD FRIEND.
HE TAKES ME OUT BACK AND SHOWS ME HIS STOCK. THE MISSILES ARE TO DIE FOR, LONG AND THIN AS CIGARETTES. "YOU CAN'T AFFORD THOSE," HE SAYS. WHAT? NOT EVEN A LITTLE ONE? NOPE. NOW I'M MAD.
WHAT ISN'T SAMMY TELLING ME? HE SAYS IT'S NOTHING, JUST HIS PRICES HAVE GONE UP IS ALL. SAMMY'S GOT A NICE HUSTLE. HE'S INDEPENDENT, BUT HE HAS TO SWIM IN THE SAME DESERT WE ALL DO. IS SOMEONE SQUEEZING HIM? COULD ONE OF THE BIG JEFES BE STOCKPILING ROCKETS?
I TAKE A WILD GUESS. I SAY, "WHATEVER THE KING IS PAYING YOU, I'LL DOUBLE IT." I BET MY NEW HOLEY, HURT, WOULD APPROVE. "IT'S NOT THE KING, IT'S CHAVEZ," HE SAYS. GIVES IT UP RIGHT AWAY. I SAY IF HE DOESN'T SELL ME A ROCKET RIGHT NOW, I'LL TELL THE KING ALL ABOUT IT. I WOULD, TOO. NO BLUFF.
GOT WHAT I CAME FOR.
I HEAR WAR MUSIC.
With regard
SEE YOU SOON, JEAN-PIERRE.
TO BE CONTINUED.
TALLADEGA CLIP 219 • © 新地球理事会

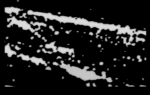

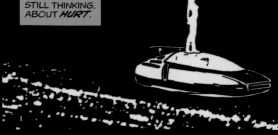

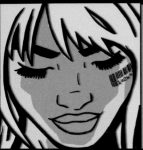

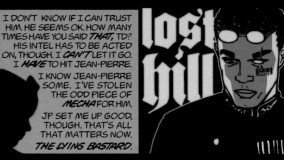

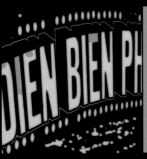

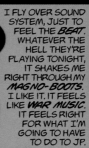

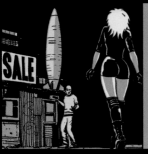

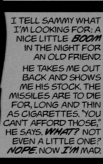

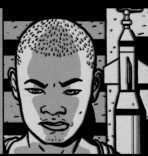

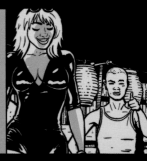

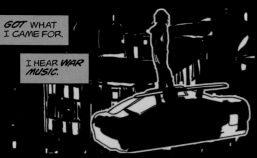

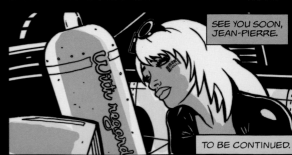

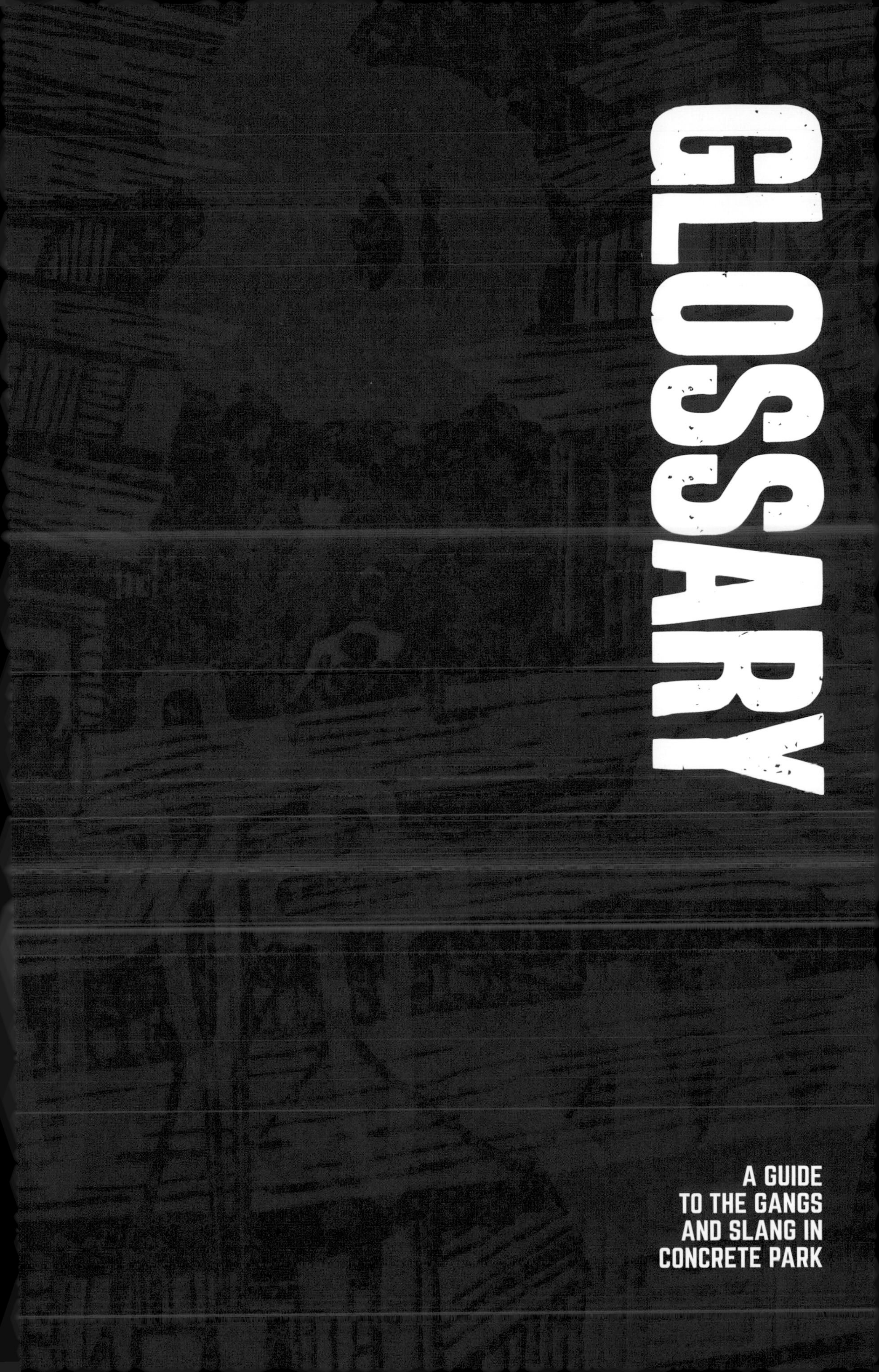

GLOSSARY

A GUIDE
TO THE GANGS
AND SLANG IN
CONCRETE PARK

THE GANGS OF SCARE CITY

GIGANTE

Motto: "*Construimos.*" ("We Build.")

Gigante was the first gang—and is still the biggest gang—in Scare City. They have the sweetest deal with the NEC and they have the most powerful radio tower, which broadcasts the city's most popular station—Radio Gigante—thirty-two hours a day. Their unseen leader's name is Chavez. It's always Chavez. The name is titular, like *Kaiser*. The current Chavez, the seventh of that name, is the most unusual in this unusual line. He uses Radio Gigante as his pulpit, and on his daily show he broadcasts a radical call for peace in Scare City. As with so many other prophets of peace, a bad end for him is almost a foregone conclusion.

POTATO KING

Motto: "Famous Worldwide."

When he came to Oasis, he was a skinny but ambitious exile. His time in the mines made him tough and turned him into a leader. Today, at over eight hundred pounds, he is the biggest living thing on the surface of Oasis. Even in the planet's 0.9g, it takes two men to prop him up when he stands. He has cornered the market on alcohol in Scare City, and both he and the gang that follows him go by the name *Potato King*. Seeing his "King" label on a bottle of liquor means at least you won't die from the contents. Unless you want to. In a world where nothing grows, the Potato King has found a way to produce things that look, cook, and ferment like potatoes, an impressive and profitable achievement. He denies the rumors of cannibalism.

LAS CRUCES

Motto: "Three Sorrows."

Las Cruces is a mystery among the gangs of Scare City. The newest of the gangs, Las Cruces is building its strength through vigorous recruiting and aggressive business practices. "Aggressive business practices" means, in this context, murder. The leader of Las Cruces is a chain-smoking alien who only appears to be a human named Silas. He is actually one of the most powerful beings on the planet, a godlike spirit from when Oasis was young. What is his agenda? How many of his human cat's-paws must die before he gets what he's after?

M-80s

Motto: "Proof God Exists."

What little the Potato King doesn't own of the alcohol business in Scare City, the M-80s do. The M-80s' leader, Luca, is an old friend of the King . . . or she used to be. In these dangerous days, no one can say for sure who's safe. The M-80s is an all-woman outfit, a rarity among Scare City's gangs. From their tiny piece of turf in the Shoulder, they project a lot more power than their small numbers would warrant. That's because of Luca.

LOST HILL

Motto: "Don't Sleep."

Lost Hill is the second-largest gang in town. It's also in possession of the best strategic location, an enormous mesa at the edge of town from which they will never be dislodged. Their good fortune in having that location is also a curse, however. They have only so much room for growth. Thus, Lost Hill has a well-earned reputation for secretly initiating strategic partnerships with other gangs, only to betray them in the end, all with hopes of getting more "living room." Their motto, "Don't Sleep," is both a reminder of their own vigilance and an admonishment to all not to sleep on them.

BAMA

Motto: "Calamity."

More of a cult than a gang, Bama stands out as an insane, nihilistic group—even by the crazy standards of Scare City. Their leader, Fontaine, is a madman with a method, a paranoid visionary responsible for some of the darkest deeds ever done on Oasis. The gang lives in the desert, shunning the temptations of the city. Other gangs trade with the New Earth Council for money, influence, and power. Bama doesn't trade, doesn't want money, doesn't want influence, and doesn't want power. What, then, do they want?

According to NEC estimates, there are over one hundred smaller gangs, sets, and militias in Scare City.

CONCRETE PARK TERMS AND SLANG

A

ABDIDAS

n. A disparaging word encompassing all the fake-ass clothes and shoes made and sold on Oasis or brought used from Earth. *Also adj.* Fake, bogus, counterfeit.

B

BÁI MÙ

adj. Stupid. (Chinese, "white eyed, blind." On a desert planet with two suns and not enough sunglasses, this takes on a whole new meaning.)

BALLER

n. Someone who's got game.

BANGER

n. Gang soldier.

BAR 'N' GRILL

n. The identifying barcode mark of slavery tattooed on every exile's face.

BEM BOLADO

adj. Clever, cool. (Brazilian Portuguese, "well thought up.")

BHENCHOD

n. A contemptible person. In use all over the Indian subcontinent for eons, and in use now all over Scare City. Indians claim it; Pakistanis claim it. Wanna fight? Call someone *bhenchod*. (Hindi, "sister fucker.")

BIDI

n. A homemade cigarette. Silas smokes bidis. (Hindi.)

BINDASS

adj. Cool; carefree. A term of approbation, originally denoting a cool and carefree person, as in: "Check out my man Raj." "*Bindass*." "*Bindass*." Now, just an all-purpose word like *cool* that fits in any part of a sentence, as in: "See you." "*Bindass*, man, see you." (Hindi.)

BLUR

adj. Dense, stupid. As in the expression "*blur* like *sotong*" ("stupid as a squid"). (Malay.)

BRACE

v. To get arrested by the New Earth Council, resulting in injury or sometimes even death, as in, "A couple of bangers got braced last night. They won't be back." From the punning *NEC-brace*. See also **NEC-bone**.

BUMBACLOT

n. The king of curse words. (Jamaican, "ass wipe, ass cloth.")

C

CHARANGA

n. A loud-ass old car or truck. Also, a loud-ass gun. (Cuban Spanish, a type of dance band.)

CHEATERS

n. Sunglasses.

CHECKS AND BALANCES

n. The nine-foot-tall biomech cops of the New Earth Council. Part human, mostly machine, they once were gangsters. Injured, mutilated, arrested, the subjects of hideous medical experiments, they found themselves rebuilt into fearsome law-enforcement mechs.

CHOLA

n. A Latin gang girl, the female counterpart of a cholo. Arched eyebrows and gelled hair are a must. So is a razor. A chola is down for her barrio.

CHONGA

n. A gang girl with a Miami style, a somewhat less serious variant of a chola. If a chola is down for her barrio, a chonga is down for her hair gel and her barrio, in that order.

CINNABUN

n. A crazy person, mentally challenged. Also adj., as in, "This shit is cinnabun." (Anglo-Arabic, from Arabic *cinnadebun*, "to fly with the crazy eye.")

D

DAI LO

n. Big man, boss. Sometimes used sarcastically. (Cantonese slang.)

DALIT

n. An untouchable. On Oasis, the term takes in handicapped or differently abled people, outcasts within a world of outcasts. All parts-people could be considered Dalits, while not all Dalits are parts-people. (Hindi.)

DESAPARECIDOS

n. The missing. The exiles on Oasis. One of the hardest things for the exiles to accept is that successive waves of young humans have landed on this penal colony in space with no more knowledge of its existence than the first arrivals had, indicating that most people on Earth have no idea what the New Earth Council is doing or where huge numbers of Earth's poor youth are disappearing to. The young exiles are truly the forgotten ones. (Spanish.)

DESCANSO

n. A roadside marker or memorial to a victim of a shooting or an accident. (Spanish, "place of rest.")

DESI

n. A person from the Indian subcontinent, such as India, Pakistan, Bangladesh, or Sri Lanka.

DHIMMI

n. A second-class citizen; a little person; someone unaffiliated with a gang and therefore unprotected. (Arabic slang, from *ahl al-dhimma*, "people of the contract," the name for tolerated unbelievers in a Muslim state.)

DONNO GO WHERE

expr. Lost. (Malay pidgin, "I don't know where it went.")

E

EL EXILIO

n. The Exile. As in, "This is day whatever-the-fuck of El Exilio." Just as in prisons everywhere, most of the exiles on Oasis keep a running count of the days they've been there. The difference is there will be no parole; there will be no return home from El Exilio. (Spanish.)

EYEBORG

n. Biointeractive sunglasses with implants. Very helpful on sunny Oasis, very hard to come by. Also, synecdochic for people who wear these glasses and implants, as in, "What you lookin' at, eyeborg?"

F

FANAGALO

n. A pidgin miners' language based on Zulu, with English input, that spread from the mines of South Africa to the mines of Oasis.

FAVELA

n. A slum neighborhood; a barrio. See also **solar**. (Brazilian Portuguese.)

FIFTEEN

n. An AR-15, a much-prized assault rifle.

FILMI

adj. Looking like something out of a Bollywood movie, as in: "All new, all live filmi girls!" A term of art used to promote the charms of prostitutes. (Hindi.)

FRAUDBAND

n. NEC radio stations, which are notorious for broadcasting shit. Also, any bogus information.

G

GÀN NI MA

expr. "Fuck your mother." (Chinese.)

GA6

n. An outcast. It stands to reason a planet full of exiles would have multiple words in many languages for *exile, outcast, unwanted*, etc. Pronounced "gat." See also **olvidados**, **desaparecidos**. (Arabic.)

GAT

n. A gun.

GHORA

n. A gun. (Mumbaiya Hindi.)

GOD WINK

n. Something taken as evidence that a higher power is at work; a coincidence.

GUJU

n. A person from the Indian state of Gujarat who is good at business. *Also adj.* Admirable, as in, "You got him to pay what? Damn, son, that's *guju*!"

GULTI

n. A native speaker of Telugu from the Indian state of Andhra Pradesh, home to a subculture of engineers and software developers.

H

HACK-MECHA

n. A low-grade, improvised, or ad hoc prosthetic limb or other body part. *Also adj.* Used to describe a situation where the wiring is not up to code, as in, "That peace treaty won't last; it's just hack-mecha."

HANGER

n. A gang associate or second-class wannabe; a punk. See **banger**.

HOLEY

n. A friend or associate from the mines, a boon coon.

HOLEY-ER THAN THOU

expr. Used to describe someone who did more mine time than you, or someone who just cops that annoying, bullshit attitude.

HOPE ON A ROPE

n. Your ace holey. Someone who's absolutely got you. The friend who'll pull you up when you're down a cold, dark hole. (Miners' slang.)

HUDNA

n. A cease-fire. (Arabic.)

J

JHEELO

n. A zero. Someone who can do nothing, who has nothing, who is nothing; i.e., pretty much all the human exiles on Oasis. (Malay.)

JINETERA

n. A prostitute. (Spanish, "female jockey.")

K

KANJANI

expr. "How are you?" Common Fanagalo greeting among those who have served time in the mines; i.e., everyone in Scare City.

KEPLER 56-B

n. The original name of the planet Oasis. First identified (and immediately covered up) by German astronomers in 2007, it was named after the greatest of German astronomers. The existence of this (relatively) close, Earth-like world was kept secret for years. As evidence of vast ice deposits at the planet's poles mounted, a secret initiative was begun, complete with unmanned, and then manned, missions of exploration.

KIRK

n. The man, a badass, a stud, an interplanetary love god.

KOS SHE'R

n. Bullshit. (Farsi, "pussy poem.")

L

LOST AND FOUND

n. A church, mosque, temple, or place of worship.

LUPANGO

n. A slang name for the planet Oasis, originating with East African exiles. (Kiswahili, "prison.")

M

MADARCHOD

n. A despicable person. See also **bhenchod**. (Hindi, "motherfucker.")

MBUSHI

n. A derogatory term for someone living (or trying to live) in the desert wastes outside Scare City. (From Kiswahili *bushi*, "bush," someone too foolish to come in out of the wilderness.)

MIKEY

n. An untraceable phone. Often used as a proper noun, as in: "Who's calling?" "Mikey."

MOFONGO, THE BIG

n. Derogatory name for the Potato King, the Puerto Rican who, at 800+ pounds, is the biggest single living thing on the planet Oasis.

MOOK JUNG

n. A slow or stupid person. (Cantonese, "dummy," the wooden training dummy from a million kung fu films.)

N

NAAFI

n. A lazy person. (South African acronym, "no ambition and fuck-all interest.")

NEC-BONE

n. Human New Earth Council cops and workers. A despised group; collaborators; the lowest of the low. *Also v.* To arrest and maybe fuck someone up.

NEC-BRACE

v. To arrest and definitely fuck someone up all the way.

NEW EARTH COUNCIL

n. The human raj on Oasis. Shrouded in secrecy from its inception (at the time of the discovery of what was then known as Kepler 56-B, in 2007), the New Earth Council grew from a small initiative of the EU countries into a full-blown military government of the new world. The NEC has jurisdictional power to arrest, try, and transport anyone in the selected Earth demographic (young and poor). The NEC operates the massive ships that take the young human exiles on their two-year voyage to Oasis, and it directs all mining operations there.

O

OLVIDADOS

n. Forgotten ones. The human exiles on Oasis. (Spanish.)

P

PABLO

n. A drug dealer.

PARTS-PERSON
n. One with bionic or robotic implants or prostheses, from limbs to adrenaline pumps to hearts.

PATTY
n. Street money issued by an independent bank. Indie banks live and die on reputation, just as their Earth counterparts do, but without any sanction or backup from civil authorities. Also *hairy patty.* (Mumbaiya Hindi slang, *hari patti,* "green notes," as opposed to the red notes of the New Earth Council.)

PINCHE
adj. Fuckin', rotten, no-good, worthless, contemptible, nasty, filthy. The greatest all-purpose slang word on two planets. Thus *pinche puto,* "worthless fuck"; *pinche cabrón,* "no-good asshole"; etc. But on Oasis, *pinche* is used every day, all day, in the ubiquitous exile expression, "It's *pinche calor* today, holey" ("It's fuckin' hot") or just, "*Pinche calor.*" Everybody—black, white, Asian, bot, whatever—says this. (Mexican Spanish.)

PROCIDIGAAADE
expr. Jargon, "Proceed to gate." For reasons that are unclear, many of the public-address announcers in the ice mines of Oasis are either Malays or have adopted their characteristic weary slur. Thus the announcement, "Lot 47, proceed to gate 12," becomes "Lah for-senn, procidigaaade twel-lah." In Scare City's twisted alleys and tangled favelas, street directions fall into this comical singsong: "Go up the hill, procidigaaade Sugar Street, left at the sign, procidigaaade ring-road . . ."

R
RANDI
n. A prostitute. Used as a proper name, it is a great insult, as in, "Shut up, Randi, nobody asked you shit." (Hindi.)

RED, REDS, RED BILLS, RED NOTES
n. New Earth Council–issued money.

S
SALAAMBRO
n. Arab.

SAMZDOT, SAM'S DOT
n. Forbidden information. Originally referred to forbidden digital information, but could be in any form. (From Russian *samizdat.*)

SANGOMA
n. Street healer, as opposed to a real doctor. (Zulu, Xhosa.)

SCARE CITY
n. The universal name for New Earth Correctional Colony City Number Two on the planet Oasis.

SMEAR
n. A cell culture, virus, or other bioactive building-block material for genetic design. What chips are to computing, smears are to life engineering.

SOLAR
n. A slum. (Brazilian Portuguese.)

SOTONG
n. A stupid person. (Malay, "squid" or "cuttlefish.")

SQUEEZE
n. The gang tax or surcharge on any transaction. You don't pay squeeze, you don't do business.

STEVE
n. A new arrival on Oasis; a rube; fresh meat. Everybody has been Steve at one time or another. The point is to not stay Steve. (Rhyming slang, "Steve Naive," from Steve Nieve, the Attraction.)

T

TAPORI
n. A street-smart kid. (Hindi.)

TSOTSI
n. Thug, gangster, no-gooder. A word which lent its name to a whole category of languages, *tsotsitaals* (mixed gangster creoles). The language of Scare City is growing into its very own *tsotsitaal*. (South African Sesotho.)

U

ULABU
n. A potent homemade beer primarily brewed and sold by Kenyans and other East Africans. You don't want to know what they make it with, but it does the job. *Also excl.*, as in (after knocking one back), "*Ulabu!*" (Kiswahili slang.)

X

XANA
n. Pussy. (Brazilian slang.)

XOTA, XOXOTA
n. See **xana**.

Y

YALLA-GANG
n. A small, unaffiliated kidnapping gang. (From Arabic, *Yalla, yalla!*, "Come on! Let's go! Hurry!")

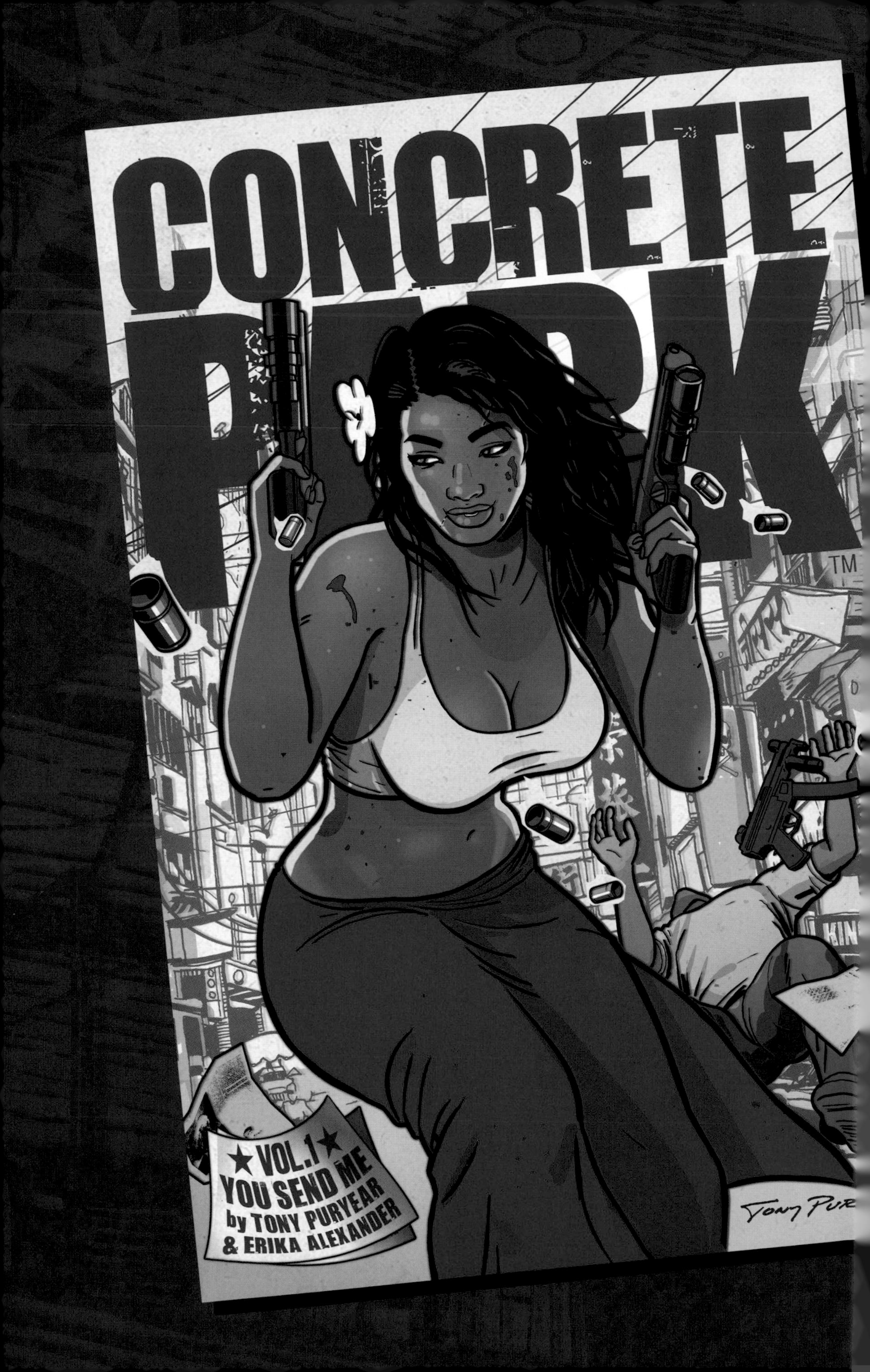
CONCRETE PARK
TM
★VOL.1★
YOU SEND ME
by TONY PURYEAR
& ERIKA ALEXANDER

Concrete Park Volume 1: You Send Me
YOUNG, VIOLENT, AND TEN BILLION MILES FROM HOME.

When Earth's outcasts are exiled to Scare City—a vast outpost on a distant desert planet—they must find a path to redemption or be destroyed by their own violence. A dark, sexy sci-fi saga by Tony Puryear (*Eraser*) and Erika Alexander (*Living Single*), *Concrete Park* is filled with unforgettable protagonists, a colorful supporting cast, redemption, romance, hope, and nonstop action presented in an exceptional, vibrant style. *Concrete Park* Volume 1: *You Send Me* collects the critically acclaimed graphic novel from the pages of *Dark Horse Presents* into a "director's cut" hardcover featuring new pages and bonus materials!

A *Best American Comics 2013* selection!

ISBN 978 1 61655-530-6 | $12.99

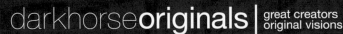

darkhorse**originals** | great creators
original visions

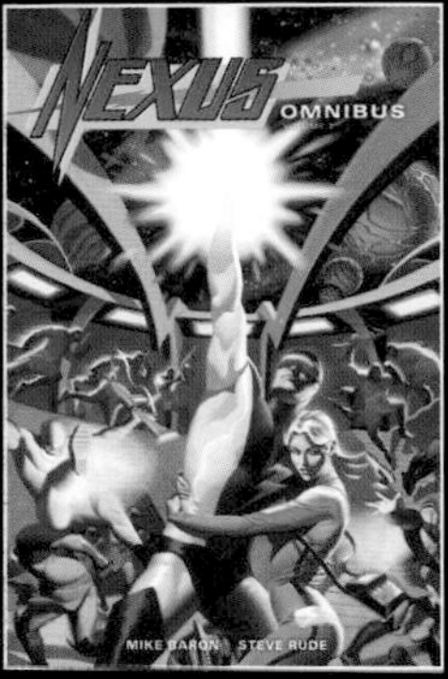
NEXUS
OMNIBUS
MIKE BARON STEVE RUDE

NEXUS OMNIBUS VOLUME 1

Steve Rude and Mike Baron

A multiple Eisner Award–winning series that defined the careers of acclaimed creators Steve Rude and Mike Baron, *Nexus* is a modern classic. In 2841 Nexus, a godlike figure, acts as judge, jury, and executioner for the vile criminals who appear in his dreams. He claims to kill in self-defense, but why? Where do the visions come from, and where did he get his powers?

ISBN 978-1-61655-034-9 | $24.99

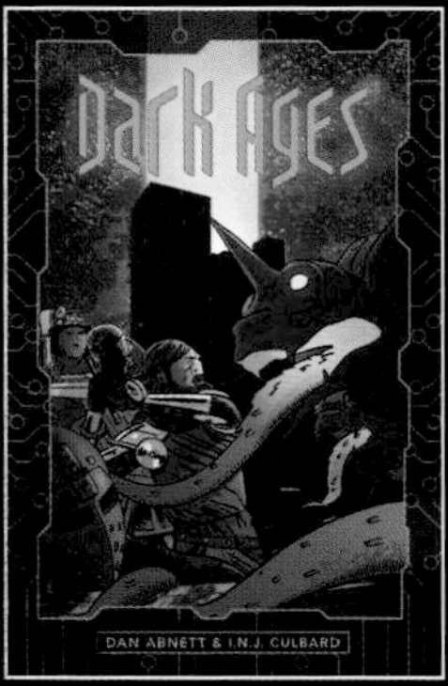
Dark Ages
DAN ABNETT & I.N.J. CULBARD

DARK AGES

Dan Abnett and I. N. J. Culbard

1333: The known world is locked in a holy war. As a godless mercenary company slogs across Europe in search of sustenance and coin, they encounter a demonic force born not of hell, but from beyond the stars!

ISBN 978-1-61655-602-0 | $14.99

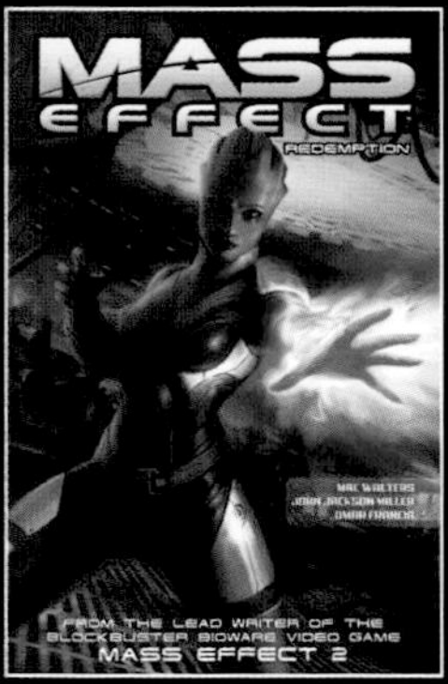
MASS
EFFECT
REDEMPTION
FROM THE LEAD WRITER OF THE
BLOCKBUSTER BIOWARE VIDEO GAME
MASS EFFECT 2

MASS EFFECT VOLUME 1: REDEMPTION

Mac Walters, John Jackson Miller, and Omar Francia

Collecting the four-issue miniseries, *Mass Effect* Volume 1 features essential developments in the *Mass Effect* gaming saga, plus a special behind-the-scenes section with sketches and more.

ISBN 978-1-59582-481-3 | $16.99

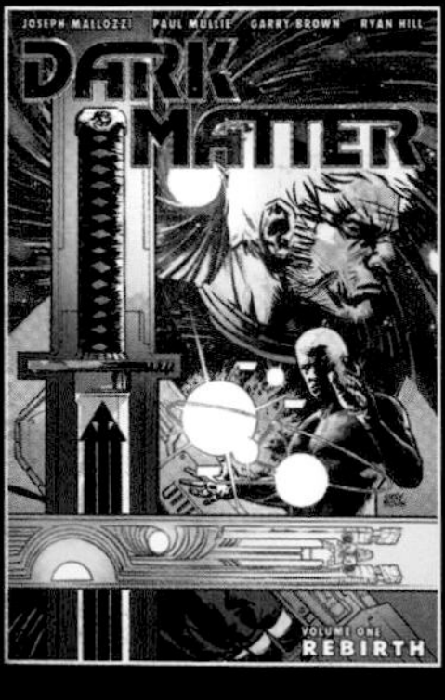
JOSEPH MALLOZZI PAUL MULLIE GARRY BROWN RYAN HILL
DARK
MATTER
VOLUME ONE
REBIRTH

DARK MATTER VOLUME 1: REBIRTH

Joseph Mallozzi, Paul Mullie, and Garry Brown

Sci-fi action from the writers of *Stargate SG-1*! The crew of a derelict spaceship awakens from stasis in the farthest reaches of space. With no recollection of who they are or how they got on board, their only clue is a cargo bay full of weaponry and a destination that is about to become a war zone!

ISBN 978-1-59582-998-6 | $14.99

PARIAH

Aron Warner, Philip Gelatt, and Brett Weldele

Genetically engineered teenage geniuses known as Vitros are labeled a terrorist cell after an explosion at a military weapons lab. The Vitros are rounded up and left on a decrepit satellite orbiting Earth. Now they must band together and use their supergenius abilities to get back to Earth safely.

Volume 1 ISBN 978-1-61655-274-9 | $14.99
Volume 2 ISBN 978-1-61655-275-6 | $14.99

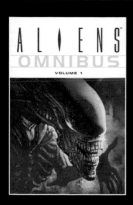

MORE SCIENCE FICTION

FROM DARK HORSE BOOKS

ALIENS
OMNIBUS
VOLUME 1

ALIENS OMNIBUS VOLUME 1

Mark Verheiden, Mark Nelson, Sam Kieth, and Den Beauvais

Dark Horse Comics took the industry by storm with its release of *Aliens*, a comics series that for the first time captured the power of film source material and expanded its universe in a way that fans applauded worldwide. Now, the first three Dark Horse *Aliens* series are collected in a value-priced, quality-format omnibus, featuring nearly four hundred story pages in full color.

ISBN 978-1-59307-727-3 | $24.99

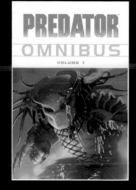

PREDATOR
OMNIBUS
VOLUME 1

PREDATOR OMNIBUS VOLUME 1

Mark Verheiden, Dan Barry, Chris Warner, Ron Randall, and others

Trophy hunters from another world, hiding in plain sight, drawn to heat and conflict. A historical scourge, lethal specters, powerful, savage, merciless. Utilizing their feral instincts and otherworldly technology in the sole pursuit of the most dangerous game . . . Man.

ISBN 978-1-59307-732-7 | $24.99

THE
TERMINATOR
OMNIBUS
VOLUME 1

TERMINATOR OMNIBUS VOLUME 1

James Robinson, John Arcudi, Ian Edginton, Chris Warner, and others

Terminators—indestructible killing engines hiding inside shells of flesh and blood. Tireless, fearless, merciless, unencumbered by human emotion, dedicated to the complete eradication of mankind. *The Terminator* is one of the finest examples of bringing top comics talents to the expansion of a premier action/adventure mythos.

ISBN 978-1-59307-916-1 | $24.99

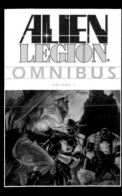

ALIEN
LEGION
OMNIBUS

ALIEN LEGION OMNIBUS VOLUME 1

Alan Zelenetz, Frank Cirocco, Chris Warner, Terry Shoemaker, Terry Austin, and Randy Emberlin

Footsloggers and soldiers of fortune, priests, poets, killers, and cads—they fight for a future Galarchy, for cash, for a cause, for the thrill of adventure. Culled from the forgotten and unwanted of three galaxies, they are trained to be the most elite, and expendable, of fighting forces. *Alien Legion Omnibus* Volume 1 features over three hundred story pages of the groundbreaking series!

ISBN 978-1-59582-394-6 | $24.99

AVAILABLE AT YOUR LOCAL COMICS SHOP OR BOOKSTORE! • To find a comics shop in your area, call 1-888-266-4226.
For more information or to order direct visit DarkHorse.com or call 1-800-862-0052 Mon.–Fri. 9 AM to 5 PM Pacific Time. Prices and availability subject to change without notice.

EXPLORE THE MANY WORLDS OF THE EISNER AWARD–WINNING CREATORS OF *DAYTRIPPER*—

GABRIEL BÁ AND FÁBIO MOON!

"[De:Tales is] a perfect blend of fluid storytelling and contemporary style . . . A+." —Tom McLean, Variety

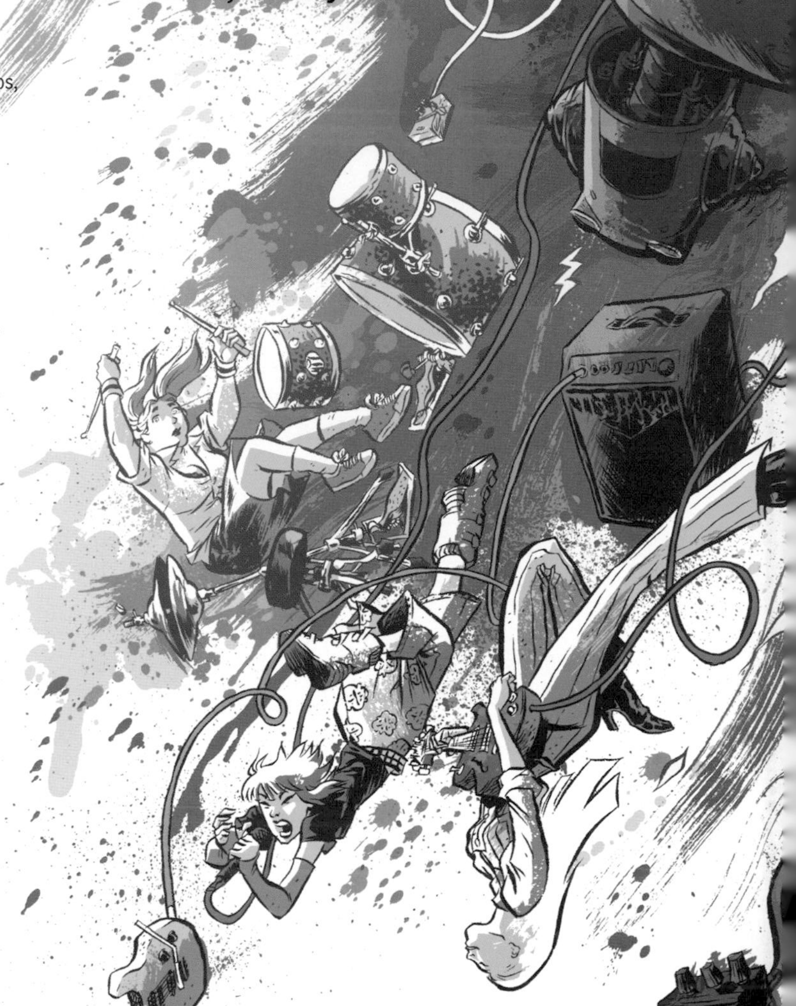

PIXU: THE MARK OF EVIL
Created by Gabriel Bá, Becky Cloonan, Vasilis Lolos, and Fábio Moon
ISBN 978-1-59582-340-3 | $17.99

B.P.R.D.: 1947
Written by Mike Mignola and Joshua Dysart
Art by Gabriel Bá and Fábio Moon
ISBN 978-1-59582-478-3 | $17.99

MYSPACE DARK HORSE PRESENTS
Volume 1
ISBN 978-1-59307-998-7 | $19.99

SUGARSHOCK
One-shot comic
Written by Joss Whedon
Art by Fábio Moon
$3.50

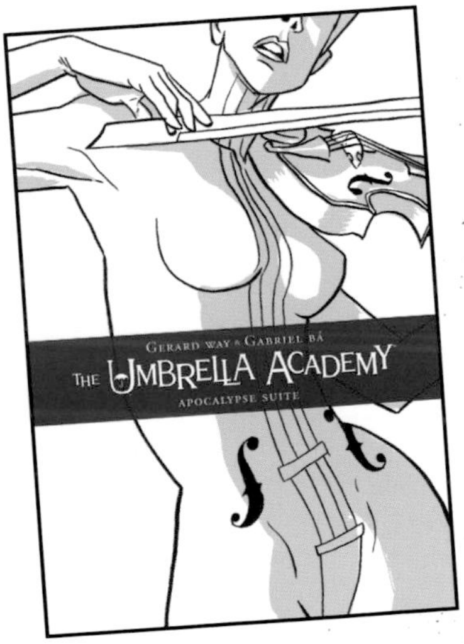
GERARD WAY & GABRIEL BÁ
THE UMBRELLA ACADEMY
APOCALYPSE SUITE

THE UMBRELLA ACADEMY: APOCALYPSE SUITE
Written by Gerard Way
Art by Gabriel Bá
TPB: 978-1-59307-978-9 | $17.99
Ltd. Ed. HC: 978-1-59582-163-8 | $79.95

THE UMBRELLA ACADEMY: DALLAS
Written by Gerard Way
Art by Gabriel Bá
TPB: 978-1-59582-345-8 | $17.99
Ltd. Ed. HC: 978-1-59582-344-1 | $79.95

DE:TALES
Story and art by
Gabriel Bá and Fábio Moon
ISBN 978-1-59582-557-5 | $19.99

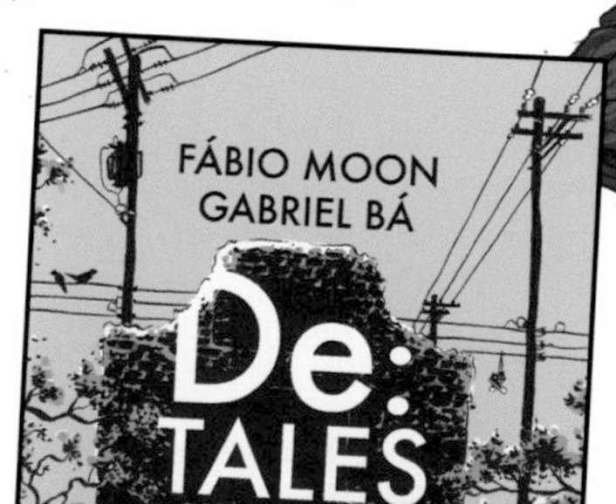
FÁBIO MOON
GABRIEL BÁ
De:
TALES

AVAILABLE AT YOUR LOCAL COMICS SHOP OR BOOKSTORE! • To find a comics shop in your area, call 1-888-266-4226.
For more information or to order direct visit DarkHorse.com or call 1-800-862-0052 Mon.–Fri. 9 a.m. to 5 p.m. Pacific Time. Prices and availability subject to change without notice.

ALSO FROM DARK HORSE BOOKS

JEREMIAH OMNIBUS VOLUME 1
Hermann
One of Europe's most revered comics classics comes to America! At the end of the twentieth century, the United States is overcome by race hatred, and the ensuing civil war leaves only a few million survivors and a shattered society. Forced by circumstances into a series of violent moral compromises, innocent Jeremiah and his cynical friend Kurdy attempt to find their place in the postapocalyptic world without descending into savagery.

978-1-59582-945-0 | $24.99

THE MANARA LIBRARY VOLUME 1
Milo Manara with Hugo Pratt
The first of nine volumes, The Manara Library Volume 1 collects two of Manara's seminal works in a magnificently appointed, deluxe hardcover edition. The sweeping epic Indian Summer, a collaboration with celebrated creator Hugo Pratt, is collected here along with Manara's The Paper Man, both translated by Euro comics expert Kim Thompson.

978-1-59582-782-1 | $59.99

THE INCREDIBLE ADVENTURES OF DOG MENDONÇA AND PIZZABOY
Filipe Melo and Juan Cavia
What do an overweight Portuguese werewolf, a seven-year-old girl who's actually a six thousand-year-old demon, and a downtrodden pizza boy have in common? In this smash-hit import, the unlikely team bands together to ward off occult evils, Nazis, and impending global doom! Featuring an introduction by An American Werewolf in London director John Landis!

978-1-59582-938-2 | $12.99

THE WEDNESDAY CONSPIRACY
Sérgio Bleda
Think you've got problems? Meet the patients in Dr. Burton's Wednesday afternoon support group: Violet carries a jar of demons. Roger can read minds. Akiko talks with her dead parents through the bathroom mirror. Joe is an exorcist. Brian is pyrokinetic. And then, of course, there's Charles. They've been thrown together by the luck of the draw, stuck with supernatural powers they don't want and can't control. But when something begins to pick them off one by one, the surviving members of the Wednesday Conspiracy find themselves the last, reluctant line of defense between the reincarnation of an ancient evil and the fate of the world.

978-1-59582-563-6 | $19.99

AVAILABLE AT YOUR LOCAL COMICS SHOP OR BOOKSTORE! • To find a comics shop in your area, call 1-888-266-4226.
For more information or to order direct visit DarkHorse.com or call 1-800-862-0052 Mon.–Fri. 9 AM to 5 PM Pacific Time. Prices and availability subject to change without notice.

DarkHorse.com   All works © their respective creators. Dark Horse Books® and the Dark Horse logo are registered trademarks of Dark Horse Comics, Inc. All rights reserved. (BL 5019)

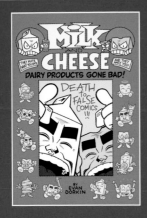

MILK AND CHEESE: DAIRY PRODUCTS GONE BAD

Evan Dorkin

The Eisner Award–winning dairy duo returns in this deluxe hardcover collecting every *Milk and Cheese* comic from 1989 to 2010 and a staggering array of extras, supplements, and bonuses.

ISBN 978-1-59582-805-7 | $19.99

RESET

Peter Bagge

If you could relive major events in your life, would you try to make things better—even if your best attempts only make things worse? Or would you set your most twisted fantasies into motion? A hilarious new hardcover graphic novel from Harvey Award–winning writer/artist Peter Bagge!

ISBN 978-1-61655-003-5 | $15.99

CHIMICHANGA

Eric Powell

When Wrinkle's Traveling Circus's adorable little bearded girl trades a lock of her magic beard hair for a witch's strange egg, she stumbles upon what could be the saving grace for her ailing freak show—the savory-named beast Chimichanga!

ISBN 978-1-59582-755-5 | $14.99

BUCKO

Jeff Parker and Erika Moen

After discovering a body in an office bathroom, Rich "Bucko" Richardson becomes suspected of the murder. A quest to find the real killer becomes a romp through the wilds of Portland, Oregon. After taking the Internet by storm, Jeff Parker and Erika Moen's dirty, funny murder mystery is now a hilarious hardcover book!

ISBN 978-1-59582-973-3 | $19.99

THE BEST OF MILLIGAN & MCCARTHY

Peter Milligan and Brendan McCarthy

One of comics' most fruitful collaborations gets its due in this deluxe collection of hard-to-find gems from Peter Milligan (*Hellblazer*, *X-Statix*) and Brendan McCarthy (*Judge Dredd*). This volume is the ideal starting place for new readers!

ISBN 978-1-61655-153-7 | $24.99

RECESS PIECES

Bob Fingerman

When a science project goes wrong, only the prepubescent children are spared the fate of zombification—which doesn't mean they're immune from being eaten alive! Bob Fingerman (*Beg the Question*, *You Deserved It*) dishes up a grisly combination of Hal Roach's *Our Gang* and zombies.

ISBN 978-1-59307-450-0 | $14.99

THE BOOK OF GRICKLE

Graham Annable

As befits his classically trained animation background, Graham Annable's fluid art pulses with life, in stories that practically jump off the page. Alternately poetic and hilarious, *Grickle* presents a strange twist on the everyday with heart and humor.

ISBN 978-1-59582-430-1 | $17.99

DARK HORSE BOOKS

AVAILABLE AT YOUR LOCAL COMICS SHOP OR BOOKSTORE • To find a comics shop in your area, call 1-888-266-4226.
For more information or to order direct: ON THE WEB: DarkHorse.com / E-MAIL: mailorder@darkhorse.com / PHONE: 1-800-862-0052 Mon.–Fri. 9 a.m. to 5 p.m. Pacific Time.

DarkHorse.com   Milk & Cheese © Evan Dorkin. Reset™ © Peter Bagge. Chimichanga™ © Eric Powell. Bucko™ © Jeff Parker and Erika Moen. MILLIGAN & McCARTHY Collected Works © Pete Milligan & Brendan McCarthy. Recess Pieces © and ™ Bob Fingerman. Book of Grickle © Graham Annable. Dark Horse Books® and the Dark Horse logo are registered trademarks of Dark Horse Comics, Inc. (BL 5059)

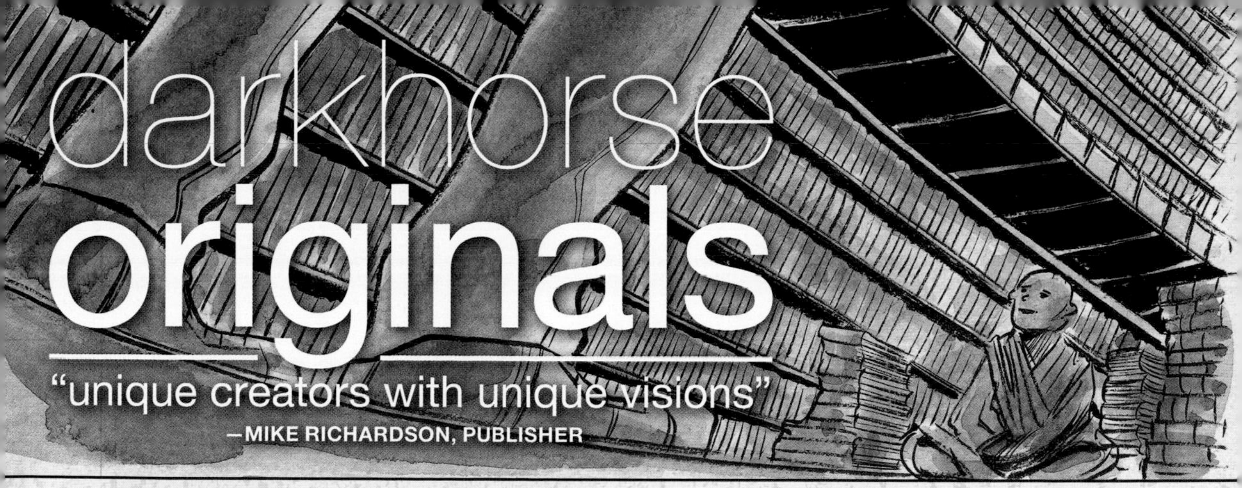
darkhorse
originals
"unique creators with unique visions"
—MIKE RICHARDSON, PUBLISHER

BLACKSAD
978-1-59582-393-9 | $29.99

BLACKSAD: A SILENT HELL
978-1-59582-931-3 | $19.99

MIND MGMT
Volume 1: The Manager
978-1-59582-797-5 | $19.99
Volume 2: The Futurist
978-1-61655-198-8 | $19.99

RESET
978-1-61655-003-5 | $15.99

CHERUBS
978-1-59582-984-9 | $19.99

BRODY'S GHOST
Book 1: 978-1-59582-521-6 | $6.99
Book 2: 978-1-59582-665-7 | $6.99
Book 3: 978-1-59582-862-0 | $6.99
Book 4: 978-1-61655-129-2 | $6.99

NINGEN'S NIGHTMARES
978-1-59582-859-0 | $12.99

EVERYBODY GETS IT WRONG! AND OTHER STORIES: DAVID CHELSEA'S 24-HOUR COMICS
978-1-61655-155-1 | $19.99

3 STORY: THE SECRET HISTORY OF THE GIANT MAN
978-1-59582-356-4 | $19.99

365 SAMURAI AND A FEW BOWLS OF RICE
978-1-59582-412-7 | $16.99

THE ADVENTURES OF BLANCHE
978-1-59582-258-1 | $15.99

BEANWORLD
Volume 1: Wahoolazuma!
978-1-59582-240-6 | $19.99
Volume 2: A Gift Comes!
978-1-59582-299-4 | $19.99
Volume 3: Remember Here When You Are There!
978-1-59582-355-7 | $19.99
Volume 3.5: Tales of the Beanworld
978-1-59582-897-2 | $14.99

BLOOD SONG: A SILENT BALLAD
978-1-59582-389-2 | $19.99

THE BOOK OF GRICKLE
978-1-59582-430-1 | $17.99

BUCKO
978-1-59582-973-3 | $19.99

CHANNEL ZERO
978-1-59582-936-8 | $19.99

CHIMICHANGA
978-1-59582-755-5 | $14.99

CITIZEN REX
978-1-59582-556-8 | $19.99

CROSSING THE EMPTY QUARTER AND OTHER STORIES
978-1-59582-388-5 | $24.99

DE:TALES
HC: 978-1-59582-557-5 | $19.99
TPB: 978-1-59307-485-2 | $14.99

EXURBIA
978-1-59582-339-7 | $9.99

FLUFFY
978-1-59307-972-7 | $19.99

GREEN RIVER KILLER
978-1-59582-560-5 | $24.99

INSOMNIA CAFÉ
978-1-59582-357-1 | $14.99

THE MIGHTY SKULLBOY ARMY
Volume 2
978-1-59582-872-9 | $14.99

MILK AND CHEESE: DAIRY PRODUCTS GONE BAD
978-1-59582-805-7 | $19.99

MOTEL ART IMPROVEMENT SERVICE
978-1-59582-550-6 | $19.99

THE NIGHT OF YOUR LIFE
978-1-59582-183-6 | $15.99

NOIR
978-1-59582-358-8 | $12.99

PIXU: THE MARK OF EVIL
978-1-59582-340-3 | $17.99

SACRIFICE
978-1-59582-985-6 | $19.99

SINFEST: VIVA LA RESISTANCE
978-1-59582-424-0 | $14.99

SPEAK OF THE DEVIL
978-1-59582-193-5 | $19.99

UNCLE SILAS
978-1-59582-566-7 | $9.99

AVAILABLE AT YOUR LOCAL COMICS SHOP OR BOOKSTORE!
To find a comics shop in your area, call 1-888-266-4226

For more information or to order direct:
On the web: DarkHorse.com
E-mail: mailorder@darkhorse.com
Phone: 1-800-862-0052 Mon.–Fri. 9 AM to 5 PM Pacific Time

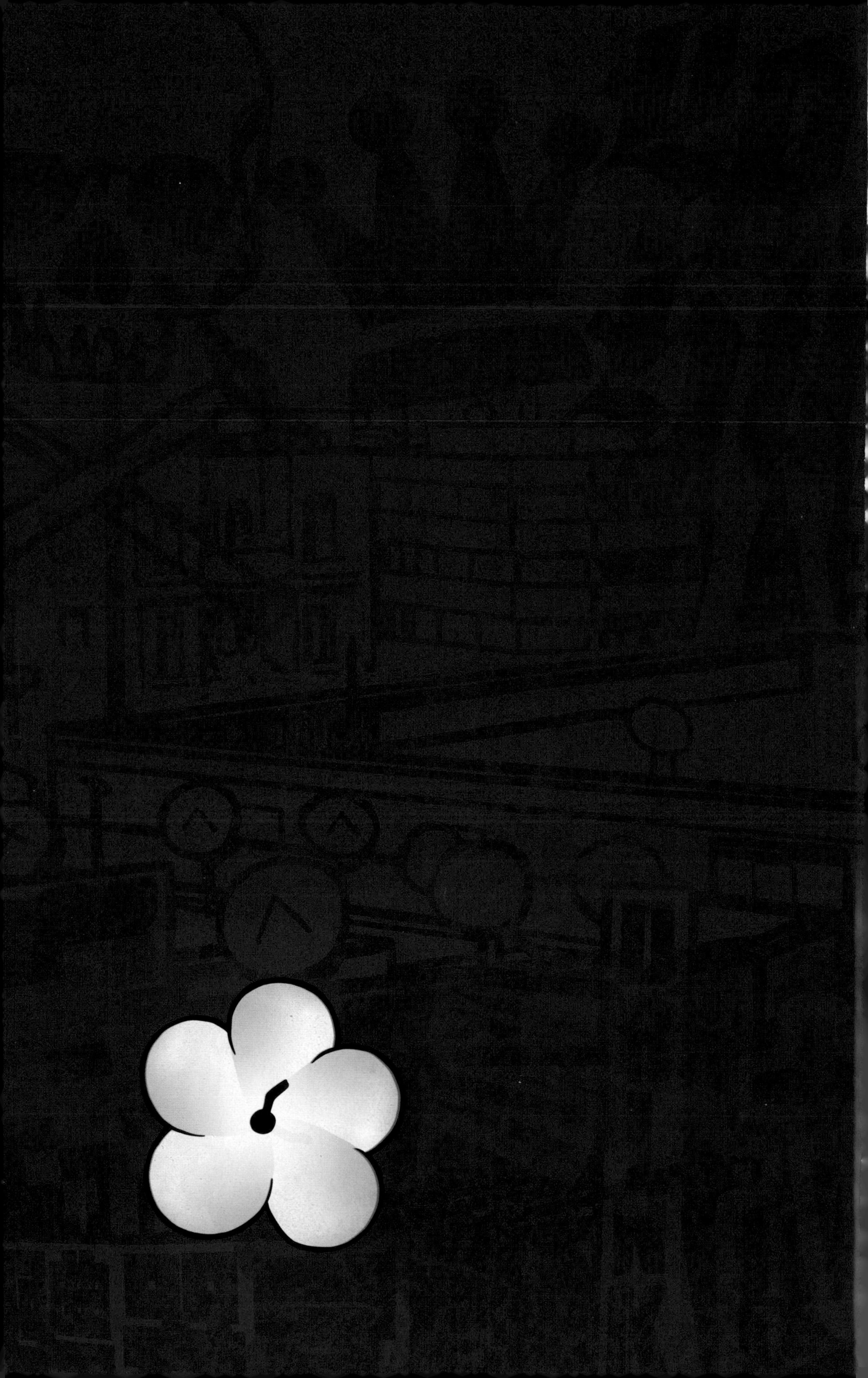

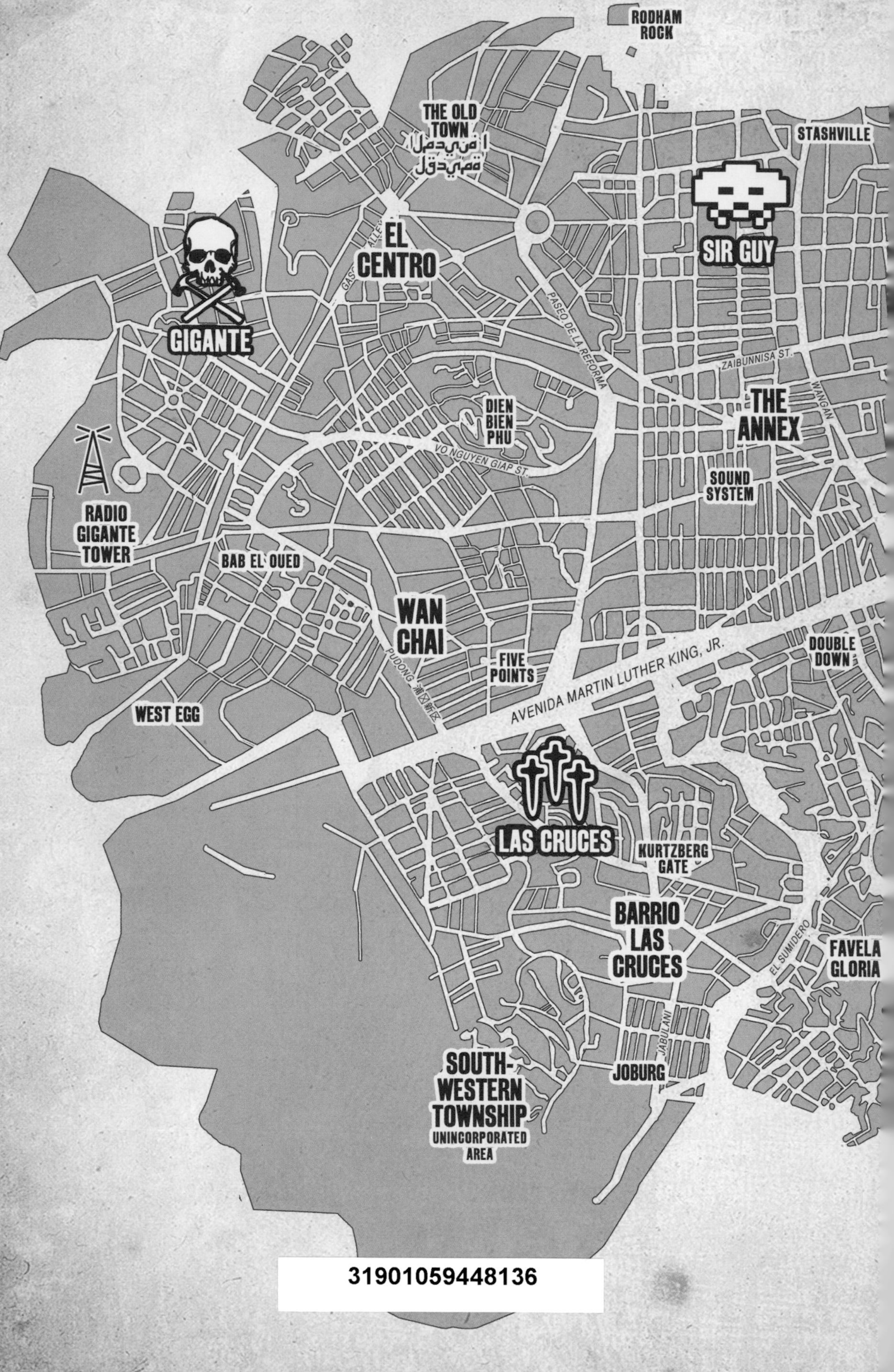
RODHAM ROCK
THE OLD TOWN
STASHVILLE
EL CENTRO
SIR GUY
GIGANTE
PASEO DE LA REFORMA
ZAIBUNNISA ST.
WANGAN
THE ANNEX
DIEN BIEN PHU
VO NGUYEN GIAP ST.
SOUND SYSTEM
RADIO GIGANTE TOWER
BAB EL OUED
WAN CHAI
PUDONG 浦东新区
FIVE POINTS
DOUBLE DOWN
AVENIDA MARTIN LUTHER KING, JR.
WEST EGG
LAS CRUCES
KURTZBERG GATE
BARRIO LAS CRUCES
EL SUMIDERO
FAVELA GLORIA
JABULANI
JOBURG
SOUTH-WESTERN TOWNSHIP
UNINCORPORATED AREA